Louis Garnier, Eudist

Dog Sled to Airplane

A HISTORY OF THE ST. LAWRENCE
NORTH SHORE

Translated from the French
by . . .
HÉLÈNE A. NANTAIS, B.A.
and . . .
ROBERT L. NANTAIS, B. Ph., B. L. S.

1949

Thorold, Ont., November 8, 1948.

Dear Father Garnier,

During the month of August you thoughtfully sent me a copy of your excellent little book *Du Cométique à l'Avion*, and it is just recently that I have had an opportunity to examine it carefully.

The story is most interesting and fascinating, and I am happy to have this occasion of extending to you my heartiest congratulations upon the production of this history of the endeavours of the Eudist Fathers and this record of events and places on the North Shore which, of course, is very dear to me because of our operations there and because Mrs. Schmon and I spent several years living there.

This is the kind of work that will enable the Nation's historians to give prominence in years to come to a tale that reveals the difficulties under which was inaugurated a section of Canada that is fast increasing in importance, and in the development of which the Order of the Eudist Fathers has so worthily contributed in encouraging the people and in imparting to them guidance in their spiritual, moral, and economic welfare.

With my thanks for so kindly remembering me and trusting that your book will enjoy a wide distribution, I remain with best respects and wishes,

Yours sincerely,
Arthur A. Schmon

Reverend Father L. Garnier,
Baie Comeau, P. Q.

Laval-des-Rapides, P. Q.,
March 14th, 1949.

Rev. Fr. Louis Garnier, c.j.m.,
Baie Comeau, P. Q.

Dear Father Garnier,

All your friends and superiors will rejoice with the appearance of this English edition of your recent history of the North Shore.

I'm sure many tourists, Canadian and American, will be delighted to read something on the development of a region that is only beginning its history and is destined to play an important part in the life of the Province of Quebec. The book is very opportune, and what is more, it is interesting and well informed.

May it obtain a wide circulation and help the people of the North Shore to know and love their country better, to appreciate their Missionaries ever more deeply.

Fraternally yours in Christ,

A. D'Amours, c.j.m.,
Sup. prov.

TABLE OF CONTENTS

	PAGE
Acknowledgments	VI
Note by the translators	XI

CHAPTER ONE
The Pioneers 1

CHAPTER TWO
The first Missionaries 16

CHAPTER THREE
First contacts of the Eudists with the North Shore . 29

CHAPTER FOUR
Fishing 46

CHAPTER FIVE
Hunting. — I 69

CHAPTER SIX
Hunting. — II 97

CHAPTER SEVEN
The postal service 102

CHAPTER EIGHT
Travel on the North Shore 114

CHAPTER NINE
Attempts at progress 131

	PAGE
CHAPTER TEN	
Progress. — I	145
CHAPTER ELEVEN	
Progress. — II	160
CHAPTER TWELVE	
Progress. — III	175
CHAPTER THIRTEEN	
Progress. — IV	197
CHAPTER FOURTEEN	
Anticosti	213
CHAPTER FIFTEEN	
Religious and moral life on the North Shore . .	227
CHAPTER SIXTEEN	
The leaders of the flock	255
Bishop Gustave Blanche	255
Bishop A.-P. Chiasson	260
Bishop J.-M. Leventoux	263
Bishop N.-A. Labrie	271
CHAPTER SEVENTEEN	
The future prospects for industry	284

NOTE
BY THE TRANSLATORS

H E who offers this book to the public first came to the North Shore on August 27, 1903 and worked for ten years as a missionary with Father Joseph Gallix at Natashquan, and following thereon for twenty seven years at Rivière-au-Tonnerre, visiting his parishioners over a distance of sixty miles between Magpie and Pigou.

Naturally, many of the events which form the history of this distant place are to be found stored in the memory of such a witness. At the suggestion of the Reverend Father Louis-Philippe Gagné, curé of Baie Comeau from 1936 to 1946, and in compliance with a formal instruction from His Excellency Bishop N.-A. Labrie, this missionary, in spite of his advanced years, 74, has very ably attempted the setting down of his recollections in this book, *Dog Sled to Airplane*, of which the original French edition first appeared in August, 1948.

These recollections proved quite a success among the French-Canadians of the North Shore and it has, therefore, been thought desirable to translate and offer them to the English speaking population. It is hoped that this English version will prove as interesting to the readers thereof as was the French version to those who read it.

The way of life of the early settlers on the North Shore, their trials and tribulations on hunting expeditions into the forest and fishing trips on the waters of the Gulf, the heroic apostolate of the missionaries of whom four lost their lives in the icy waters of Labrador, the journeys by dog sled, progress in the social, moral, religious, and commercial spheres up to the present gigantic transformations in the field of industry ; all these form a central theme of which it is hoped the public will gain some appreciation through the reading of these notes and recollections.

This is a worthy effort at bringing to life the history and recording the developments that half a century have brought to such an out of the way region ; of which developments the chief have been the creation by the Catholic Church of a new diocese, that of the Gulf of St. Lawrence, and the formation of important industrial centres in which work has already been begun around the vast mining territory of Ungava, Seven-Islands, and Havre Saint-Pierre.

H. N.
R. N.

CHAPTER ONE

THE PIONEERS

**The Newfoundlanders. — The men from Berthier.
The Magdalen Islanders. — The Gaspesians.
The choice of village sites.**

O<small>N</small> February 23, 1943, His Excellency Bishop N. A. LaBrie, Vicar Apostolic of the Gulf of St. Lawrence, gave a conference in the Hall of the Knights of Columbus of Quebec City. In the course of his lecture, he afforded his listeners such interesting and such precise details concerning the North Shore that it has been deemed most proper to assign them first place in these *Notes and Recollections*.

"If we consider the North Shore as co-extensive with the apostolic vicariate of the Gulf of St. Lawrence, then it begins at the Portneuf River and ends at Blanc-Sablon, a distance of 709 miles. This constitutes my spiritual domain, to which must be added Anticosti Island. You will readily see that this North Shore is not so far north that one must shiver just to think of it. Quebec City is near the 47th parallel of latitude, and the North Shore, as a whole, extends very little above the 50th, ending on the 53rd. Its general direction is rather from east to west, and it ends far east of the longitude of Halifax. Our climate is therefore under the influence of both the Gulf Stream, which gives us our mild winters, and of the cold currents from Belle-Isle, which account for the fogs and the coolness of our summers.

"These seven hundred and nine miles may be divided into three zones. The first, extending from the western limits to Seven Islands in the east, can be compared with the South Shore, enjoying much the same climate as Rimouski. The second, comprising the area between Seven Islands and Natashquan, enjoys even milder winters than the first zone, and can pride itself on a serene sky, rather calm days, and moderate snowfalls. Its very cool summers are the delight of certain constitutions. People who like ice and snow can go on to Blanc-Sablon. Even in August they will see ice borne by the waves. I have seen immense icebergs stranded in thirty-five fathoms of water (210 feet), splendid battlemented castles, with stalactites visible in their grottoes, where the light plays the whole gamut of shades from purest white to richest indigo.

"The North Shore as a whole, being entirely of granitic formation, is one of the oldest lands in the world. One must except, however, the Mingan and Anticosti Islands, which are linked with the Appalachian range and are of calcareous and fossil formation. The Laurentians, which form the backbone of this region, wander along the whole of its length, now running towards the interior, now returning to refresh themselves in the green waters of the Gulf, and, after Natashquan, finally entering the waters and forming, by their summits, an archipelago of thousands of islands and islets. This last region constitutes a geologist's paradise, for few countries can give us a better idea of the cataclysms which shook the globe in prehistoric times. Glaciers have deeply grooved the granite surface. Earthquakes have broken up mountains into parallel ranges, and immense longitudinal faults have created passages where the largest ships can navigate, while other crevasses have made fjords as picturesque as those of Norway."

This division into three zones holds also for their vegetation. Further information on this subject will be given in these *Notes and Recollections* in the chapters on the colonization of the North Shore. As to the natural beauties which may be viewed by the tourist all along its shores, they are as varied as its heavily wooded or starkly bare islands, its grey or white rocks, and its beaches covered with fine russet sand or with the jet black ilmenite that has been deposited in many places. Which part of the North Shore should get the preference for the summer resorts of the future? Pointe-aux-Outardes, Godbout, Baie Trinité, Pentecost, Sainte-Marguerite, Seven Islands, Moisie, Matamek?... Mr. J.-E. Chabot, an artist who visited the shores of the second zone twenty years ago and recorded some of the beautiful scenes with his camera, had these photographs published with considerable success in a Montreal newspaper, *La Presse Illustrée*. A Frenchman wrote to his brother, a missionary in this region : "Your country is ravishing, your photographs exhibit scenery that could be taken for certain landscapes of Brittany along the English Channel, so popular with the tourists of France and Great Britain."

If we study the ethnographic side, it seems well proven that Jacques Cartier, after crossing the Strait of Belle-Isle, landed at a place to which he gave the name of Brest, probably the "Old Fort" (*Vieux Fort*) of today, and erected on Canadian soil the first cross bearing the *fleur-de-lis*. It also seems certain that Basque fishermen built at Brador some fishing establishments, interesting remains of which may still be seen. Could not these fishermen, still preceding Jacques Cartier, have reached Seven Islands, where Basque Island and Pointe-aux-Basques, both of which are well-known today, seem to testify to their passage in these places? And then there is the port of Brest, founded by a man named Aubert from Dieppe, a real port around which some two hundred families settled. A governor very likely directed the colony while a chaplain looked after the spiritual interests. A short-lived colony it proved to be, which lasted, as the French poet says, *ce que durent les roses*, the life span of a rose. Europe would not colonize that "land of Cain", as Jacques Cartier called it. It was so far from *la doulce France*! The French did return, in later years, but as Canadians, more familiar then with navigation on the Gulf.

How did these communities of Canadians, who eventually became parishioners of the Eudist fathers in 1903, form themselves? Beautiful pages of history could be written on the origin of each of these settlements. How many instances of courage, of devotion, of Christian charity, even of heroism, could be told the grandsons of these incomparable pioneers! There are a few episodes concerning the origin of these Labradorian villages worthy of recall in these notes.

In 1820 there were no European women in Labrador. Among the very first residents were courageous fishermen from the Isle of Jersey and Newfoundland. To be sure, it is their descendants that we see actually in

Photo Paul Provancher

THE AUTHOR,
Missionary on the North Shore since 1903

CHARLES ARNAUD, O.M.I.,
Missionary of the Montagnais for 50 years at Bersimis

this district, families named Jones, Robertson, Wilcott, Collier, Kennedy, Court, King, Russell, Foreman, Organ, Gallichon.

About the same time, also, daring fishermen from Berthier and the surroundings, probably drawn by the memory of the great Labradorian expeditions of Louis Jolliet, Seigneur of Anticosti and of the Mingan Islands, decided to attempt the great adventure. These skilful sailors and sea wolves, as were so many of the residents along the banks of the St. Lawrence, set sail in their little schooners, which they managed with great dexterity. Weeks passed by on this long and hazardous journey, and the season had far advanced when the men from Berthier entered the Bay of Brador, eight hundred miles away from their village. They were surprised to find plots of cleared land around the Old Fort, the seaport of long ago, and there they pitched their tents. Newfoundland fishermen living near there showed them racks of fine cods and shanties filled with salted fish. There had never been such excellent prizes taken in Berthier! Subsequently, they went to work with lines and nets, but alas, without any success: in the Strait of Belle-Isle and in the neighbouring bays to the west, one must be there when the fish penetrate into the Gulf waters! They had arrived too late! In desperation, a few of them unfurled their sails for the return trip, although they must face the eight hundred miles before them with the added dangers of the frequent storms and the high winds of the fall. Others hesitated, and thinking they would have better luck in the spring when they would be on the spot for the passage of the schools of fish, decided to spend the winter in their improvised camps, hunting rabbits and fur-bearing animals. During the summer they worked at first for the Newfoundlanders, who already had a long record of experience in that region. Then they worked on their own and succeeded in making magnificent catches, thus allowing them to make substantial savings. Now was the time to erect a few dwellings to house their families. Amongst the Catholics, the sacred bonds contracted at the altar are not to be broken. Accordingly, in spite of the enormous distance to be navigated, the wives, accompanied by their children, embarked to join their husbands, keep house, and take part in the labour of these intrepid fishermen. Friends and relatives of these pioneers soon followed. Thus, about forty families originally from Berthier had settled in that territory that is today under the ecclesiastical jurisdiction of His Excellency Bishop Scheffer, O.M.I. A few names are well-known there : Labadie, Morency, Beaudoin, Lavallée, Maurice, Marcoux, Bilodeau, Lessard, Nadeau. To this list must be added the Maugers, who had come directly from Jersey. Protestant in origin, they have become Catholics. The Blais, Collards, Guillemettes, Merciers, Galibois, Métiviers, Babbuts, Andersons, Osbornes, Sturberts, founded Romaine and other small communities. Those who now people the pretty villages of Kegashka, Muskuaro, Romaine, Itamamiou, Harrington, Baie-des-Moutons, Tabatière, Tête-à-la-Baleine, St. Augustine, Bonne-Espérance, Notre-Dame-de-Lourdes, Blanc-Sablon, to name only the more important ones, are, therefore, the descendants of these sailors from Berthier, Newfoundland, Jersey, and also Gaspé, whose long voyages aboard their sailing schooners and barges would frighten our contemporary inhabitants of these places. If you take the boat at Natashquan and follow the shore as far as Blanc-Sablon, you will see these settlements, picturesquely situated facing the sea, some on barren rocks, others on the shores of a river or around a rocky beach protected by islands. Their inhabitants lead an upright, Christian life, following their satisfactorily remunerative vocation. Nothing, now, could entice them to leave these places that they love and cherish as much as the farmer loves and cherishes the land on which he was born.

In 1784, fishermen from Nova Scotia, New Brunswick, and the Baie des Chaleurs appeared at Romaine and Kegashka where they set up fishing establishments. But they did not linger long on this north land. There were no fixed and stable settlements on the North Shore until some valiant Acadians came and settled there. Sailing their light schooners, these excellent navigators had no fear of long sea voyages nor of bringing with them their wives and children and all their belongings, if necessary.

In 1852, the Acadians of the Magdalen Islands were suffering much from misfortunes and their desire for freedom. "The plagues of Egypt," they complained, "have befallen us. The first three are the poor harvests the landlords, and the merchants, while the other four have been brought by the men of the law. Since lawyers have come to the Islands, living here has become intolerable."

A new administrator, John Fontana, judged obsolete the human and equitable methods of his predecessors. By his odious partialities he antagonized even the most patient. From 1854 to 1865 about one hundred and twenty five Acadian families left their country once and for all. A few chose to stop at Kegashka but stayed only a short while.

Jean Vigneault, Victor Cormier, Pierre Lapierre, ("Gros Pierre"), the four Vigneault brothers, Paul Landry, Louis Talbot, made a happier choice when their preference fell on the pretty village of Natashquan.

Farther up the Gulf, twelve miles to the west, is the village of Aguanish, and close by, that of Île-à-Michon. Aguanish has its own little history. It was founded in 1849 by Xavier and John Rochette. The two brothers had discovered that the Aguanish and Napissipi Rivers, which abounded in salmon, should receive their attention. They straightway settled west of the Aguanish River. Victor Blais, a young man from Berthier, soon joined them. Later on, when the Acadians of the Magdalen Islands emigrated in an effort to escape the "plagues of Egypt," a cluster of families, the Gallants, Deraps, Boudreau, of which the venerable Joseph Boudreau was so widely known for the generous hospitality he freely offered to travellers, the Cormiers, Vigneaults, Noëls, Molaisons, Chevaries and Lapierres, came to establish two interesting villages where they could live happily from the results of their hunting, fishing, and gardening. At Piastrebaie, forty miles west of Aguanish, four Acadian families, the Bourques, Loyseaus, Desjardins, Devosts, and a few Canadians like the Tanguays, founded the very charming village made famous by Johan Beetz, who gave it its name.

Let us mention briefly another post, "Betchuan", where Father Boutin, the missionary at Natashquan, came in 1885 to fetch some parishioners reduced to utter poverty and misery. Fishing, which had been their principal source of subsistence, had fallen off considerably all over this region. Led by this courageous priest, these fishermen and many of the residents of Natashquan became the founders of St. Georges de Beauce, P. Q. The distance they had to cover and the means of transportation of that period give us an inkling of the hardships these people had to face. An interesting page remains to be written in the history of the colonization of Beauce County concerning this emigration of 1885.

We must now turn our attention to Esquimaux Point, the future Havre St. Pierre, a spot privileged amongst all others, where many interesting events will occur. On May 20, 1857, Firmin Boudreau, owner of a schooner, sailed from the Magdalen Islands towards Labrador in search of a land of freedom for himself and his family. Among the passengers were the families of Nathaniel Boudreau, Benjamin Landry, Louis Cormier, and François Petitpas. They halted at the Corneille River, then sailed along the shores of the Gulf up to Mingan, exploring carefully all the bays and islands. From Mingan, a small boat was sent to explore farther west ; it sailed up to Sheldrake without finding the ideal location dreamed of. At that time, a mission for the Montagnais Indians was going on at Mingan under the direction of the illustrious Father Arnaud, an Oblate Father. The sight of the chapel dominating the shores, the singing of hymns, the evening prayers said in common, the attractive little harbour so well protected from winds and tides by its sheltering island all made a deep impression on the newcomers. The general concensus of opinion was that here was a new country for them. Up at dawn, they brought their cattle ashore, and each member of the party proceeded to the choice of a site for his future home. But the poor exiles had not figured on an obstacle in the person of the representative of the Hudson's Bay Company, who, alerted, and concerned with the rights of the Montagnais Indians, formally forbade them to erect any buildings on this land, Mingan being a Montagnais reservation. They had to submit, reload their belongings, and set sail again towards the unknown. Providentially, Father Arnaud was there. Possessing a thorough knowledge of this region over which he had travelled for some time, he consoled and encouraged them by assuring them that they would find, somewhere to the east, a suitable location. Heartened, they got ready and took the direction indicated, scanning the horizon and counting the islands and passages along the way. After having carefully examined "Betchuan" its coves, and all the surrounding coastline, they felt a moment of disappointment and harked back wistfully to their own Magdalen Islands. Then one of the women came forth with an inspiration : "Why wouldn't we choose the pretty site that we saw yesterday, halfway from Mingan, with the sandy point stretching out to sea and its harbour so well protected by islands?" This suggestion struck all the travellers as a sound one. The next day, June 10, the schooner dropped anchor in the suggested port. The village of Pointe-aux-Esquimaux was soon to rise. Everybody went to work immediately. The men hastily built a few log cabins with the trunks of trees cleared from the site, poor dwellings indeed, that the women left willingly in the evening to congregate at Firmin Boudreau's, chat of the day's events, and compare the broken skyline of the new country with the vast horizons and the blue waters of their native land.

One evening brought bad news : the *Mariner* was lost, thrown against the shoals of the Sheldrake River by the wind ! Nevertheless, the men did not remain idle. Fishing was good. The saintly Father Arnaud came from Mingan, eager to call on his new friends. He visited them in their poor dwellings and invited them to attend a mass which he proposed to sing the next day, feast of St. Peter, at Firmin Boudreau's house. Each and all were present, crowded in the small space, but attentive and reflective before the family table, which served as the altar. They entreated God to take possession of the new land and never more to withdraw the blessing brought by this devoted priest. In the evening, as a memento of this event, Father Arnaud caused a cross to be erected at the foot of the hill, on the site chosen for the future church, and consecrated the mission to St. Peter and St. Paul. This first public prayer had been listened to, for the fish abounded and the colony prospered.

As we hark back to the beginnings of each of the villages of the North Shore, although we do not have equally precise details as to the origin of each of them, unfortunately, why could we not imagine that events followed the same pattern ? Schooners similar to the *Mariner* were built at Pointe-aux-Esquimaux, Natashquan, and other places. They ventured out among the ice floes of the Gulf almost up to Newfoundland in search of seals, Hunting seals proved very profitable the first years and contributed greatly in encouraging these pioneers to stay at their outposts. In other places, they were content to hunt fur-bearing animals and fish for cod. Wherever it was possible, they captured salmon at the mouths of rivers where it was then very abundant.

All the villages west of Pointe-aux-Esquimaux, Long Point, Saint-Jean, Magpie, Rivière-au-Tonnerre, Dock, Sheldrake, Chaloupe, Rivière-aux-Graines, have had much the same beginnings.

In these communities, companies had fishing establishments where they would bring fishermen during the summer from Gaspé and the Baie-des-Chaleurs for the catching and drying of cod. At that time fishing was quite abundant in all these localities. That is why many of the fishermen, attracted by the beautiful catches made on the North Shore, decided to settle there. There was also a variety of sites from which one could contemplate at leisure, at all hours of the day, the waves of the sea, now calm, now agitated. Small harbours formed by the rivers offered fine shelter to the schooners. And so these fishermen settled all around this region, which seemed more attractive to them than their former homes on the South Shore. Here they followed their calling of the sea, happy to be free to work on their own account. They came from Grande-Rivière, Saint-Godefroy, Paspébiac, Caraquet, Lamecque, the Magdalen Islands. Some of the wide variety of names which they carried were : Méthot, Giasson, Vibert, Beaudin, Leblanc, Lebrun, Blaney, Cody, Poirier, Girard, Boulé, Chapados, Delarosbil. In 1881 the most important of these villages, Rivière-au-Tonnerre, was entirely destroyed by fire. How were these inhabitants, forced to seek refuge in sheds and in the boats of the harbour, able to keep their courage in the face of this terrible loss ? It was a time of great misery

THE PIONEERS 13

and great charity, all working together, in brotherly collaboration, to rebuild the village which quickly rose from its ruins.

When, in 1895, Henri Menier became the owner of Anticosti Island, he imposed a new way of life upon its inhabitants. He bought all the houses and cultivated land. He drove no one off, but all became his subjects and had to pay an annual tax to this new king. Fifteen families, the Bezeaus, Dignards, Noëls among them, wishing to regain the freedom they had enjoyed before his coming, emigrated to Rivière-au-Tonnerre and other localities.

Seven Islands is situated seventy miles west of this village. A few Acadians, Dominique Giasson, Édouard Vigneault, the Montignys, for instance, were attracted by the majestic beauty of the immense Bay around which the Lévesques, Brochus, Smiths, and others had already settled. A mere hamlet at first, Seven Islands rapidly became the most important settlement of the whole region.

Going up the Gulf to Sainte-Marguerite, Pointe-aux-Anglais, Îlets-à-Caribou, Pointe-des-Monts, one meets many families noted for their hospitality : the Thériaults, Langlois, Jourdains, Bilodeaux, Poulins, Labries, and Fafards. Father Alfred Poulin, a missionary of the North Shore since 1928, was born at Baie Trinité on March 2, 1902. As its pastor, he founded one of the finest parishes in Saguenay County.

At Pointe-des-Monts looms forth one of the oldest lighthouses of the Gulf. Built in 1830 under the English regime, it has always been considered as one of the most important to navigation. "The round and white form of the lighthouse stands out with pride and in relief against the background of the forest. Its light, which was placed in its upper story, was surrounded by a thick glass. Seventeen powerful lamps, each having a silver reflector, projected their rays in every direction for miles around." (Mme Fafard-Lacasse). A little farther up the Gulf, by the side of a splendid beach, in an enchanting and sunny site, the Labries, who gave the North Shore its present bishop, the Savards, Morins, Moreaus, and the Comeau brothers, one of whom was the celebrated Napoléon-Alexandre, have founded the most attractive of the Labradorian villages, Godbout. Then there is Pointe-aux-Outardes, which still remembers Jean-Baptiste and Ferdinand Ross, the Tremblays, Jeans, Malouins, Morins, Côtés, Maltais, and Hémons, all great hunters and fishermen and even farmers. Fifteen miles to the west, there is the famous hamlet of Betsiamites, the great Indian reservation, where a few Canadians lived continually and from which ventured forth so often the valiant and fearless mail carriers of a bygone era, David Miller, his sons Frank, Alexander, and Oscar, abetted by David Malouin.

We do not forget either the timber camps of Pentecost and Manicouagan, the industrial centres of that age, but so modest and so small compared to the modern town of Baie Comeau and the other camps opened later on.

Finally, there are the Montagnais posts, the most ancient of all, the same today as they were then, as we follow the North Shore from west to east : Betsiamites, Seven Islands, Moisie, Mingan, Natashquan, Muskuaro Romaine, and Saint Augustine.

We have given an all too brief and imperfect description of the principal villages which existed in 1903 on the immense and irregular North Shore of the Gulf of Saint Lawrence. The most stark solitude surrounded them. They were separated by the then enormous distances of ten, twenty, forty miles. It is easy to imagine what sorrows and worries beset the hearts and minds of these pioneers who had neither the airplane nor the radio to bring them the solace and comforts which we know today. It must be said that the isolation and its accompanying hardships have been made lighter for everybody by the remarkable spirit of Christian charity which has always prevailed on the North Shore. In all the villages one finds friendly cooperation and mutual help. The traveller, whoever he may be, wherever he may hail from, whatever the time of day or night he may knock on the door, is always assured of a hearty reception. Welcomed with a smile, invited to share the common fare, he is considered one of the family so long as circumstances prevent him from resuming his journey. It can only be hoped that this virtue, set above all others by Christ, will be always practised on the North Shore as well as it was by these early pioneers.

CHAPTER TWO

THE FIRST MISSIONARIES

Father Lecourtois, eudist. — Aunt Pélagie. — Father Ternet. Father Arnaud. — Father Nadeau. Father Villeneuve.

How did spiritual assistance reach the pioneers of the Gulf of Saint Lawrence?

It is a matter for surprise that, in these notes, whose purpose it is to retrace briefly the work of the Eudist Fathers on the North Shore, we are able to mention the name of a Eudist Father who preceded the contingent of 1903 by more than a hundred years.

On June 30, 1794, Bishop Hubert of Quebec wrote that four French priests had just arrived in the city. The oldest was only 31 while the youngest was 27. Their countenances radiated zeal and learning. One of them, François-Gabriel Lecourtois, went to the seminary temporarily. On September 28 of the same year, Father Lecourtois, who was then ministering to St. Vallier, was put in charge of the parish of St. Nicholas, on the south shore of the river. Four years later, Bishop Denaud sent him to Rimouski, granting him extraordinary powers over the region between Rimouski, Gaspé, and the King's Posts, the name by which the Indian settlements on the north shore of the St. Lawrence were known at that time.

THE FIRST MISSIONARIES 17

This Father Lecourtois was a Eudist, a former professor of philosophy at the seminary of Valognes in Normandy, who had fled to England in order to escape the revolution of 1793.

Is it not a source of joy and pride for the Eudist of 1946 to see a brother Eudist sent by the Bishop of Quebec to that difficult post, because of the bishop's conviction that he would exhibit the same zeal as at St. Nicholas and Rimouski?

On January 10, 1807, Father Lecourtois became the first resident pastor of La Malbaie. He built the church that is still standing there and had all the gold needed to decorate it sent from France. He also gave to this church an enormous lamp, a holy-water basin, a monstrance, and cruets, all in sterling silver. His former church of Rimouski equally received a lamp from him, a holy water basin, and cruets, also of sterling silver. As he had no relatives in Canada, he often said that is heirs would be God and the poor. During his life he gave 36,000 francs to the Seminary of Nicolet and left about an equal sum in the hands of insolvent debtors. While making his rounds of the King's Posts he used to cover the whole of the North Shore, braving the dangers of navigation on the river. When, for the first time, he visited Muskuaro, a village some 500 miles east of La Malbaie, he found a tribe of Montagnais there who had never yet seen a priest.

In a letter which he wrote to his bishop in 1805, he did not complain either of the fatigue or the physical sufferings attached to his ministry. He simply deprecated his inability to go to confession oftener than once a year. Bishop Plessis deemed it necessary to demand of him that he look after his health and take whatever care and precaution it might require.

Twenty-nine years of this hard apostolic labour brought him to the end of his journeys on the North Shore. Bishop Panet wrote in a letter (January 10, 1826) : "Father Lecourtois' health is rapidly deteriorating." He had to resign his duties and preoccupy himself solely with preparing himself for his heavenly reward. He died on May 21, 1828, at sixty-four years of age, and was buried in the church of St. Lawrence on the Isle of Orleans. Father Arthur Gallant, Eudist missionary of Sainte-Thérèse-du-Colombier, had the praiseworthy idea of preserving the memory of his presence on the North Shore on a commemorative plaque in the chapel of the Jérémie Islands. It reminds one of this glorious predecessor of the Eudist Fathers of 1903, worthy emulator, also, of many Jesuit missionaries, who were the first apostles among the Montagnais, and again of their successors, the Oblate Fathers.

It would be very difficult, in this modest work, to draw a complete picture of the religious history of the very first years. A report on the missions of Quebec, written in March 1864, notes that Father Parent was named missionary of Mingan and St. Augustine in 1770 and of Romaine in 1773. Father Parent died at Natashquan on April 7, 1784 and was buried there.

From 1820 to 1852, that part of the North Shore which stretches from Belle-Isle to the Saint-Jean River was under the jurisdiction of the Bishop of Newfoundland. There were no resident priests before the advent of Father Théberge who, in 1883, spent the winter at Anse-des-Dunes in the old Labadie homestead. Nevertheless, priests from the South Shore did not hesitate to

THE FIRST MISSIONARIES 19

cross the Gulf aboard the little sailing schooners of the times whenever their presence was required on the North Shore. Thus, in 1847, Father Desruisseaux sailed from the Baie-des-Chaleurs with a large group of Acadian fishermen in a schooner under the command of Captain Woodings. They reached the harbour of Kégashka on June 13. Everybody there attended Sunday mass said by this missionary and served by Pierre Thibodeau. From that date on, priests from the Magdalen Islands or from the Gaspé peninsula visited this district every year. The Oblate Fathers, who had been looking after the Montagnais for many years, did not neglect the Canadians that they came by within their orbit of ministry. Annually, during the summer, they visited them several times.

Again in 1859, Father Charpenay conducted a mission at Esquimaux Point and concluded it with a temperance crusade which met with much success. In many villages, men or women substituted for the absent priest by reciting the beads at the hour of the mass. At Esquimaux Point, one pious lady, known to everybody as Aunt Pélagie, deserves having her memory kept alive. The conversion and baptism of Charles Lebrun, originally from Jersey, were due to this zealous Christian. The people who had known her used to say that she was their pastor. Every evening she would assemble her "parishioners" at Madoise's for the beads and other prayers. On Sundays there was more solemnity. Her face, then radiant with sincere piety beneath her unpretentious hood, impressed even the most heedless. She would lead the congregation in the singing of the *Kyrie*, the *Gloria*, and the Vespers, ending with the sailor's favorite hymn :

> Chère Dame de la Garde,
> Soutenez de vos bras,
> Et nos vergues et nos mâts.
> Fortifiez le bordage,
> Les câbles et les haubans,
> Pour faire tête à l'orage.
> Conservez à tous moments,
> Tous nos pauvres bâtiments,
> Conservez-nous l'artimon,
> La boussole et le timon. *

During the evening, after the religious side had been taken care of, the singing continued with all the old songs from Marseilles, such as the tragic ballad of St. Alexis, of St. Suzanne, all naive and touching songs that tend to disappear today. They even sang war songs like *The capture of Sebastopol.*

> Marchons, marchons
> Au son du clairon,
> Soldats, soldats,
> Livrons le combat. **

---

* Dear Mistress of the Sea,
 Sustain with thine arms,
 Both our yards and our masts.
 Strengthen the bulwarks,
 The ropes, and the shrouds,
 To withstand the spiteful storms.
 Protect at all hours,
 All our poor vessels.
 Keep safe the mizen-masts,
 The helm, and the compass.
** March, march,
 To the sound of the bugle,
 Soldiers, soldiers,
 Let us fight the battle.

SCENIC GRANDEUR

Photo Paul Provancher

*Msgr. F.-X. BOSSÉ,
first Apostolic Prefect of the North Shore, 1882-1892*

THE FIRST MISSIONARIES 21

These examples of deep religiousness and good Christian living help us to understand the scene related by Father Huard in his book, *Labrador and Anticosti*.

In the fall of 1860, many fishermen from Esquimaux Point travelled to Quebec to sell the season's catch of fish and buy provisions for the winter. Meeting a priest on the street whose edifying appearance inspired them with confidence, they asked him if he would hear their confessions. The priest replied that he was a stranger in the city, that he had just come from the missions of Upper Canada and was on his way back to his native France. His place on the boat was already reserved and paid for, and his luggage, moreover, had been brought aboard the vessel, which was to sail on the morrow. Nevertheless, he was willing to confess them, he said, provided they would accompany him to the archbishop's palace, where he would ask for the necessary jurisdiction. His Excellency the Bishop, moved by the justifiable complaints of these poor fishermen, prevailed over Father Ternet in winning him over to their cause. This priest, instead of returning to his native land aboard the comfortable steamer, sailed for the unknown solitudes of the North Shore aboard a fishing schooner. The first boats returning from Quebec announced the good news. Father Ternet was to become the first resident pastor of Esquimaux Point, where he remained for two years.

The North Shore depended on the diocese of Quebec until 1867. In that year, it fell under the jurisdiction of the bishop of Rimouski. The resident missionary of Esquimaux Point took charge of Anticosti Island and all the posts comprised between his parish and

Seven Islands. The villages between Seven Islands and Pointe-des-Monts received an annual visit from the Oblate Fathers, the missionaries of the Montagnais. They made the rounds every winter, wearing snowshoes, and preceded by two men to beat the trail and carry the portable altar. These journeys were surely long and hard ones for them.

If we except Tabatière, Natashquan, and Esquimaux Point, the post of Moisie was the only one on the North Shore to possess resident missionaries before the prefecture was established. This privilege was due to the exploitation of its iron mines by Lamotte and Viger, and later on by the Molson Company.

The Church is too vigilant a mother to abandon any of her children. Bishop Langevin of Rimouski was the first bishop to make a pastoral visit over all of the North Shore[1]. In 1875, he sailed in a schooner along most of the coast, encouraging the missionaries, blessing several new chapels, even confirming a man 99 years of age. Exhausted from this wearisome journey, he convinced his colleagues in the episcopate of the difficulty of properly administrating this territory, which was virtually cut off from the outside world during the winter. Negotiations finally brought results in 1882. The North Shore was then constituted into an apostolic prefecture with Father F.-X. Bossé, a pastor of the Gaspé Peninsula as its titular head. The following year, Father Bossé was raised to the dignity of a Roman Prelate. The son of a teacher, ordained since 1863, matured by a long experience in the ministry and

---

[1] Bishop Mullock of Newfoundland had already visited Blanc Sablon in 1852, and Bishop Baillargeon of Quebec had gone as far as Mingan in 1853.

THE FIRST MISSIONARIES

in missionary work, vigorous in health, a man of talent and of a real evangelical spirit, Monsignor Bossé was ideally suited for the difficult task that was entrusted to him. He set himself to work with great zeal and an almost feverish activity. For ten years he laboured unceasingly to organize and develop his spiritual domain. His outstanding achievement was the creation of primary teaching in his prefecture, and to this he devoted all his care and attention from the very first. For a time, he entertained the idea of opening a seminary and even had lessons given to some young men. Mgr Ross, the future bishop of Gaspé, was one of these. But the life of adventurous liberty of the fisherman is not very compatible with the necessary discipline of studies : Mgr Bossé had to give up his project. He also realized how precarious and uncertain is a recruited foreign personnel and so diverted his attention and drive to founding a boarding-school for girls. In spite of all the difficult transactions to be made, the obstacles and delays to be overcome, the cares and extra work it imposed on him, he succeeded in establishing his boarding-school and getting nuns to take charge of it, the Grey Nuns, the only sisters who "overcame the terror inspired in Quebec and vicinity by the very name of Labrador, a wild and isolated land." The nuns would educate good wives and mothers, a real, a salutary piece of progress.

It is often said that the Church has made French Canada what it is by preserving its faith, its language, its customs, and its traditions. This axiom is true even on the North Shore, due to the diligent and now uninterrupted labour of its bishops and priests who devote themselves to the salvation of souls, valiantly seconded by missionary sisters. In 1892, however, Mgr Bossé still lacked the necessary personnel. After ten years of hard work, finding it impossible to recruit a greatly desired clergy, he retired and ceded his prefecture to the diocese of Chicoutimi. From 1892 to 1903, Bishop Labrecque very actively looked after the North Shore. Thrice he travelled over the whole of this territory, gave it priests, and left a memory of his kindness and devotion that still remains. The account written by the celebrated companion of his travels, Father Huard, in *Labrador and Anticosti* is still read with interest. It was Bishop Labrecque's suggestion to the Holy See that this territory be entrusted to a religious congregation which could assure a regular religious service.

Although we do not propose, in these Recollections, to retrace the complete history of these years of activity on the North Shore before the arrival of the Eudists, a beautiful history for the priests who succeeded one another on the North Shore at the request either of the Labradorians or of their bishops, it is a particular pleasure to recall two names, that of Father Nadeau, missionary at Magpie from 1888 to 1894, and Father Villeneuve, pastor of Seven Islands from 1896 to 1903. Father Nadeau has remained among the most famous of these missionaries. He was a practical, energetic, resourceful man. He always drove his own dog team and did not balk before long trips on foot or on snowshoes. During the summer, he captained a little schooner used for the service of the missions. Long Point owes him its first chapel, built in 1889, and Rivière-au-Tonnerre its second chapel built in 1891. An oft-told anecdote, typical of this country, illustrates the charity and love of souls of this missionary. The

THE FIRST MISSIONARIES

Count of Puyjalon, having withdrawn himself to Île-à-la-Chasse, in a solitary tent which had become weather-proof by the icy snow which adhered to it, "was relishing the strange happiness of feeling alone in the woods", as he expressed himself, "far from fools and especially from those who pass as wits". A terrible blizzard was raging above the woods where he was camped, "crushing with its furious gusts of wind, the tops of spruces already laden with snow and ice." No man used to the north country would have dared start out on a trip that night. Yet, that very day, Father Nadeau had suddenly left his rectory at Magpie for an unknown reason. Forty-five miles lay between him and his destination as he set out with snowshoes through the thick snow that continued to fall. Overtaken by nightfall while he was on his way, he stopped to build a fire "which roasts you on one side while you freeze on the other" and slept under the open sky. Finally, during the second night of this dangerous journey, he stumbled heavily into the tent of the Count of Puyjalon. The following dialogue was narrated by the Count : —

—" 'What ! Is it you ?'

—" 'Of course it is I,' answered my pastor, for it was indeed he.

— " 'Are you coming to hunt in my trapline ?'

— " 'No, I am making my rounds.'

— " 'Your rounds !' I thought he had lost his mind.

— " 'I'm hungry,' he said, 'would you have anything good to eat ?'

— " 'I have some rabbit and partridge, even a trout, if you'd prefer that, and a bit of good whiskey.'

— "I began to prepare the meal," continues the Count, "and while the partridge was cooking, and the water boiling for the tea, I gazed upon my friend who had fallen asleep on my bed of spruce boughs."

After a few moments of rest, Father Nadeau took the food that was offered him, then smoked his pipe. The Count rolled a cigarette, and dared question him a second time as to the reason for this unexpected visit. His answer was evasive, he spoke about how much he would have liked to go on a hunting trip with his friend. Unfortunately, a Montagnais woman whom he named, was desperately ill in Mingan. "She may do the great portage, I'd have to be there," he said. The following morning, after breakfast, he started on his way back, walking with difficulty through the soft snow in which his snowshoes sank six to eight inches. A month after, the Count discovered the answer to the enigma. A hunter stopped on his way to bring him a letter from the post office of Long Point. Madame de Puyjalon expressed her worry therein and inquired after the health of her husband. There had been a rumour throughout the province that the illustrious hermit of the north had been stricken down by a serious illness in his lonely tent in the distant forest. His pastor, also, had heard the bad news. And that is why one day, alone, without any equipment other than a hunting axe, without sufficient provisions, he had braved the distance and the frightful weather, risking his life so as to bring divine consolations to this solitary soul. Having found him in good health, he had left him without telling him the reason for that heroic undertaking. Now one can well understand the final word of the Count of Puyjalon in this affair : "I think of him sometimes, when the thick snow falls and the wind bends the trees of the forest ; then my eyes become moist."

THE FIRST MISSIONARIES 27

Fortunately for us, Father Victor Tremblay has recorded from his interview with Father Abraham Villeneuve incidents which paint an admirable picture of the life of the missionaries on the North Shore before 1903. Father Villeneuve spent one year on Anticosti Island and, in 1895, replaced Father Maltais at Seven Islands. Four missions fell to his care : Seven Islands, Moisie, Sainte-Marguerite, and Les Jambons. To reach Sainte-Marguerite, a varied route then lay before the traveller : nine miles by water, one mile of portage, and five miles on foot on the beach. "We did not find it long," said Father Villeneuve, "we were used to long distances on the North Shore." Ten times a year, while awaiting construction of the first chapel, he sought hospitality at Mr. Thériault's, the lifelong friend of the missionaries. Seven Islands took up seven months of his time ; and Moisie, the remaining five months. These communities are eighteen miles apart, and did not have very many white people, but the Montagnais frequently had recourse to Father Villeneuve for christenings, visits to the sick, and burials. Thus, this courageous priest often made use of the dog sled and snowshoes and undertook long trips on foot, thereby courting danger. "During my nine years of sojourn on the North Shore," he stated, "I have had numerous accidents, the principal causes of which were cold, imprudence, or poor guides. I have been many times in danger of death and am consequently very grateful to Divine Providence for the protection afforded me."

Father Villeneuve was an outstanding builder. Sainte-Marguerite owes him its first chapel. At Moisie, he finished the pastor's humble dwelling and gave

Seven Islands a church and a rectory. He deserves our gratitude for having so well prepared the way for the Eudist Fathers who, in 1903, became the successors of these valiant priests from Chicoutimi.

CHAPTER THREE

FIRST CONTACTS OF THE EUDISTS WITH THE NORTH SHORE

Departure from France. — Rimouski. — On board the *King Edward*. — Eudist Fathers at work. Daring oarsmen. — The whistle of death.

O<small>N</small> the morning of August 18, 1903, twenty-nine Eudists, about to sail for Canada, assembled at the Eudist headquarters in Paris. It was the day of leave-taking from the spiritual family and of that kind of joy and peace that no persecution can take away from priestly souls obsessed only with the idea of a Paradise to be gained. The following day, August 19, which was the feast of the Venerable Jean Eudes, after having celebrated holy mass, they exchanged their robes for the habit of a clergyman and then departed. At Dieppe, the moment came for the final goodbye to their native France where they first saw the light of day and which some of them were never to see again.

Could not these exiles have said, with even greater truth than the great outcast of 1815 : "A few traitors less, my beloved country, and you would still be a great nation ?"

After crossing the English Channel, they made a pleasant trip through England, got a glimpse of the vast capital city of London, and embarked at Liverpool on the *Tunisian*, a ship of more than 10,000 gross tons and capable of sixteen miles per hour, the largest steamer, the floating city of that era. The crossing of the sea was a new experience to them all, and it was a fine voyage during which "the wide Atlantic rocked them in the folds of its azure mantle." The spiritual exercises of the Congregation were faithfully observed. On Sunday there was a general reunion of Catholics around this numerous clergy, and as the angry waves prevented the priests from celebrating mass, they recited prayers in common and chanted the *Credo*, the *Ave Maris Stella*, and a stirring hymn. During a charity concert, which was a tradition of all oceanic crossings, one of the missionaries sang French songs that were warmly applauded.

On August 26, the twenty-nine missionaries beheld with joy the hospitable land of Canada to which Providence had led them, and in the afternoon of this memorable day, they disembarked from the *Tunisian* and landed on the wharf of Rimouski. Father Blanche, who had preceded his comrades into Canada by a few months and has found for each of them some field of apostolic activity, awaited them with a happy and hearty welcome. All the passengers stood on the footbridge, looking with an amused curiosity at these Catholic priests, wearing clergymen's clothes, still surprised to see themselves thus apparelled, and experiencing very understandable emotions upon setting foot on this unknown land. Trunks and suitcases greeted them in one big heap on the landing ! Some of them were even sent to the wrong destinations and reached their proprietors but several months later. In 1946, the survivors of the group could still recall having spent part of the night sorting out their belongings and trying to bring some order out of this jumble. Furthermore, many of them had received from their Very Reverend Father Le Doré an obedience that Father Blanche felt obliged to change.

It was this Father's task to indicate to each member of the party his itinerary for the next day. Some were to go to Valleyfield, others to Woonsocket and to the Dakotas in the U.S.A., to Sainte-Anne-de-la-Pointe-de-l'Église in Nova Scotia, to Tobique in N.B., Fathers Leventous and Le Guyader to Chicoutimi. As for the twelve first Labradorians, it was understood that they would leave the following day aboard the little steamer *King Edward* for the North Shore of the St. Lawrence. This huge territory, as has been explained, stretches from south of the Portneuf River to Blanc-Sablon, a distance of seven hundred and nine miles. Fifty villages of varying importance, built along the shores of the Gulf of St. Lawrence, shared at that time a population of nine thousand Catholics, of which twelve hundred were Montagnais. These villages, frequently built on the banks of rivers with either narrow or exceedingly wide mouths were sometimes separated from one another by enormous distances and obstacles of all kinds. One still meets with lowlands and swamps, bleakly bare or thickly wooded mountains of all shapes and dimensions, and here and there, beaches of fine sand. Thus, in sailing along the coast a traveller can admire a very appreciable diversity of scenes, both picturesque and imposing.

On August 27, 1903, the caravan of twelve missionaries wended its way towards the North Shore under the direction of Vicar General Gendron, a former pastor of Esquimaux Point and an excellent guide, whose advice and information about the country were of the greatest value to everyone in the party. The steamboat's stop was at English Bay not far from Baie-Comeau, which is so well-known today. The crossing from the south to the north shore had been ideal, and on the way the passengers sang the *Ave Maris Stella*, the *Ave Maria* and songs by Botrel !

The moment to disband was now at hand. The *King Edward* dropped anchor at a short distance from the shore. Immediately a little tug belonging to the company, which was exploiting timber for sawing at Manicouagan, drew near the steamer to receive the expected missionaries, Fathers Auguste Brézel and Louis Garnier, and to take provisions aboard for the lumber camp six miles away. It is difficult to describe the feelings of these missionaries. A great sadness pervaded their whole being. Was it because of the last handshake given to their comrades, from whom they felt suddenly cut off, or because of this new solitude, which now enveloped them on all sides? Not a single house around this huge bay ! All one could see was spruce and firs, surrounded by mountains also covered with the same sylvan species of evergreens. The two newcomers remained taciturn all the way. Captain Gaudreau and the mechanic Pascal Martel, who later became their fast friends, must have had a poor opinion of their future eloquence !

The boat turned into the vast estuary of the Manicouagan River, and everywhere the same landscape presented itself to them, made even more sombre by the approaching darkness. This dismal sight, so new to both of them, depressed them. Finally, two hours after having left the *King Edward*, they set foot on the tiny pier of Manicouagan. The first trustee of the mission, Abel Martel, welcomed them, took charge of their suitcases, and led them to the hill, which dominated the river and the thirty houses of the settlement, and on which were built the rectory and a small unfinished chapel. He seemed very happy to meet two French priests and was a little surprised to see Father Brézel, whose cassocks had been sent to the U.S., dressed as a clergyman ! Abel Martel they soon perceived, was a man just like those they knew in Rennes or Fougerolles ! The ice was broken ! The missionaries recovered their faculty of speech. They had become the missionaries of Manicouagan and of the neighbouring villages !

Although the new country bore no resemblance to any part of France, the people reminded them of the best of their native Frenchmen. Father St. Gelais welcomed them with open arms, introduced them to the principal personalities of the village and made them more familiar with the topography of the new territory which they would have to travel over.

The following day Fathers Nonorgues and Laizé were greeted at the wharf of Pentecost. They were favourably impressed by the activity of the regular labourers and lumbermen, who were working at the prosperous lumber camp. The village was built on a graduated slope, on the side of a long green hill. Two beautiful rivers flowed leisurely, one above and the other at the foot of one of the most picturesque hamlets on the North Shore.

At Seven Islands, where they found a valiant predecessor of the Eudist Fathers, Father Abraham Villeneuve, Fathers Conan and Brochard were entranced with the magnificent bay which spread itself before their eyes, this immense harbour, which could accomodate the whole of His Majesty's British Navy. Already, a sizeable group of Canadians and Acadians, all good-natured, gay, and polite folk, had built trim dwellings along the shore. Hard by, about five hundred Montagnais were living in that enchanting site that had long been their home.

That locality will always remain a favourite with the missionaries throughout the years.

At Rivière-au-Tonnerre the reception for the Fathers proved enthusiastic and full of surprises. On Sunday, August 30, around four o'clock in the afternoon, small boats sauntered out to meet Fathers Robin and Louis Héry, and from each of them, volleys of shots were fired as a salute. It is said that Father Pihan, an ex-African soldier, famous among his comrades, seized an old breech-loading rifle, which he had brought with an eye to future hunting trips, and answered these marks of rejoicing with powerful detonations from the ancient firearm. But once ashore, a few disillusionments lay in the wake of the joyful arrival.

Entering into the rectory, the new occupants found it entirely empty. Wine and wafers were lacking for mass ! Father Blanche ordered supplies, and Father Robin also made a few purchases in order to remedy the general penury that awaited him. There was an extraordinary hustle and bustle about the village when this discovery was made. Fortunately, Father Gendron, aware of this local scarcity, had requisitioned wine from Seven Islands and had asked two Sisters, who were on the boat, to make some wafers. A generous hospitality was tendered to the Fathers by a family, and some kind ladies furnished sheets and blankets for the expected beds. Finally, as all the rooms of the rectory were filled to the ceiling with articles, which were being brought continually from the boat, Father Robin decided to set himself up as a merchant of beds, mattresses, furniture, dishes, and kitchen utensils. The good Father must have been quite amused at this unexpected vocation, but he was quite annoyed at another turn of events. While packing in Paris, somebody had the bright idea of packing all the cassocks in a common trunk. Would his cassocks and those of his colleague ever reach them? That long remained a subject of discussion at the rectory.

Twelve miles east of Rivière-au-Tonnerre is Magpie, a striking village built along an abrupt cliff and protected by a section of the Laurentians. Fifty houses, surrounded by gardens that were still green and shrubs yellowed by autumn, were then the dwellings of the most venturesome fishermen of the North Shore.

This mission, one of the oldest, was entrusted to Fathers Étienne and Joseph Gallix, one, an uncle, the other, his nephew.

The people were very happy to welcome the two missionaries. But, alas! there, also, the rectory was bare! The first meals were taken at Albert Dupuis'. The indispensable furniture and linen were borrowed. As the far-sighted Father Blanche had shipped to each mission a barrel of the most urgently needed supplies, adding a five-dollar bill, they were able to use this precious reserve until the arrival of the fishermen, who graciously offered some of their catch to their missionaries.

Soon after, the younger of the two, who was known everywhere as Father Joseph, received the order to leave for the neighbouring mission of Saint-Jean so as to assure this village, as well as Long Point, a more regular religious service.

Fathers Pottier, and François Hesry arrived at Esquimaux Point on October 30 at one o'clock in the morning. Father Tremblay, the church wardens, and a goodly number of parishioners were waiting on the pier to greet the newcomers, who did not feel particularly loquacious at that hour of the night, but were pleasantly surprised to see, when daylight broke, British flags flying from every mast of the village. Father Pottier sang mass in the church, and Father Hesry in the chapel of the beautiful convent.

Father Gendron accompanied the last two of the twelve missionaries right up to Natashquan, one of the first fishing stations chosen by the Acadians from the Magdalen Islands in 1854. The first meeting with Father Dufour and the parishioners was very encouraging. How easy it would be for the missionaries to get along with a population that was particularly honest, thrifty, pious, and devoted to its priests! Upon his return from Natashquan, Father Gendron, who liked hunting and was very familiar with the neighbourhood, invited Father Hesry on a hunting trip that was crowned with success. Father Hesry — who would have believed it? — killed two young inexperienced seagulls, and Father Gendron brought back a wild duck and a half dozen terns. The birds were carefully prepared and served at the first meal. They looked superb, a beautiful golden brown in colour, but detestable in taste. " Our young boys ", wrote

THE EUDIST FATHERS IN 1908:

1st row: Rev. Fr. Savary. Bishop G. Blanche, Rev. Frs. L. LeDoré. A. Divet
2nd row: Rev. Frs. E. Jandret. Delanoe, E. Gallix. G. Blondel, P. Brochard
3rd row: Rev. Frs. J.-M. Locintoux, A. Brézel. R. Kerdelhué. L. Héry. F. Hesry. J. LeStrat

Father Pottier, "lay snares in the forest and on the islands, and every morning they come back loaded with rabbits." For ten cents, two persons can enjoy a rabbit stew. More experienced hunters would bring in a fine wild duck and an eleven pound bustard.

Thus the twelve new missionaries took over the posts to which they had been assigned and, in a general way, under favourable auspices.

Two of the missionaries, Fathers Travers and Robin soon went to Baie-Sainte-Claire on Anticosti Island. A little later, Father Hesry accepted a transfer from his beloved Rivière-au-Tonnerre to Blanc-Sablon, where he was to spend twenty-one years of solitude in that immense territory.

One can easily imagine what their occupations were. They exercised their ordinary ministry at the principal mission where their residence had been established. Every Sunday in each of these localities, the ordinary offices, mass and vespers, were performed. Moreover, many took advantage of that day to assemble the children for catechism, to preside over the reunions of congregations, the Sacred Heart League, the Ladies' Society of St. Anne, the Children of Mary, etc. The villages that had no resident pastor were visited one by one by the missionaries, quite regularly so until 1918, when the Congregation had to recall half of the personnel, leaving in most missions only one Father. Visits to the lumber camps required a more or less lengthy absence, depending on the number of camps on their territory.

Everywhere, the ministry was discharged with zeal and regularity. Never was a call from the sick left without an answer, even though sometimes enormous distance (fifty, even sixty miles) separated the Labradorian rectory from the far-off mission.

In addition to this consoling and interesting ministry among devout and devoted parishioners, almost everywhere manual work was necessary. They had to cut firewood in the forest, saw it into a convenient length, build simple, rustic fences around the garden, clear some land, or construct some system to bring water up to the rectory, such as the amusing funicular conveyance devised at Manicouagan for hauling up a few pails of water. One curate dug a well thirty feet deep with only a rope, a windlass, and ordinary pails for equipment, and mobilized his arms and those of the school children for help. A vegetable garden was a necessity everywhere, as the big towns were distant, the funds very limited, and vegetables so necessary to one's health. Then there was the good example to be given to others. The Honourable A. Taschereau, former Prime Minister of the Province of Quebec, wrote to one of the Fathers these words of praise concerning Father Divet, who was for twenty-seven years pastor of Seven Islands : "I have met many of your colleagues on the North Shore, Father Divet, in particular, who was always busy with the care of souls and of his garden !"

Some of the missionaries were young, inexperienced, little prepared for the type of travelling that awaited them. This North Shore was so different from their old and beautiful France ! Sometimes, the parishioners found them too daring and imprudent. For example, one can read this in the *Écho du Labrador*[1]

---

[1] *Écho du Labrador*, Eudist bulletin that gave news of the labours of the missionaries, served as an agent of contact among them, and was published during their first years on the North Shore.

FIRST CONTACTS... 39

November, 1903 : "With the authorization of my pastor, I left one Saturday at eleven in the morning to hold a mission at Pointe-aux-Outardes. Three young men readied a boat, and in an hour we reached the other shore of the Manicouagan. The residents, including Mr. and Mrs. Lebel, stood aghast at learning that I had made up my mind to travel on foot the twenty-one miles of beach that stretched before me. Out of pity, an old lame horse was harnessed for me. Six miles farther, at the Chouinards, a young man offered to accompany me. I refused, saying that I had walked considerable distance before... All went well until about six in the evening. The sea was at low tide, the little rivers easily crossed. But suddenly, the time I had been gone seemed long, very long, and there seemed to be no end to my road... A sudden thought dismayed me with the approach of night. I had been told that I risked passing Pointe-aux-Outardes without seeing its houses, that I was being imprudent. At "Grosse-Pointe", I came across a fresh path. A very narrow trail made by animals led up into the forest. I began following it and very soon lost my way in the woods. Frantically I tried to find my way back to the beach, a long, hard, endless search... Finally I got to it, weak, worn out, a nervous wreck, and alarmed to discover that some precious books, that I had been carrying under my arm, had disappeared. Being once again in the open, I recovered my wits and continued my journey with courage. At last, around nine o'clock in the evening, an opening appeared leading from the beach up the hill, a road, a real one this time, that brought me straight to the house of Alexander Tremblay. One can imagine the surprise of the family at the sight of this new missionary, whom they welcomed and cheered up as best they could." Nightmares have often recalled to this missionary that it would have been more prudent for him to have accepted the services of a good guide in such unfamiliar territory. Nevertheless, not satisfied with this memorable journey, the same missionary got the idea that a bicycle would be a good mode of travel on the wide beaches. By coincidence, there was a good whell for sale, perhaps that of a discouraged cyclist. The purchase was made. Alas ! two trips, during which adverse winds made the vehicle useless, and the narrowness of a track, which the soft sand made quite resistant, convinced the too ardent cyclist that it was best to give up that mode of locomotion. Would it not be more advisable to turn to water travel and use a boat equipped with good oars and a sail to take advantage of a favourable wind ? All the Eudist missionaries have had occasion to familiarize themselves with this manner of boat travel with oars and sail.

At Mistassini, a tiny outpost situated sixteen miles from Manicouagan, the only inhabitant of the place had not seen a missionary for four years. Even though I was uncertain as to which mission he belonged to, Pentecost or Manicouagan, I decided one day to try the adventure. A young man, one of my pupils to whom I was giving a few lessons, offered to accompany me. The mission's boat, a beautiful new one, was ready, and we departed. All went well at first, so long as we stayed in the river's estuary. But, as we progressed into the open waters of the Baie-des-Anglais, the vastness of the waters surrounding our frail vessel and the threat of a possible storm set out hearts pounding. We

FIRST CONTACTS... 41

rowed with all our might and succeeded in reaching shore, at Michel Hémon's, just in time, and with perspiration streaming down our faces. This gallant hermit received us in a very friendly manner, but as he did not particularly appreciate company, I understood from certain hints of his that it would be better if we could leave the next day after mass. That morning I tasted smoked seal meat, and, after a cup of tea, rowed as fast as I could to round the neighbouring cape and then skim along, all sails aloft, through the Baie-des-Anglais. But there it was impossible to continue... We spent the night in a camp that was strategically situated for us. The next day, we completed our journey very smoothly by hugging the shore back to the mission. I was proud of having covered a distance of thirty miles rowing a boat, and later on I liked to boast about this feat of my younger days.

Father Le Strat, missionary at Manicouagan from 1905 to 1907, who admired this feat, was the protagonist of an even more spectacular adventure :

Théophile Jean, merchant at Rivière-aux-Vases (Ragueneau today), fell from a ladder one day and lost consciousness. He so frightened the people around him that they sent a telegram summoning a missionary from Manicouagan. The younger of the two, Father Le Strat, was designated to answer the call. As the men were all working at the lumber camp, it was difficult to obtain a guide or companion. How was he going to get across the thirty miles of sea ? Would it not be better to stop overnight in one of the few houses along the way and put off until the next day the second half of the trip ? But it was a matter of assisting the sick ; nothing could stop the missionary. Father Le

Strat took a few sandwiches and a bottle of fresh water, hurried through the village, and set off in his canoe, rowing as hard as he could. After a few minutes' stop at Mrs. Lebel for light refreshment, he continued on his solitary way, following the shore. Without stop or rest he covered the twenty-one miles between Pointe Lebel and Pointe-aux-Outardes. Meanwhile, Louis Tremblay had left Rivière-aux-Vases in a boat also, to meet the Father. He waited for a long time on the sandy beach of Pointe-aux-Outardes, uneasily pacing up and down. At eleven o'clock in the evening, he suddenly heard a shrill mysterious whistle coming from the open sea and echoing over the waves. Louis Tremblay was terrified : "It is the whistle of death," he said to himself and began praying for the repose of the soul of his friend, who had died without receiving the last rites ! Just then Alexander Tremblay arrived to welcome Father Le Strat and invite him to his home for a brief rest, if he so desired He, also, had heard the sinister recurring whistle. "Ah !" he exclaimed, "that's Father Le Strat, he can't be far" . . . and he shouted at the top of his voice to show the Father that somebody was waiting for him on the beach. The whistle of death !... Come now !... It was only Father Le Strat whistling through his fingers to let them know he was there !

Later this dear comrade was fond of relating the story of the whistle of death and of teasing the too superstitious Louis Tremblay about his nocturnal scare. That particular evening, though, was no time for banter. The Father ate a sandwich, took a drink straight from his bottle of fresh water, and took his place in Louis Tremblay's boat. At Rivière-aux-

Vases, everything was under control. Théophile Jean had recovered from his momentary lapse of consciousness. In the morning he assisted at the mass that was said in his house and received communion with the other members of his family, thanking God for the protection with which He had favoured him. That day, the missionary rested himself at Pointe-aux-Outardes. The following morning he returned, winning a bet that he had made before leaving with the people of the locality, who were sure that he would be stopped by the low tide at "Petites-Rivières" and forced to spend the night in the open on the shores of the Gulf of St. Lawrence... He was able to get across by going sufficiently out towards the sea and was back that same evening in the rectory of Manicouagan, tired, but happy in the sense of having fulfilled a duty and successfully accomplished a hazardous journey.

How many similar instances could not be recalled, if the missionaries had not been too prone to hide their most praiseworthy actions and to look upon as very ordinary undertakings what seem to us well-nigh impossible!

One can read the following in the *Écho du Labrador* of December 1, 1903: "The missionaries had the pleasure of receiving, this very first fall, the visit of the Reverend Father Gustave Blanche, Provincial of the Eudists, recently named Apostolic Prefect." It was a joyful event for all to see this good Father who, from then on, devoted himself exclusively to his new country.

The entire North Shore rejoiced, and everywhere the warmest welcome was extended to him. The people were eager to make the acquaintance of the "new

Monsignor" and tendered him tokens of the most sincere respect and highest consideration. In spite of the brevity and intimate character of this first visit, the Reverend Father was everywhere received with the highest honours. After a few days at Natashquan with the dauntless Fathers Pihan and Divet, he went to Esquimaux Point where Father Pottier was proud to show him around his well-organized mission. A short stay at Magpie allowed him to ascertain, in contrast, the less well-favoured state of that post. Then, for lack of a boat, he had to remain three weeks in Rivière-au-Tonnerre, where the excellent Father Hesry had just taken charge, succeeding Father Robin, whose stentorial voice was now supplementing the powerful church "organ" of Esquimaux Point.

Seven Islands at last welcomed the venerated Visitor, who was amazed at the activities of this city of the future.

Pentecost pleased him with its modest yet enchanting appearance. Only our rather shabby dwelling detracted from the first favourable impression. Eight days were spent in studying present conditions and elaborating plans for the future; then, after keeping the presses of the *Écho du Labrador* busy with his first prefectoral circular, he left us, well pleased and with good memories of his trip, to return to Chicoutimi, where he had taken up domicile.

In this first journey, Father Blanche had guided the nuns of Kermaria, the Daughters of Jesus, who had left France for Canada, driven to exile, like so many other Congregations, by the persecution of Combes. They, also, were gratefully welcomed by the entire population. To have nuns in all the more important villages teaching school, looking after the rectory, seeing to the decoration of church and altar, taking care of the vestments, what an unexpected blessing for all the North Shore !

Heartened by this visit of their Father, guided by his advice for the task to be accomplished, the missionaries set to work with renewed ardor.

Each one devoted himself to his post, without aspiring for any other, looking upon this North Shore as their country to which they must give the best of themselves for the good of souls and the greater glory of God, as worthy followers of Saint Jean Eudes.

We shall see them at work throughout these recollections. We shall see them, in particular, deeply interested in the livelihood of the majority of the people on the North Shore, namely, fishing and hunting, whose economic importance in the Gulf of St. Lawrence district accounts for the following two chapters.

CHAPTER FOUR

FISHING

Seals. -- Cod. -- Porpoises. -- Caplin.

FISHING is what mainly attracted to the North Shore of the Gulf of St. Lawrence the valiant Canadians, Acadians, and Newfoundlanders who became its first inhabitants.

The Count of Puyjalon, the "Man of Labrador", whose life and activities have been so admirably recorded by Damase Potvin in his absorbing book, *Puyjalon, le Solitaire de l'Île-à-la-Chasse*, travelled during many years all over the North Shore. Time and again he visited every corner of this territory and went up all the rivers in his canoe and by portage. He discovered that salmon were to be found in every one of them and that they travelled very far up those rivers where they were able to jump the falls. The accounts he wrote and the remarkable reports he made attracted public notice. Fishing permits authorizing individuals to spread nets in the mouths of these rivers and along the neighbouring banks at distances specified by the Department of Maritime Fisheries were thereafter more freely granted. Goodly profits were gathered at certain seasons, and holders of permits wanted to retain them henceforth for themselves and their children. On the other hand, these excellent fly-fishing waters also drew American and Canadian sportsmen, who found there the most restful and attractive form of relaxation. The telegraph often reported the glee and the rivalry of clubs that are now well-known. Twenty, thirty, thirty-five catches in one day ! Where in the world could one find luckier fishermen ?

As the rights to salmon fishing in certain rivers, however, had been granted to these gentlemen to the prejudice of the inhabitants of the neighbouring localities, these protested, demanding their share of the wealth lavished by Providence at their very doors. The Eudist Fathers, from time to time, found themselves obliged to work towards a solution of this problem, which became more and more troublesome as the population of their missions increased and the means of earning a living decreased.

The Honourable Edgar Rochette and Dr. Arthur Leclerc, both former Members of the Legislative Assembly for this district, could serve as witnesses in this matter. Our efforts finally produced excellent results. Amicable agreements were reached between the parties concerned, and an annual sum was paid by the clubs to the inhabitants, who consented to putting their nets away in favour of the sportsmen.

Today, everybody is satisfied, and the North Shore remains a much-sought paradise of the enthusiasts of one of the most pleasant diversions on earth.

This sport, however, is reserved for those graced by fortune : salmon fishing will support only a fraction of the population. Cod will occasion a revenue more readily accessible to all, but, as it must be waited for, the former inhabitants of the Magdalen Islands, who had been used to trapping seals either by throwing nets out for them or taking these animals by surprise on the ice, emitted the familiar cry : "To the ice floes, let us go to the ice floes." Conversation then became animated, plans were made, and schooners of thirty, forty or fifty gross tons built, in spite of countless inherent difficulties resulting from the lack of communications and the scarcity of necessary materials. Thus, these regular fishermen became, in March and April, the fearsome hunters of seals. Their expeditions to the ice floes have been so spectacular and have left such vivid memories to this day that it is impossible to abstain from writing on this episode of valour and heroism.

Every spring after their arrival on the North Shore in 1857, the Magdalen Islanders, who settled at Esquimaux Point, Natashquan, Betchuan, Westavaka, Muskuaro, staged a seal-hunt. About the middle of February, the crews of the schooners began preparing for the hunt. New schooners were built, old ones repaired, the interior of each boat put to order, part of the hold filled with the necessary wood, and purchases of flour, salt pork, lard, fats, beans, biscuits, and other provisions were made. These expenses of $150. to $200. were evenly distributed among all these men who strove together, suffered hardships together, and then shared the profits and losses of the hunt, a virtual cooperative along the St. Lawrence, long before the present grand-scale movement for cooperatives got under way. At that time of the year, the harbour was covered with ice at least two feet thick. Equipped with special saws, the hunters cut this ice in order to form a channel more than two miles long. While the saws bit into the ice, the old French Canadian songs were wont to awaken the echoes of neighbouring rocks and islands. To a sprightly tune, the words would pour forth :

"The sheep upon the plains, digue dindaine,
Began to hum a song, digue dindé."

With each rhythmic stroke of the saw came the crack and tinkle of breaking ice. All gay fellows in this group ; the sea that awaits them loves gay sailors. As piece after piece of ice broke away from the immense surface, it was sunk deep enough to be carried off by the current and leave a free space. Once the channel was opened, the schooners were dragged into it one after the other and placed in Indian file. From that moment on, the older men among the crews stayed on board, while the younger men went ashore every evening to visit their betrothed for a few pleasant hours of banter.

Around the fifteenth of March came the *au revoir* to wives, children, fiancées, and the beginning of the long voyage to the floating ice of the Strait of Belle-Isle. To tack skillfully against the winds, to keep a straight course and a sharp lookout for stray icebergs in the Gulf, such were the duties of every member of the crew.

Up very early, always on the alert, these men could not be too choosy or too exacting at meals. Whether the journey was long or short, it was the cook's duty to see that the provisions would last. Nobody liked to be forced to seek refuge in some out-of-the-way settlement of the region, a fate that had once befallen the crew of a wrecked schooner. Hence, it was best to content oneself with simple and inexpensive food : pancakes, for example, made with flour and lard mixed in water. A facetious cook once pretended having heaped up enough pancakes on the table during a fishing season to reach the top of the mizen-mast !

With time they came upon the vast ice floes they had been looking for. In the distance, with the aid of field glasses, one could see dark moving masses, seals! Quickly the hunters donned their heavy white trousers, white hoods, and white caps, then, armed with clubs bearing an iron or steel spike, they began the long-awaited battle at dawn. Strategy consisted in surrounding the seals and suddenly pouncing on them. Once the alarm was given, the area was like a frog pond into which children have thrown stones. The hunters advanced with precaution, hiding behind some jutting ice or crawling along the edge of the ice. When the circle was completed, they stood up suddenly, and the massacre began. The younger hunters would rush forward, hitting the animals a sharp blow on the snout. Instinctively, the seals would simulate death, staying on their guard the while with their big bright eyes watching. Thus they thought themselves safe. The other hunters would approach at that psychological moment, striking right and left with all their might, killing them while the survivors shrieked and thrashed about, not knowing where to go. Presently they would come together, piled on top of one another, in the hope that the ice would break under their combined weight, if it happened to be a bit soft. If this last resource failed them, it was the end, for this concentration made the kill even easier. A few who managed to escape would scramble down the crevices of the ice. "After five hours, we stopped through sheer weariness. We had killed more than eighteen hundred seals," wrote Placide Vigneault in the ship's diary (1886). "The following day we removed the skins. It was a horrible butchery. We were covered with blood... No matter ! our hunt guaranteed an excellent season, and the cook could take the livers, hearts, and a few choice pieces from the younger animals and offer his friends a more varied menu and some tasty dishes. As a sort of trophy for our victory, we put up our empty barrels to mark the route and the location of the catch."

Such strokes of fortune were rare ; the lesser "manna" was more the rule. Still there were some magnificent catches : as many as 2,800 in one day.

From the foundation of Esquimaux Point up to 1900, 184,102 seals evaluated at more than $616,803.00 were caught by its flotilla. But after the fat years came the lean years. In 1881, the schooners from Esquimaux Point had taken 24,149 seals ; in 1895 they captured only a few hundred. Five years later, only four schooners went out, and they took absolutely nothing. This last failure brought the industry to an end on the North Shore and left a free hand to the Newfoundlanders, who were now using steamers for hunting seals and so did not risk being engulfed by the ice floes. The days felt very long when the schooners were held immobilized by the ice. Then the crews used to play cards, not for money, however, for they did not keep any on board, but for pieces of tobacco or matches. A piece of chewing tobacco was often divided into twelve pieces, with matches near them, and these served as the stakes in a game that provoked laughs and caused much merriment. Even the older sailors doted on this childish pastime.

On the other hand, on such journeys where they were constantly beset by perils, these fearless sailors thought of their God. All without exception fulfilled their Easter duties before leaving. At sea they faithfully recited their prayers, and every evening they assembled in the main room to say the beads in common. If, perchance, one of their number fell asleep at the hour of common prayer, he was sure to be rudely awakened by the deafening noise of falling metalware, which a hidden string released from afar at the right moment. This practical joke, which is still mentioned in conversations, testifies that these men had not lost their good spirits in spite of the fact that they had to earn their living and that of their families by a labour which today seems so difficult and dangerous. One can imagine the happiness of those returning and of those waiting on the shore on the day when, after having safely navigated through the immense fields of ice floes, the schooners appeared on the horizon, all sails full blown. As they approached and were recognized, one could hear the firing of guns from on board. One shot meant one hundred seals taken ! Two shots, two hundred seals, etc. What manifestations of joy if the shots were repeated ten, twenty times !

Seal hunting was dangerous. Of the twenty six schooners which made up the fleet of Esquimaux Point in its best days, six of them, according to the historian, Placide Vigneault, were crushed between icebergs or lost at sea in some other manner.

An admirable Christian spirit reigned among these enterprising men. Those who underwent shipwreck were always helped and rescued in time, because of the great charity and brotherly love which prompted them to watch over one another and be ready for any emergency.

What about the economic side of seal-hunting ? Was it very profitable ? Naturally, all the schooners were

Photo Féd. Nat. Mét. Bât. et Mat. Constr.

CHAPEL OF JÉRÉMIE ISLANDS,
built in 1735 and restored by A. Gallant, Eudist, in 1939

RIVIÈRE-AU-TONNERRE
(*Thunder River*) . . . *and its attractive little harbour*

not equally fortunate. There were ups and downs. Some came back without a single skin. Then the flag would hang at half-mast, as for sickness or death. But many trips were quite lucrative, if one judges by the gold pieces of French louis which were still in circulation in 1903, authentic witnesses long kept in the wool stockings of some thrifty families. Right up to 1915, a good old man, Isidore Landry, then 93 years of age, used to change some twenty-dollar gold pieces to pay his Mass stipends. "Le père Isidore" had known what it was to make voyages to the ice floes from Natashquan to Newfoundland.

Hard work still awaited the hunters on their return to the village. The preparation of the skins for the market, the melting of fat with the most rudimentary equipment required a lot of patience and fortitude around the iron cauldrons from which arose a strong odour.

During the month of June, the schooners, accompanied by fishing boats, once more set out to sea for the great cod fishing expeditions. Once the fishing area was chosen, the barges left the schooners to go out and return to them with their catch of cod, abundant or meagre according to weather conditions or their own good or bad luck.

In the fall, one or several of the schooners were designated to carry to Quebec the products of the whole village's hunting and fishing and to fetch some provisions.

When the Eudist Fathers took charge of their missions, the great seal hunts had already become adventures of the past. Only cod fishing was being practised all along the North Shore.

In June, the barges of Esquimaux Point and of Natashquan used to meet for a fishing expedition known as "fleet fishing". "Cod running at Natashquan". The news flashed over the telegraph! Immediately, eighty, perhaps a hundred barges took to the seas and scattered over an area of 3 or 4 miles facing the mouth of the great Natashquan River. Such expeditions were very popular for a while and brought joy as much to the hearts of the missionaries who prayed as to the hardy fishermen, who sought from the sea bread for their families!

In the evening, when the white sails would appear within sight of the harbour, the return of the fishermen became the main subject of conversation. "The Richards are the best cod fishers; their barge has unloaded two thousand cod on the piers of the Robin Company". "William Cormier, nicknamed "Bat-le-Diable" (Beat the Devil) because he could have won a cod fishing contest against the devil himself had he dared challenge him, has topped all his competitors again". "The men of Natashquan have been defeated by those from the upper country!" Hundreds of similar observations flitted about from tongue to tongue in the village.

In the posts situated west of Esquimaux Point, going up the Gulf towards Godbout, fishing was carried on in June in the bays of Long Point, Magpie, Rivière-au-Tonnerre, Sheldrake, around the reefs and close to the shore. From the middle of July till the first days of November, the fish gradually withdrew from these places. The fisherman must go after them first three or four miles out, then six, eight, ten miles near banks and in shallows which must be found. Fishing out at

FISHING 55

sea, in the unknown ! How useful to our fishermen would have been the thermometers of Commandant Beaugé, which indicate whether or not the fish can live in any given place in the water. At dawn the barges left the little cove or the great harbour their habitual shelter. Formerly, they were activated by a solid pair of oars or by sails; nowadays they carry a powerful motor. They used to travel all over the waters of the St. Lawrence, as vast as a sea. At some moment the captain of the barge would catch sight of a point or cape, an opening in the rocks, his guiding-mark, the "alignment." He has found the spot he has been seeking. His experienced eye did not deceive him. The anchor was dropped and all went to work.

Father Brochard, one of the first missionaries of 1903 and one whose untimely death snatched him away from the affection of his comrades and from the Labradorian missions to which he had devoted himself body and soul, has left a very accurate description of this line fishing, so long practiced on the North Shore.

"The two men who man these barges stand motionless, silent, their arms inflexible from holding their lines, their downcast eyes dulled by the monotonous movement of the waves, always on the watch, waiting to feel the tugging at the hook of the ravenous cod which, forty or sixty fathoms below, circles the tempting bait. Suddenly the line is agitated ! Quickly, it is hauled up, the fish emerges on the crest of a wave in a curving flash of silver seen in the sun's reflection, and the cod falls to the bottom of the boat. The sailor presses his foot on it, and it opens its jaws to release the hook. New bait is affixed, and once more the line sinks under water." And so the hours passed, with a repetition of the same movements, adding more and more fish to the pile. It was time to head for the harbour when the south wind rose and the tide was about to come in. The lines were then reeled in and the anchor, embedded in the clay bottom, was hauled up by sheer strength of the wrists. The three sails would fill out in the wind, and the boat would glide rapidly over the glittering waves... The two fishermen, seated at the helm, would contemplate the day's catch while puffing on their pipes. There, on the bottom of the boat, lay the cod, some still moving, others inert, limp, their huge mouths open, half revealing the bait, which had enticed them to their undoing. Soon the sails drew nearer, the boats would congregate and enter their home harbour.

"From the door-steps of their home, the children watched for their father's return : having recognized him, they would rush out to meet him. After a quick glance to see whether "the flat" (boat) carried a good load, all set to work dressing the fish. Everyone had an assigned task. The boys would seize the cod by the gills and throw them on the table, the mother or the daughter opened them, the helper removed the liver and broke off the head on the edge of the table with a sharp blow ; the father and owner of the barge, his gloved hand covered with blood, removed the vertebrae with his knife and split them lengthwise. The fish were then allowed to drop into a container of water. Around the table of operation the little children removed the tongues by slitting the gullet at the risk of cutting their little pink fingers. And the dogs, wandering from group to group, ate with crackling sounds whatever useless remains were left over, while the gulls circled majestically over the barges." In many places one could see men contending with these voracious birds for the precious spoils, throwing them with pitched fork onto their ox-drawn carts. There was nothing better in the spring than this fertilizer for the gardens and meadows.

Was cod ◆fishing very remunerative on the North Shore?

We have already seen that, in 1885, Father Boutin, missionary of Natashquan, moved by the poverty which he saw around him, prevailed upon forty families to emigrate to Beauce County. Their descendants in the lovely village of. Théophile are now benefiting from the privations and hardships endured by their ancestors in this extraordinary exodus. A severe depression was felt that year at Natashquan and in the surrounding villages.

In the course of several years, the Robin, Colas, and LeBouthillier Companies of the South Shore set up fishing establishments in numerous localities : Long Point, Rivière-Saint-Jean, Magpie, Jupitagan, Riche-Pointe, Le Dock, Rivière-au-Tonnerre, Sheldrake, La Baleine, La Chaloupe. These companies brought fishermen from the south and employed them during the summer. A popular saying then around the work tables was : "No fishing, no eating."

Around 1875, these nomads grew weary of this servitude. The beautiful sites on the North Shore, the little harbours to anchor their boats, the fishing so near the shore attracted them. They bought plots of land in the Mingan Seigniory and built some humble dwellings. Attractive villages, many of them still thriving, mushroomed all over this area. From then on, these people lived on credit consented to by the companies and paid off by the season's catch of fish. Nobody grew rich at this game. A few valiant fishermen, luckier than others, managed to pay off all their debts. Many were always behind in their accounts at the store. They did not complain, however, for they were not suffering. They were not well-off, so to speak, but then, does one need wealth to be happy ? At any rate, it was a real pleasure around that time to witness the sudden bustling activity in the villages when the fishing season drew near. The men spent most of their days and nights at sea. The women and children kept busy with the drying of the cod. When fall came around, schooners from Halifax and Gaspé, chartered by the companies, arrived in the harbours to fetch their load of dried cod : two thousand, three thousand hundredweight in the same little harbour.

Since 1926, especially 1927, a cruel setback has befallen the North Shore fishermen. To their bewildered eyes suddenly appeared, in the bays and coves once so full of fish, enormous schools of porpoises. Already, in 1919, a few "white backs" had been seen here and there ... nobody had paid much attention to this serious menace. But this time they showed up by the thousands, now diving, now rising to the surface, very close one to the other, covering enormous areas of two, three, four miles and more. These cetaceans followed the shores, by-passed the bays, in quest, no doubt, of caplin or the sand-eel, small fish which the fishermen used as excellent bait for cod fishing. Like a forest fire which ruthlessly burns down everything in its path, these forays drove away all fish, cod especially, as soon as the month of June came around. From then on the fishermen laid their trap nets in vain. One of these nets which, on June 8, 1927, brought its owner, Honoré Bezeau, fifty hundredweight of cod, did not take a single fish on June 9 and afterwards ; a school of porpoises inaugurated their entry on that day into the bay of Sheldrake where the nets were laid ! Nonetheless daunted the fishermen still went out to drop their lines in the usual recesses, but they returned crestfallen, without a single catch. The fish came back after four or five days, drew near the shores once more only to flee anew in the face of a fresh onslaught by their enemies. Finally, these incursions, recurring regularly from west to east, then from east to west, ended by driving them out altogether.

Commandant Beaugé, a well-known professor at the College of Sainte-Anne-de-la-Pocatière, and Professor V. D. Vladycof, a biologist of the Department of Maritime Fisheries, taught the theory that the disappearance of cod from the waters of the North Shore at that time was due to changes in the temperature of the water. We bow before these facts of science coming from such authoritative sources. Whatever the case may be, the fishermen, drawing their own conclusion from what they saw, came to believe that they had only one enemy : the porpoise. We must confess that the missionaries, first hand witnesses, also, of the disaster, shared that opinion for a long time.

When, in 1922, the provincial government decided to regain control of the fisheries of the Gulf of St. Lawrence, the Honourable J.-E. Perreault requested my collaboration in the organization of fishing on the North Shore. Indeed, whatever help I could furnish was very limited, very laborious, and, alas ! always without any apparent success ! But, as I was constantly in contact with an important group of fishermen, living amongst them, well aware of their needs and the hardships they suffered, receiving at all moments of the day their well-founded complaints, I could not refuse. I availed myself, subsequently, of every opportunity to present to the Minister whatever propositions seemed most urgent to us.

Already in 1925, seeing these poor fishermen completely destitute, I obtained in an interview with the Minister and his Superintendent, Mr. F. M. Gibaut, a grant of twelve thousand dollars, which was distributed in fishing equipment and buying or exchanging barges. Every deserving fisherman who needed help received from fifty to a hundred dollars. After another visit, inspectors were appointed for the most important localities. The distribution of grants for the purchase of fishing equipment and of salt to be alloted to each fisherman, the preparation of lists of fishermen eligible for a bonus, the supervision of fish salting and of the methods to follow in the preparation of the fish, its inspection and classification, were all part of the inspectors' duties. Needless to say, these inspectors, who were at first disliked by the fishermen, proved to be of the utmost service in maintaining the good reputation of their product.

1926 ! The year of the great disaster ! No more fish, first along a distance of a hundred miles or so, then all along the North Shore.

One day, when one of the regular service boats was at anchor at Rivière-au-Tonnerre, I received an invitation from Messrs. Desmond, Wilfrid Clarke and Colonel J. M. Stanton to meet them on board. Our conversation, which lasted over an hour, revolved exclusively around the burning issue : since there was no more fish, what was to become of our fishermen ? By mutual consent we decided to send a long telegram to the Honourable J.-E. Perreault requesting him to come and see for himself, on the very premises, the gravity of the situation. A boat was immediately put at the disposition of the ministerial party, which was composed of the Minister, the Honourable A. David, Secretary of the Province, the Deputy Minister L.-A. Richard, and a few ladies. A reception for these distinguished visitors was held in the poor parish hall. The missionary read a welcoming speech in which he traced a realistic picture of our unhappy state of affairs. The Minister listened attentively and tried to inform himself by speaking with some of the fishermen present, as he had done all along the coast aboard the steamer.

A resolution was taken which was destined to have repercussions throughout the province. The Gaspesians upon hearing of it, immediately demanded for themselves the same privileges that were accorded the North Shore.

Since fishing close to the shore is a thing of the past, said the Minister, the Government will help in the building of more spacious and safer barges. After lengthy negotiations, this grant was fixed at a hundred dollars per barge, preferably built in the region.

It became a heavy responsibility from then on for the missionary, who had to endorse all necessary purchases in each case and on whom rested the final decision in the matter of barges.

A hunt for porpoises with airplanes and bombs made a lot of noise at the time and put the unsuspecting promoter of this affair in an embarrassing situation.

Colonel Stanton must recall the long evening spent in a Labradorian rectory where the fatal word, airplane, was first spoken ! In the waters of the Gulf, as vast as a sea, as stormy as the ocean, it was impossible to use nets, as once did David Têtu around the Saguenay or about the Gaspé Peninsula, nor the brushwood traps of Rivière-Ouelle, nor the Winchester rifles, useful only when the animal was caught on a sand bank, as in the estuary of the Manicouagan River, where Honoré Chouinard and other hunters carried a very successful campaign against the porpoises. Would it not be advisable to try out the new instrument of destruction ?

In an electoral compaign a member of the Legislative Assembly declared to the whole population assembled in front of the rectory that the government in power had wasted a hundred thousand dollars in this unfortunate attempt. Upon hearing these words the pastor of the locality, who had been the principal instigator of the misdeed, who had received orders to oversee the aerial operation and to limit or stop it, if necessary, felt an old remorse, which time had barely stifled, well up within him again.

One day, a delegation from the North Shore, which had journeyed to Quebec to ask for a national highway, was assembled at the Renaissance Club. The member of the Legislative Assembly who headed the delegation, the missionary, and the deputy minister who had paid the bill were all present. The poor culprit felt that this would be a splendid opportunity to attenuate somewhat the unpleasantness of this memory. Turning to the member of the Legislative Assembly he said : "Have you noticed the patience of one of your listeners, at least once ? Do you remember the hundred thousand dollars thrown to the waves with Dr. Cuisinier's bombs? It should be possible to know exactly how much this affair cost the department." "Ten thousand dollars," answered the Deputy Minister, who had understood.

Since then, the pilot and the mechanic of Dr. Cuisinier, the French airman who had undertaken the hunt, have made a rather interesting disclosure to this same missionary. "One thing was missing in the enterprise : perseverance." The bombs dropped on a school of porpoises sighted from the air off Perroquet Island threw the band into a panic, and several of them precipitated themselves onto the neighbouring coast, where hunters armed with Winchester rifles could easily have dealt with them.

What is the present state of affairs of the fishing industry on the North Shore?

East of Natashquan, especially at and around Blanc Sablon, fishing with trap nets continued after the lean years and has been getting on rather well for some time. In other districts, the scarcity of fish has lasted over a longer period. Right up to 1938, when the North Shore fishermen were permitted to work in the lumber camps, their missionaries felt continually obliged to find some new way of providing them with their daily bread.

At that time, a deputy minister, who offered new farms to young men of the province willing to clear the land, argued that it was time to take away the fishermen from their enchanting shores and direct them to the new settlements. Can fishermen be converted into colonizers? Exceptionally, yes. Generally, no.

The missionaries, who suffered indeed more than any one else to see their parishioners with their bags of flour empty and lacking other essential provisions, did not entertain such an impossible dream. But it was most assuredly from their constant solicitude that the idea arose of drying the caplin and the sand-eels. The sand-eel is well known on certain Breton beaches. It lodges itself in the sand and dives quickly back if any instrument makes it come out of its hiding place. These two fishes, the caplin in June and the sand-eel in July, enter our bays and penetrate the sands of our beaches by millions. The inhabitants capture them with nets and with seines. They serve as bait for fishing. If spread on lawns, gardens, and vegetable patches, they can advantageously replace commercial fertilizers. They are made to dry on the flat or round rocks that hem the coastline. They can be given as an excellent dog food. Finally, the most inexperienced cook can turn them into the most delicious fried tidbits.

Everybody on the North Shore knew that Johan Beetz, the famous fox-rancher, fed his animals a daily portion of dried caplin or sand-eel.

From this, the missionaries, who were anxious to seize upon every opportunity to help their parishioners, got the idea of offering this dried fish to the fur-ranchers as a new food. This project was soon put into execution. Mr. Jos. Alain, a well-known merchant in Quebec City, was one of the first persons to become interested in it. He authorized the missionary, as his representative, to pay for the fish upon its delivery at the boat. An understanding with Wilfrid Clarke assured the transportation of the merchandise at the low rate of twenty-five cents per hundred pounds. A new industry, a very modest industry, was thus born. At first, it provoked laughs and critical remarks from many quarters and sometimes offended the nostrils of tourists. Yet, it did some good and brought a little bread to the tables of the devotees of the fishing industry. It will grow, without doubt, if, as it is to be hoped, an artificial dryer come soon to add its action to that of the sun on the rocks.

At any rate, a new hope has risen in the hearts of the fishermen.

Co-operative establishments have lately been created in the larger centres. The fishermen have assembled, studied their problems, and come to the conclusion that it is to their common good to unite, to work together, to co-operate, as was attempted in 1922, but in vain, due to a lack of organization for the sale of the fish. A progress that is real and constant has resulted from these agreements among fishermen of the same village. The fisherman is paid on delivering his fish to the co-operative. He works, if he has time, at the drying or salting of the fish. He receives a reasonable salary through this cooperation. Money thus enters his pocket, a rare treat in the days of yore; it also goes out to return, he hopes, in a surprising dividend.

Would that the fish, now better prepared according to more scientific and constantly improved methods, may henceforth bring to the Labradorian fisherman a suitable income ! The fishing industry will revive and bring other numerous benefits.

"The sea," wrote Father Rovolt in his biography of the Reverend Father Ange Le Doré, former Superior General of the Eudist Fathers, who gained recognition for himself at the time of the persecution against the religious congregations, "the sea is the school of great compassion, of charity, of unfathomable mercy. The sea has a spirit of broadmindedness, of humanity, of fraternity, that those who have never sailed experience with difficulty."

How often, all along the immense North Shore, brother has helped brother, whether friend or enemy.

The man of the sea will not forget to lift his heart towards God in thanksgiving for success as well as in an appeal for succor in peril. What follows is an example amongst thousands... One evening, telegrams from the rectories of Ellis Bay on Anticosti Island, and Rivière-au-Tonnerre were exchanged, charged with the worries of all the neighbours over Albert Dignard, whose barge had been at anchor that morning in the Baie-Sainte-Claire, and had now disappeared. Was it lost ? Where could it be ? Albert Dignard and his son had, as usual, passed the night in the cabin of their barge. Suddenly, a violent storm arose. The wind, rushing from the south, blew about the barge and broke the only cable which kept it tied to its anchor. It drifted out to sea, and neither motor nor sail could bring it back to the shore. The only manœuvre possible was to let the little craft be carried out by the winds, in the heavy seas, where enormous waves threatened to engulf it at every instant ! The poor captain at the helm scanned the waves with an anxious eye, dreading to make one false manœuvre. He ordered his young son to remain in the little cabin and to put up a fervent prayer. God alone could steer the bark. Six long hours ! Suddenly, the North Shore was sighted : "Father", said the boy, worriedly fixing his eyes ahead of him, "see how white the shore looks". By this time, the boat was only one mile away from the harassed shore and constantly drawing nearer. "Keep on praying, my child", answered the father, "let us put our trust in God and in the Virgin Mary".

During the whole twenty-four mile crossing, Albert Dignard had been thinking only of the death that awaited him on the nearby reefs. Suddenly, a torrential downpour accompanied by a light southwest wind totally changed the situation. A relative lull allowed the still conscious sailor to unfurl what was left of the sail and take advantage of the new breeze. It was only the following day that an unknown barge was noticed anchored before Magpie, eleven miles from the home port. A weakness of the heart due to the too strong emotions of the day later brought the young Dignard to his death ! Hundreds of incidents of this type could be related. How often had not the Labradorian fisherman been required to make capital use of all the resources of his intelligence, courage, and energy to reach port in the midst of dense fogs or angry seas?

Has the hard labour of fishing, which sometimes creates an intense strain on the mind and nerves, shortened the days of these fishermen ? A missionary wrote in 1933 : "I see many old men in the four corners of my missions, still strong, bearing up well in spite of the depression, which is withholding from their table all the modern delicacies. I can find a good dozen proudly bearing their 85, 90, 93 springs". Are not Christian morals, simplicity of life, physical labour, life at sea, in the open, and frugal food all agents of longevity?

This chapter could therefore end with the hope that the men who ply this noble and healthful trade will become more and more numerous, bringing with the great variety of fish from the sea an important part of the food for the tables of their fellow men.

It would be regrettable if the housewives could not use the recipes, so well known amongst the devotees of fresh cod and about which Father Brochard wrote as early as 1904 : "First of all, there is the common method of cooking it in water and serving it with potatoes in the same sauce. It is the dish of hearty appetites and bad humour, or of trouble in the household. But when the family sky is cloudless, it is hashed in butter, and the potatoes are browned." You know all this as well as the familiar milk sauces. What you do not know about, however, are the tongues of cod, rolled in flour and fried in deep fat like doughnuts ; the jowls, baked in the oven ; and the livers of cod that you have seen only as a liquid at the pharmacist. And when you must coax your pretty little babies to make them swallow a few drops, we enjoy cod livers as a delicacy and think of the old saying : *corruptio optimi pessima* (the corruption of the very best things is the very worst kind.) Why must science thus spoil nature ? I was forgetting the national dish, the native recipe, unknown to all outsiders : One cuts a piece of cod dried on the racks and eats it slowly, relishing its yellowed, lightly salted flesh. How often have I not met children, walking to school, enjoying a cod's tail.

And, as the production of cod is too abundant for local consumption, it is sent far away to Quebec, to the United States, to Brazil, through the medium ever more and more efficacious, let us hope, of the Cooperative of the United Fishermen.

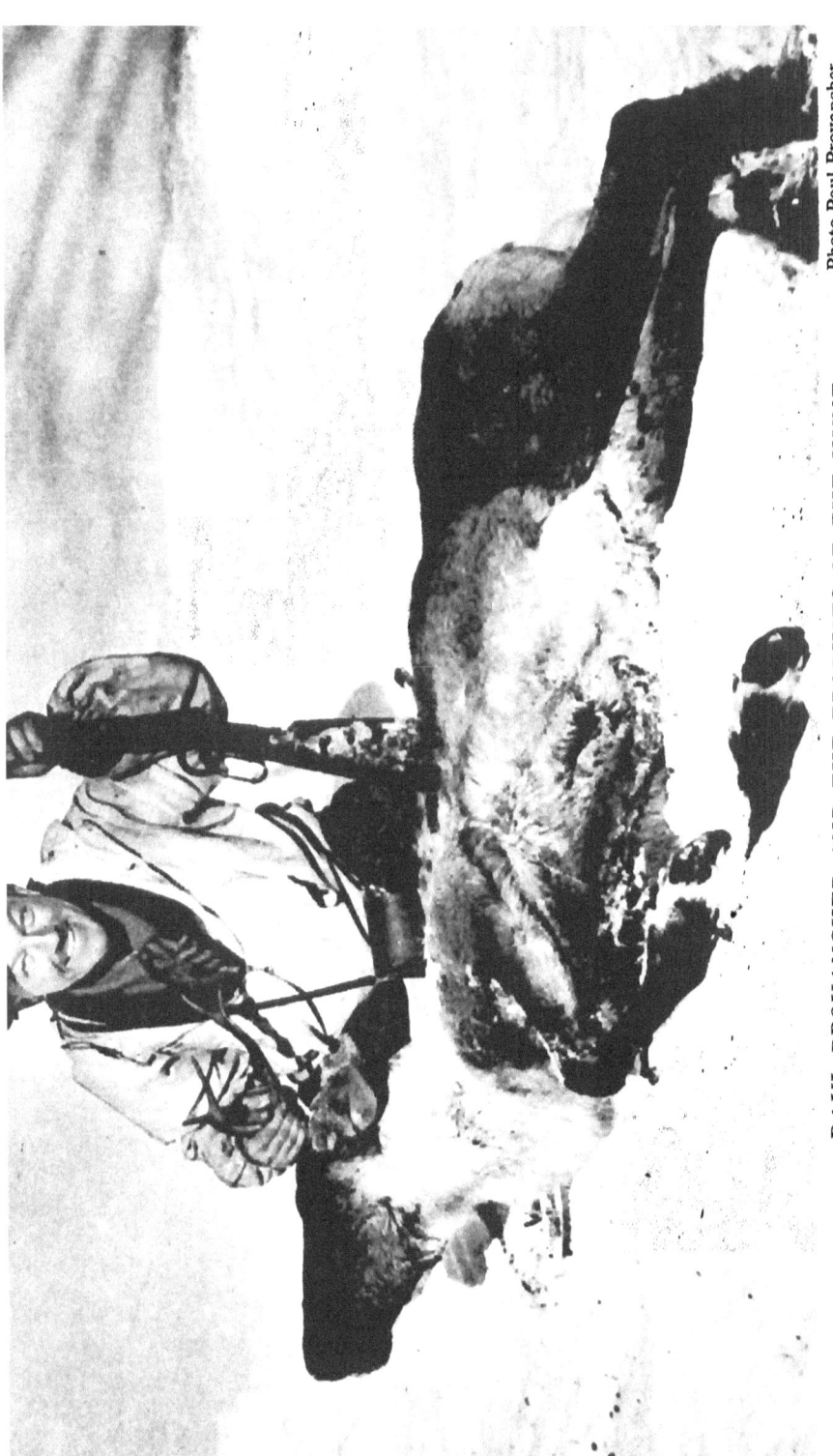

PAUL PROVANCHER AND THE TROPHIES OF THE HUNT

Photo Paul Provancher

MONTAGNAIS CHILDREN
WITH MOTHER AND GRANDMOTHER

CHAPTER FIVE

HUNTING

I

**The Indians. -- The white man. -- The sale of furs.
Forest tragedies.**

THE hunting of fur-bearing animals in the winter occupies a considerable portion of the population of Labrador. As the Eudist Fathers had to keep in continued relation with the trappers, a few details on this subject are in order.

The sole inhabitants of this vast region originally and until the arrival of the merchants and fishermen, were the Montagnais Indians. A peaceful tribe almost without a history, one may wonder whether they ever had to fight in order to remain masters of their vast solitudes. The names of Esquimaux Point and of Baie-des-Esquimaux would imply that the Eskimos had at some time or other visited and inhabited Labrador. A bloody battle may have taken place in the vicinity of Havre Saint-Pierre, and the Eskimos, less numerous, perhaps, than their adversaries, may have been defeated, and may have retreated to the bleak country of igloos where they are still living.

One question naturally comes to mind : How came the Montagnais of Labrador to be converted to Catholicism?'

Many heroic episodes could be related concerning the hundred and thirty one years (1651-1782) of missionary work among the Montagnais by the Jesuit Fathers. After very laborious journeys undertaken with Indians into the depths of the forests, journeys of which only the missionaries could give us an adequate idea, evangelization began to take on a practical aspect. Father Crespieul, one of the pioneers of this apostolate, built a chapel at Papinachois, near the present site of Bersimis where, as early as 1680, converts assembled for the mission. Another church was built at Îlets-à-Jérémie in 1735, a very humble chapel apparently, since thirty-two years later Father Labrosse found it necessary to endow this post with a more suitable place of worship. Meanwhile, Father Coquart in 1747 had erected the first chapel at Tadoussac.

Reverend Father A. Gallant, the Eudist missionary colonizer of Sainte-Thérèse-du-Colombier, having become deeply interested in the little chapel of Îlets-à-Jérémie, had it restored in 1939. On the altar and all along the walls of this ancient sanctuary he has laid out many a touching reminder of the first days of the mission. One cannot help, when praying in this hallowed spot, but dwell upon the devotion and sacrifices of these first missionaries who, long ago, prayed, confessed, preached, and offered the holy sacrifice within these walls.

A dozen priests or so from the diocese of Quebec succeeded the Jesuit Fathers among the Montagnais during the following half century (1782-1844). One of them, Father Boucher, fought against the sale of liquor to his parishioners and won the title of "Apostle of Temperance." A Eudist is prominent among the names on this list : Father François Le Courtois. During two or three of the finer months of the year this Father always left his parish of Rimouski and later, La Malbaie, to make the rounds of the New Lands or King's Posts, where the Montagnais congregated for the missions.

Then came the Oblate Fathers. The pastor of Saint-Sauveur, Flavien Durocher, initiated their labour in 1845.

All the Oblates have left excellent reminders of their work at Bersimis, but Father Arnaud, the great apostle of the Montagnais (1850-1909) and Father Babel (1851-1911) are particularly famous. Both of them resided constantly with the Indians, lived their lives and, like the Jesuit Fathers, accompanied them on their journeys through the illimitable forests.

It is difficult for an outsider to picture the hard life led by these missionaries. They travelled up the rivers, paddled canoes, carried their share of baggage in the narrow portages, slept under tents in the snow, and ate the common food, which was mostly game.

Apart from the material side, due to the intelligent and zealous action of the missionaries, who won over the sympathy of all, a great task was accomplished. The "man of prayer" took every opportunity to learn the language of his flock and converse with them on all subjects within their orbit of comprehension. He taught them the catechism ; the eternal truths penetrated their well-disposed minds little by little, bringing them a peace and joy heretofore unknown. Many pagans were converted. Due to these heroes, who spread the Good News, gradually all the Montagnais became Christians.

Once this work of conquest was accomplished, the Oblate Fathers organized the Indian missions so as to sustain the spiritual life among these roamers of the wild woods in the best manner possible. From then on the residence of the missionaries was fixed at Bersimis, and the mission was henceforth known as Our Lady of Betsiamits. Every summer one of the Fathers set out from Bersimis to visit the Indian reservations now concentrated at Seven Islands and Moisie, Mingan and Muskuaro : the Indians from Natashquan, Romaine, and St. Augustine met at Muskuaro for the mission.

It was these missions that were entrusted by the Holy See to the Eudist Fathers eight years after their arrival on the North Shore. Two young priests, Father Pétel, intelligent and devoted to his work, but of a frail constitution, and Father Jean Le Jollec, particularly chosen for this work, spent the winter of 1910-1911 with the Oblate Fathers, who were kind enough to initiate them in their ministry. From 1911 the Eudist Fathers officially took over all the Indian Reservations on the North Shore.

As for their comrades of 1903, an entirely new life opened for them. The Montagnais language is difficult, as nothing in either the French or English languages approximates the glossary in use among the Indians. They must work hard all through the long winter so as to adequately discharge their duties to their parishioners, to understand them and be understood by them.

Father Pétel has described one of the first Midnight Masses which he attented at Our Lady of Betsiamits. This very interesting narration gives a fair idea of the apostolic field in which the Eudists were to work.

HUNTING

"I knew that there were surprises in store for me in this Christmas celebration among our Indians. Let me tell you that I have never witnessed a more pious Midnight Mass. Christmas is the feast of the Indians, as it is the feast of children, speaking to their eyes and acting upon their imaginations! They think about it long beforehand. Many return from the woods purposely for it, undertaking a long, hazardous journey of two weeks, even a month! Eight days before Christmas a Montagnais woman told me: 'Father, I can't do anything, I just keep thinking of the night when we pray.''

"Some kind nuns, who are now attached to this mission, worked on the decoration of the church. Picture the finished crib with the Holy Child lying on a bit of straw, the Blessed Virgin and St. Joseph lost in adoration, the ass and the bull breathing on the Babe to keep Him warm, some shepherds paying homage and offering their gifts, and others playing the flute while tending their sheep. Above the grotto, a group of chubby angels are singing hymns. Nothing is lacking, and Father Brézel, in spite of his artistic talent, would not be able to equal this splendor in his humble chapel of Manicouagan. Artificial flowers of all colours, gold, silver, blue, white, red, etc... are crowded on permanent shelves, in a somewhat dubious array, dominating the main altar: candelabras and lamps of all colours are scattered here and there, on tables, stands, window sills, wherever there is a free space. Runners are hanging on the walls bearing inscriptions: *Gloria in Excelsis Deo — Venite Adoremus.*

"And our dear Indians are speechless with admiration. One of them told a parishioner of Father Brézel:

'Come to our church, it is like in the cities . . .' Another Indian, entering the church for the first time, asked whether he was in heaven. The Indians have little appreciation for gold intrinsically. They like anything that dazzles, that makes noise ; however, tastes differ. Half an hour before time the church is full. With eyes and mouths wide open the Indians look at the candles being lit. The curtain that veils the crib is drawn. 'Oh how beautiful it is !' Our two bells ring merrily, pealing out the Good News : 'The Saviour is born ! *Venite Adoremus.*' My confessional wicket closes on the last penitent. The Mass begins, and all the Indians, men and women, sing the Royal Mass by Dumont in their own language. One can feel the warmth in their voices ; it is their soul that is singing. During the *Gloria*, the bells once more scatter their gay and vibrant peals, and two little altar boys agitate their little three-tone bells with frenzy. All the choir boys are proud of their red cassocks, capes, and caps.

"Are Indians good singers? The men are not particularly gifted, but the women have accurate and clear voices : only once in a while does one hear a nasal twang. The singing is usually slow and solemn, but one must not expect a perfect ensemble. Each singer begins when he is ready and stops at will. At first, a few timid voices are heard, soon swelled by others ; from time to time a new voice arises while another disappears. It is more in the style of a fugue, but after all, isn't the fugue a popular style of music ?

"The Montagnais language, being soft and harmonious, is easily set to music. The alphabet comprises only twelve letters, the harshest being excluded. Here is a transcription of the *Confiteor* showing the way in

which our Indians pronounce Latin : 'Compiteol Teo omnipotenti, peatoe Malia sempel piljini.' But what I really enjoyed hearing was our suave hymn sung in Montagnais at the moment of communion : *Le voici l'Agneau si doux.* I give the refrain as a matter of interest :
> "Shash uashkuts utshiparo
> Stimamerimatau
> Ka Tiperimat irnu
> Kie Anjeriu."

"During the second mass, all our old Christmas hymns are sung, one after the other, without interruption : *Il est né le Divin Enfant,* etc.

"The Indians who were too far distant in the forest to be able to return also celebrated Christmas in their own way. Each family, seated about the stove, under the canvas tent, sang Dumont's Royal Mass, and the melodious Christmas *Gloria in excelsis Deo.*

"If Christmas is particularly a day of prayer and hymn singing, New Year's is the day of visits and kisses.

"As early as five in the morning, even before, the visits begin. The Indians run from house to house, exchanging New Year greetings. Who could estimate the number of kisses given and received ? At the house of the chief, whose distinctive mark is a large medal, which he proudly wears on feast days, there is open house all day. Everybody is invited to come and eat.

"After the High Mass, there is a real invasion of the rectory kitchen : everyone wants to wish the "Black Robes" a happy New Year.

"In the evening, there is dancing. The dancers get in single file around the table, a man, then a woman, alternately, and a round begins to the beat of Indian made drums. The men jump from one foot to the other successively and the women jump with both feet. With every jump the dancer utters a grunt similar to that of a woodsman sinking his axe into a tree. But soon the movement gathers momentum, the tempo quickens, the exclamations turn into wild yells and war whoops. The dance ends only when the last dancer has fallen, exhausted."

We can gather from these lines, written by one of our missionaries, Father Pétel, whose death came but too soon, the role which these Fathers were called upon to fill in the Montagnais mission.

The long winter months were spent at Bersimis in the rectory built by the Oblate Fathers, a pleasant residence where there was never a lack of things to do. Whatever leisure time was left after the exercise of the ministry in the village and the neighbouring missions was consecrated to the study of the Montagnais language.

A considerable group of Canadians, women and children who remained at the mission, the Sisters in charge of the schools, a few men who had become more interested in working in the timber areas than in roaming the forests in search of furs, relied on the missionaries for spiritual help.

The great majority of the Montagnais Indians penetrate into the woods during the fall. They leave at the end of September and travel towards the great River, the preferred route of the trappers. The whole family gets into its birch bark canoes. The men, women, and older children take turns at paddling and the light canoes skim silently over the still waters of the river. Upon reaching the first rapids or the first fall, they all take to the narrow trails of the portage, each carrying his share of provisions, till they get above the fall or the rapid. Often, many trips over the same portage are necessary, and the men travel back and forth until everything has been brought over. In the meantime the women and children pitch the tents, set up the stoves, and gather dry wood for fuel. This trip to the hunting country may last a month, even two months. The Indian is never in a hurry, as the fur, in general, is of good quality only in December.

In the spring, the Indian families make the return trip in the same way. Three or four months are devoted to the trapping of marten, mink, beaver, otter, lynx, and fox. It is to be hoped that the provisions brought from the mission, the trout and other fish caught in the rivers and lakes, the rabbit, partridge, porcupine, and beaver will provide enough food for every one during these long months. Hunting provides the only means of living : no hunting or poor hunting means want and misery. The credit granted to the Indians by the merchants in the fall has to be sufficient to carry the family through the winter. Conflicts have sometimes arisen in Indian villages between the merchants and the trappers. Often, the missionaries have had to appeal to the Federal Government to preserve their Indian charges from misery and famine. To leave the forest too soon, to return to the Reservation before time, would endanger the health of all, particularly the children, for life in the woods and the fresh air which they breathe are their main protection against tuberculosis and other similar diseases.

Unfortunately, this mode of travelling and the dispersion of the Indian families over a boundless territory do not permit the missionary to follow his spiritual children during the hunting season. But all take leave of the priest before their departure, requesting his benediction and the assurance of his prayers. "In the woods," they tell him, "we shall pray for you, Father, so that you may have good health and remain with us for a long time." They take a good supply of medals, rosaries, scapulars, prayer books, and hymn books with them. The exterior world, the agitation and merry-making of the cities, how far all that is from the mind and heart of the Indian ! The Indians pray to God and lift their thoughts towards Him in the morning and at mealtime ; in the evening, the beads are recited in common by the family. On Sundays, the hunters rest in their tents, and at the hour when the faithful attend Mass in the churches the Montagnais take their prayer-books and sing the *Kyrie*, the *Gloria*, and the *Credo* of Dumont's Mass, followed by their favourite hymns.

When a child is born, the parents take the greatest care of him, and should he become sick, they never fail to baptize him. If he dies, he is piously laid in a little coffin, which is deposited in the high branches of a tree, if necessary, to ensure it against all harm, and is carried to the mission in the spring to be buried in the cemetery. The same procedure is followed for an adult. Should an adult fall gravely ill and die, often he will insist upon making a confession, before dying, to the most respectable person in camp, begging that person to repeat everything to the missionary, giving him all the details of his sickness and his dispositions in the face of death.

HUNTING

Back at the mission weddings are celebrated to the accompaniment of noisy rejoicings and endless feasting. Dancing the famous "macoucham" is never omitted. When a young Indian is strong enough to carry the family canoe, he is considered old enough for marriage, and as soon as the missionary comes, the bride is chosen without further ado.

One great feast, which is looked forward to by all and without which no mission is held, is always celebrated with the greatest fervor. It is the feast of the Blessed Virgin, or the "Procession of the Indians". On the morning of that very solemn Sunday, the whole village arises very early. The interior of the chapel is adorned with its richest decorations and the exterior covered with clusters of flags and pennants. On both sides of the road that runs through the village towards the forest, young birches and aspens are symmetrically planted and enhanced with bright colored ribbons and streamers. Triumphal arches loaded with fragrant pine branches stand along the route of the venerated Madonna. When the statue of the Virgin emerges from the chapel, the whole Indian population advances in two parallel lines, the men on one side, the women on the other, towards the outdoor altar erected at the edge of the forest. The aged and the sick are carried to the chapel. The children occupy the center of the two lines left free by the parents. On both sides of the altar a guard of honour, composed of the young men of the tribe, stands at attention ready to fire a salute on the arrival and departure of the procession.

Numerous boats come from the neighbouring villages, bringing to this feast pilgrims who are always impressed by the sight of these serious and pious countenances, reflecting a faith comparable to that of our best Christians.

Trials have occasionally befallen these missions, losses which have deeply affected the Congregation of Jesus and Mary, and also, as the Almighty often permits, works dedicated to His glory.

Father Pétel, for example, lost his life on the ice as he set out on a mission. (Further details of this death will be given in the chapter dealing with travels on the North Shore and their dangers).

The first Eudist pastor of Manicouagan, the Reverend Father A. Brézel, perished in the waters of the Bersimis River as he was attempting to reach, by dogsled, a group of Canadians living west of the river, for the celebration of the feast of the Immaculate Conception. Despite all efforts to learn the cause and circumstances of this tragedy, it has remained a mystery. Could the Father have neglected to take the precautions which had been urged upon him? As likely as not. Being a zealous apostle and an artistic decorator, he probably forgot the dangers which threatened him while absorbed with plans of flower decorations for the altar of the Virgin. It may be supposed, also, that he was carried by his two dogs on a track worn thin by the action of currents. One thing is certain : the ice gave way under the weight of the *kometik* which carried the Father, and only his two dogs managed to climb out of the abyss and return to the rectory, thus giving word of their master's disappearance. The body of Father Brézel, carried away by the Gulf waters, was found the following spring on the South Shore, not far from Matane, and was buried at Pointe-au-Père. His watch indicated the precise moment of his fall into the icy waters. "Little Father Brézel" was greatly mourned by all those who had benefited from his ministry at Manicouagan, Pointe-aux-Outardes, and Bersimis. One of them told Father Pétel : "He was a devoted pastor, a saint ; unfortunately he lacked virtue," meaning that kind of virtue synonymous with physical strength to overcome obstacles, and one day, caught in the current of a river, the poor Father, who was far from being a colossus, certainly lacked that strength or virtue. But of real virtue taken in its usual sense he had a good store, as can be attested by his colleagues and parishioners. "Just imagine," wrote Father Pétel after a visit to his friend's rectory, "that this good Father Brézel, after eight years of sojourn in his present home, still had to break through ice to wash himself in the morning. I attempted sleeping there in the absence of the Father. The mercury indicated 30°. I wrapped my head in a towel and was stifling under the covers without feeling any warmth. I did not have to waken in the morning, as I had not slept at all. One is more comfortable on the Indian reservation than at the industrial post of Manicouagan !"

Two years later, in 1913, again in December, another tragedy happened. A practical joker, with no intent to do harm, brought to Father Le Jollec the untimely news that a flock of partridge had just been seen at the edge of the forest. The Father thereupon hurriedly seized a hunting gun which was cocked, ready to fire. The gun went off, instantly killing the Father. This great loss cruelly affected Bishop Blanche, his colleagues and the Indians in particular, who saw themselves deprived of a friend and a missionary already familiar with the secrets of their language.

We should not easily forget these Fathers, who remain the glory of our Society. They are praying in heaven for their successors and for the North Shore, which they loved so well.

Five French Eudist Fathers, A. Pétel, Jean Le Jollec, Auguste Tortelier, Joseph Brière, André Jauffret, respectively, devoted themselves to the Montagnais missions of the North Shore. Since 1920, five Canadian Fathers, Denis Doucet, for twenty two years, N. A. LaBrie, our future bishop, Alfred Poulin, Joachim Lapointe, Luc Sirois, carried on their work until 1946. Throughout this period the great summer mission was regularly presided over by one of them.

Occasionally, their colleagues in Seven Islands, Rivière Saint-Jean, and Natashquan generously responded to calls received from the Montagnais for baptisms, sickness, or burials. This ministry often proved difficult for these Fathers, who knew very little of the Montagnais language, but whose zeal knew no bounds.

The Eudist Fathers have given themselves body and soul to the service of these deserving parishioners, expending all their time and energy for their instruction and the care of their souls. Father Sirois, the last of the Eudist missionaries among the Indians, even set himself to the hard task of composing a grammar, *Le Montagnais sans Maître* (Montagnais Self-Taught) a valuable work about which Bishop Leventoux wrote in these terms in the preface : "Your book has been written so as to facilitate the mastery of the Montagnais language. That is its purpose, and I am sure that, due to the judicious and abundant choice of its phraseology, it cannot but fulfill it. Not only the Indians, but also their missionaries, and all those interested in linguistic studies would find it a profitable study."

Everyone knows that the Montagnais Indian lives on the returns from the furs which he brings back from the woods in the spring.

If the furs do not sell, or if the hunter falls a prey to sickness or ill-luck while in the forest, great is the resultant misery in the Indian camp. Who will then be called upon to espouse the cause of these unfortunates? The missionary always. In all circumstances it is from him that they will seek support and help. He is always happy, however, to write letters in their favour or sign official documents so as to obtain the necessary bread to eat.

The first chapels of the Indian reservations were very humble, very poor ones. The Eudists have built and maintained very suitable churches at Seven Islands, at Mingan, and even in the tiny hamlet of Muskuaro.

How often did we not hear, in infrequent meetings of the missionaries aboard boats, congratulations exchanged for certain repairs or additions to their churches and vestries? With what pleasure did not Father Sirois tell of the generosity of Mr. Joseph Simard of Sorel? This worthy layman had become aware of the needs of the mission during his trip to the Washicouté River where he and his friends used to fish for salmon. The chapel has now been repaired, and a new, though modest rectory, is now at the service of the missionary for the great summer gathering at Muskuaro of Montagnais from Natashquan, Romaine, and St. Augustine. The value of a good deed can be measured by the gravity of the ill which it cures. Here the ill seemed incurable. The value of Mr. Simard's kindness is therefore inestimable for both the missionary and the Indians.

As for the church of Our Lady of Betsiamits : considered in its architecture, style, and simple and tasteful decoration, it can be claimed among the outstanding churches of the North Shore, second only to the beautiful cathedral of Baie Comeau. It was begun by Father Brière in 1917. His Excellency Bishop N.-A. Labrie and Father Doucet improved it and gave it its present imposing aspect. All the missionaries tried to find means for the appropriate upkeep of this church and, in spite of very limited resources and great difficulties, they succeeded in completely clearing off the debts.

It was indeed a valuable gift which the Eudists Fathers made to this very deserving Indian mission, which was henceforth to return to the successors of the saintly Fathers Arnaud and Babel.

These notes close that portion of the present chapter dealing with the Indians ; some pertinent information about other trappers on the North Shore now follows.

The furs from this region have always been, and still are, among the choicest and most sought-after in Canada. Ever since the discovery of this beautiful country they have very naturally found buyers. Were not companies, given over to the trading of furs, formed in the very first days of the colony ? The Hudson's Bay Company was the first to assign agents all along the North Shore in posts where the Montagnais came during the summer to escape from the mosquitoes and flies which swarmed in the woods, and especially to

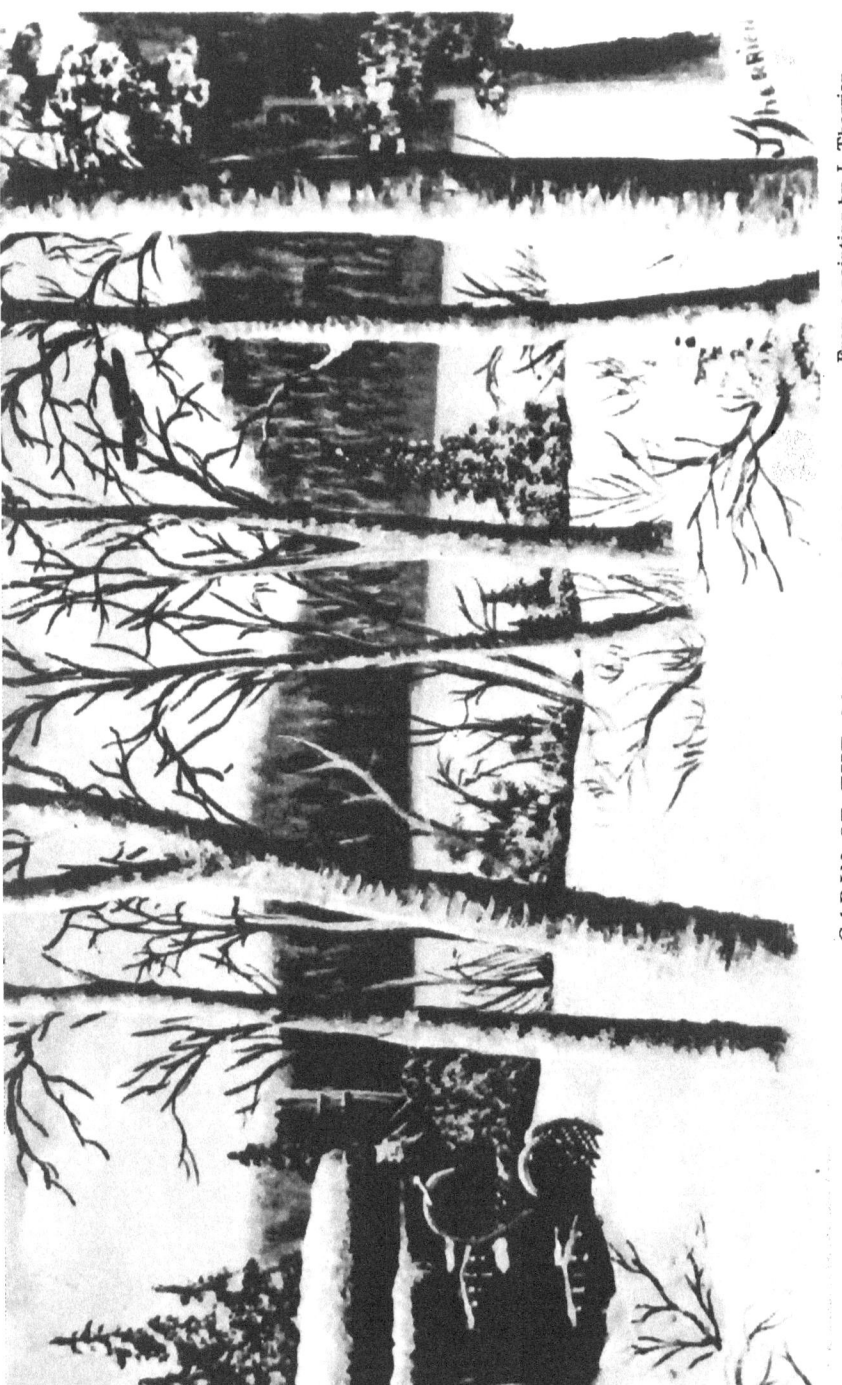

CABIN OF THE COLLIN BROTHERS
From a painting by J. Therrien

NAPOLÉON-ALEXANDRE COMEAU

THE COMTE DE PUYJALON

Dr. JOHAN BEETZ, Sc.A.V.

"assist at the mission." Its representatives stocked their stores with the provisions necessary to the trapper and his family and bartered them against the furs brought from the woods.

For a long, very long period of time there was hardly any competition in this trade.

In 1897, however, a young Belgian arrived in Canada and settled on the North Shore at *Piestebee*, a Montagnais word signifying "river of colours", and which was later spelled "Piastrebaie", a little village situated forty miles east of Havre Saint-Pierre. There, in a chalet built on the rocks, facing the sea, just out of reach of the high tide, he made his abode with his interesting and distinguished family.

Very soon, but without noising it abroad, he became aware of the real value of the beautiful furs which the village trappers brought back from the forest. Immediately he set to work to accomplish a good deed, one which he considered urgently needed.

Suddenly, it was learned that the price of fox pelts had risen sensationally. A new buyer had just travelled all along the coast. Representing the Révillon Frères Company of Paris and accompanied or preceded by the Marquis of Aigneaux, who had taken him into partnership, he stopped at all the posts from Bersimis to Blanc-Sablon and visited all the hunters. Many dogsleds loaded with furs travelled behind him. Presently, joy and ease entered into all the homes, which had known but poverty before this unexpected windfall. Up to that time the most beautiful pelts did not command much more than a hundred or two hundred dollars, and now the telegraph was flashing the news that Mr. Beetz was paying six hundred to seven hundred dollars for the best silver foxes. The story of one lucky hunter made the rounds to the effect that he received $1,100 for a black fox and that a couple of live foxes brought $1,900 to their owner.

One can imagine the benefits which accrued to the whole region, thanks to an honest and understanding buyer.

A missionary once took a census of all the furs taken in his missions of Natashquan, Aguanish, and Piastrebaie. This averaged about 160 pelts per village. Mr. Beetz found that ten per cent of these pelts were of a superior quality and paid three hundred to seven hundred dollars for each one of them.

From the day of his arrival in his new country, Johan Beetz became the friend of all : residents of the villages, travellers, and missionaries. What pleasant relaxation the missionaries found in his villa where he, his charming wife, and their children looked upon them as members of the family circle.

Very lively merriment and unaffected cheerfulness were the hallmarks of these evenings at Mr. Beetz', and in such a contagiously happy atmosphere the traveller soon forgot the fatigues of the trip and partook of the enjoyment provided for the inhabitants of the village assembled there after the prayers at church.

Johan Beetz was an indefatigable worker, always preoccupied with some pursuit that proved ever useful to his new fellow citizens.

Three years of study in medical and veterinary science in Belgium had given him a precious knowledge out of which capital was made on the North Shore. The Government of Quebec, in fact, sent him a fresh supply of vaccines and serums every six months, to the great benefit of the surrounding population.

This good samaritan, like the celebrated Alexander Comeau of Godbout, was now accomplishing a similarly fine work of charity for the eastern section of the North Shore.

In his hours of leisure, Johan Beetz pursued his favorite sports, hunting and fishing, and was proud to bring back the choicest that forest or sea could offer.

Sometimes the woodland animal was still alive in the cage where it had imprisoned itself. While touching and devouring the piece of meat placed at the back of the cage, it had closed the door behind itself. A spacious enclosure awaited the prisoner. Running water, a den for the night, a hiding place away from prying eyes, all showed the newcomer that he would henceforth inhabit a comfortable prison.

Johan Beetz made a thorough study of the habits of fur-bearing animals. For many years, and with remarkable success, he practised the breeding of these animals. In recognition of his accomplishments in this field he was awarded the title of Doctor of Natural Science. His village can be considered as the cradle of a new industry, which became very important in the Province. One knows the proportions attained by this new industry in Canada subsequent to the experiments conducted by this untiring researcher.

Every day it was his habit to withdraw in his laboratory to carry on a highly specialized study of which the layman has admired the results without understanding the secrets. "By dint of observation," he wrote, "I have finally realized a project that I had been thinking about for a long time, namely, a system of perfect mummification."

If one enters the Provincial Museum of Quebec, one will see more than four thousand specimens of his art, forming a magnificent collection of birds, fish, crustaceans, and molluscs ; nearly all are species from the North Shore. At the experimental farm of Courville, one can also admire a mummified anatomical and anatomo-pathological collection of fur-bearing animals, etc.

"I am able to preserve by perfect mummification," says Dr. Beetz again, "any dead body, with its blood, its flesh, its frame of bones, etc., as well as parts presenting special anatomical cases, even anatomo-pathological, such as cysts, purulent tumours, interior and exterior cancers, and abcesses in all stages of decomposition or of putrefaction."

All bodies mummified by this system are entirely immune to change and will not undergo any deterioration either from parasites or from variations of temperature. After forty-five years, bodies mummified by this system are still in a very good state of preservation.

In 1923, Doctor Harwood of Lotbinière, after obtaining the permission of Dr. Eudore Dubeau, requested Johan Beetz to attempt the mummification of a woman's body, which was then in the dissecting room of the Dental Institute of Montreal. Twenty one years later, this corpse was still in a perfect state of mummification. This experience was therefore conclusive.

This was a curious and interesting discovery of which no laboratory, not even that of the Sorbonne, has succeeded in coming by the secret, in spite of repeated analyses. As a matter of human and scientific progress it is to be hoped that this formula may one day be transmitted by one of our scientists to some reliable group and prove its worth in terms of service to humanity.

By his studies, based on daily experimentation, Dr. Beetz has accomplished, as Damase Potvin wrote, "a work unique in its class and of inestimable scientific and educational value."

It is not surprising that the Government decided to give to the village where all these experiments were conducted the name of Johan Beetz. It will thus remain a lasting memorial to one of the greatest benefactors of the North Shore.

Dr. Johan Beetz, Sc., A.V., Knight of the Order of Leopold II, died on March 26, 1949, at the age of 75. Both *La Presse* and *L'Action Catholique* paid tribute to this eminent Canadian scientist in these words : "Among the numerous scientific discoveries made by Dr. Beetz in the course of his long career we mention particularly that of his system of mummification which, after sundry and time-tested experiments, has proven to be the most perfect in the world."

In spite of the development of forest industries, hunting fur-bearing animals and fishing still remain the main source of income for the families living in the villages east of Havre Saint-Pierre.

The life of the trapper, so full of perils and adventures, deserves special mention in any book dealing with the North Shore. Hunting holds an irresistible attraction for anyone who devotes himself to it. In the fall, when the cold begins to be felt on the fishing banks, a nostalgic yearning for the forests fills the trapper. Then, good-bye to fishing barges and blue waves. Now is the time for the birch bark canoe and the great woods !

At first, the Canadians, lacking experience, did not dare penetrate very far. Traps were set a few miles from the village, and the hunter returned home every night. Soon, however, game became scarce along the shore and the hunter had to look for it fifty, a hundred and, today, two hundred miles away on the "hunting grounds". Due to modern progress, the hunter often has the airplane at his service, and certain merchants do not hesitate to set up well-stocked stores in the more frequented areas.

But progress is expensive in a business where profits are not always sure and never excessive.

The old methods are still the most practicable. So as to prevent baggage from becoming too bulky or too heavy, only the bare necessities must be brought : a canvas tent, a little sheet-metal stove, a few kitchen utensils, a rifle, traps, fishing equipment, some clothing and provisions for the probable duration of the stay in the forest. These last are reduced to a minimum : flour, tea, yeast, lard, matches. Many add pork, butter, a few canned goods. The hunters say that, while in the forest, they are often forced to live on "blasphemies", a well-known dish containing only four ingredients : flour, baking powder, salt, and water, cooked on the surface of the stove. As can readily be seen, the hunter would have a very monotonous dish if he could not depend on the trout, pike, and other fish of the lakes and rivers, as well as game, such as partridge, rabbit, beaver, lynx, and porcupine.

Before their departure for the forest, the hunters put their conscience in order by a good confession and communion, so as to acquire the peace and strength of soul so necessary to those who go out alone, far from civilization. Indeed, it is not without emotion that they bid good-bye to their families, missionaries, and friends. But the call of the wild is so strong that they are full of good spirits when leaving for the "interior".

All the baggage is piled into a sixteen-foot canoe, filling it to capacity. The trip begins on the river, which is at first smooth and calm of flow. Soon, an oft-recurring obstacle along the way is sighted, "the rapids". Much dexterity is then required in handling the paddles or the ten-foot poles. One clumsy manoeuvre, and everything would upset. Less dangerous than the rapids, portages, as we have seen for the Indians, all demand more or less strength, courage, and patience depending on their length. Finally, after having "jumped" the rapids, made the portages, crossed the lakes, in canoes, sleds, or even by swimming or wading when necessary, the hunting camp looms forth. Built on the shores of a lake, a river, or a creek, it usually measures about ten feet by twelve, hardly allowing enough space for a man to stand erect. In this shelter, the provisions and other baggage are stored. In other still more modest huts, scattered about on the hunting grounds of the two associates, a small quantity of provisions is stored against later excursions. One must not look for comfort in these camps. The two beds are not at all soft, but after a whole day's walking with snowshoes over plains, lakes, rivers, and in the thick underbrush of the forest, one has no trouble falling asleep even on a bed of small logs with pine boughs and branches for a mattress.

When at sundown the hunter brings back a few fox pelts, martens, or minks on his toboggan, his sleep is troubled only by dreams of better furs for the next day, or the necessity of putting more wood in the little camp stove as he begins to feel the nip of the cold. The very next day after having reached the camp, the trapper lays nets at the foot of a waterfall or in the neighbouring lake. What wonderful trout, twenty to twenty-five inches long, that are as attractive on the dinner table as around the traps!

This way of life and the requirements of his calling make of the trapper a characteristic personality. Accustomed to self-reliance, he soon acquires a taste for adventure, an amazing ingenuity in the face of danger, and an imperturbable composure, even when confronted with the spectre of death, which he sees frequently at close quarters. Life in close communion with nature, the poetry of the great woods, the majesty of mountains and immense lakes awaken in him an awareness of the almighty power of God and an inquiring and observant mind. No one better than he can arouse the interest of the missionary or of his friends upon returning from his adventurous treks into the forest. Why not disclose to the amateurs of hunting a bit of these conversations which, if they sometimes take a little too much of the missionary's time, never fail to interest him?

The trapper will tell you that the Almighty Creator has endowed each animal with a wonderful instinct and that, amongst these, the beaver is the best endowed of all. Its dwelling is amazing to behold. Built on the water in the sunniest location possible, the beaver's hut is well proportioned to actual needs. If it is wide and flattened, one can be sure that it shelters a family of five, six, or seven members. If it is smaller but higher, only one couple resides therein. The interior is always clean and well kept. Each beaver has its own bed of fine wood shavings, as well disposed as by human hand. Sometimes, the beavers will repair an old hut situated in front of the new dwelling and use it as a storage room for winter provisions. The beaver feeds on the sap of certain trees : birch, aspens, and alders. It cuts down birch trees that it has chosen, and, if the trunk be too heavy, sections it off into pieces which it can drag to its hut and place among the branches, so well piled and intertwined in a corner of its home that no storm can dislodge them. As for the dam, which keeps the water at the proper level for the conveyance of his food and for his daily exercise, it is a challenge, by its solidity and impermeability, to the knowledge of the cleverest engineer.

The flesh of the beaver is usually popular with trappers because it provides enough fat for frying.

The porcupine, well prepared and well cooked, provides a tasty dish. Like the beaver, it lives on the sap of spruce trees up which it climbs, upon emerging from its nest in the crannies of rocks, to eat at ease. The hunter only has to follow its tracks, cut down the tree atop which it is roosting, and kill it with a stick. Care must be taken not to touch the animal, for it is covered with quills, which penetrate the skin of the agressor upon contact.

Our hunters claim, also, that lynx meat can be eaten if cooked in a special way. Somewhat akin to a cat, with a similar cry, but much bigger, this animal, instead of struggling in the trap and dying of exhaustion, calmly awaits death, remaining alive up to three weeks. It crouches close to the post to which the trap is fastened, as if to attack anyone coming within range. It is very agile when pursued and will never eat frozen meat.

The missionaries have spent many a happy hour listening to narrations of adventures and discoveries of this kind.

Sometimes, also, their tears have mingled with the tears of mothers or widows whose sons or husbands met death in the whirlpools of rivers, in a lonely hut, or in some unknown place.

1890. — The bodies of Joseph Gallant and Joseph Métivier from Aguanish were found by Prudent Dion and Prosper Petitpas on a deserted island in the middle of Lake Watichou. The two bodies were lying in front of a heap of stones forming a kind of shelter. On the paddle of the missing canoe a few words were scrawled : "Died after eleven days of intense suffering."

1907. — Again at Lake Watichou ! Men from Aguanish set out in search of two of their compatriots reported missing for a long time. Under an upturned canoe the body of Honoré Deraps was recognized, with his little hunting dog beside him. As for Aristide Bourque, no one ever saw him again. His poor, inconsolable mother refused to believe in her son's death. Knowing him to be an excellent swimmer, she was sure that he had escaped from the wreck, was wandering in the forest, would be rescued by the Indians, and that she would see him again ! ! !

Sheldrake, December 3, 1924. — News of the death of Georges and Paul Bouchard reached the missionary,

HUNTING 95

who set out to visit the bereaved parents. Without doubt, they were drowned on November 17 while attempting to reach a camp on the west side of the river. The unfortunate young men, loaded with traps and luggage, must have fallen through the ice. The accident happened not far from a camp where they had just left their brother Magloire and Wilbert Touzel.

Sheldrake, 1930-1937. — Alexander Bond lost two of his brothers, his hunting companions. One was drowned in the river. Alexander himself announced the sad news to his family and to the missionary. The other died in their hunting lodge, of a liver ailment. Alexander took care of his brother, whom he could not leave to seek help. He assisted him in his last moments, encouraging him, and praying with him. When death came to the solitary cabin, he laid out his brother, remained a whole night praying beside the body, and, having secured the cabin against prowlers, turned his steps towards his seaside village. His first visit was to the rectory to acquaint the missionary, his best friend, of his loss. With a few men he returned as soon as possible to the cabin to bring back the body of his beloved brother by dog sled and have him buried in the cemetery.

December 6, 1946. — Norbert Boudreau, the son of Sandy Boudreau of Rivière-au-Tonnerre, died of pleurisy at Manitou Lake on Christmas Eve. Young and still lacking the prudence of a man of experience, he drank the icy waters of a creek while on a hurried round of his traps. Death did not come suddenly. Assisted by his father, who repeated with him the act of contrition and other prayers, he prepared himself for it and accepted it with resignation, offering his sufferings to God for the recovery of his ailing mother. The unfortunate father had to leave his son alone for twenty-four hours in order to find some help at the nearest hunters' camp. He and the hunters succeeded in bringing his son on a homemade sled up to Lake Manitou. A plane, requested by telegram to speed the sick boy home, was unable to come. A few days after Christmas, a sled, drawn by the dogs of Anthony Wright from Manitou to Rivière-au-Tonnerre, brought home the body of another victim of fur-hunting.

Everyone in Seven Islands remembers the death of Wilfrid Chiasson. After several months' absence, he began the journey back to his family, eager to show the finest lot of furs that ever hunter brought back from the forest. Death overtook him, however, on the Moisie River, which closed over another victim of the Labrador waters.

Among all the tragedies of the forest the most gripping is certainly the death of the two young Collin brothers from Long Point of Mingan. We shall recount it at length in the second part of this chapter.

CHAPTER SIX

HUNTING

II

The tragic death of Willie and Edgar Collin.

ON August 19, 1936, Willie Collin, who was 24 and his nineteen-year-old brother, Edgar, two fine young men of the North Shore, left their village of Long Point of Mingan and proceeded in the direction of "Lac Croche", two hundred miles off in the forest, where they were planning to spend the winter hunting fur-bearing animals. Two older more experienced hunters from their village, Georges Méthot and his nephew, Médard, had established themselves a little farther to the north. They visited the Collin brothers on December 9 and agreed to return in three months so as to go back to the village together. On the proposed date, the Méthots left their "hunting grounds" and, five days later, arrived at their friends' camp, which they found buried in snow and strangely silent. Two pairs of snowshoes hung at the door, according to the trappers' custom. They tried to open the door, but without success, for it was locked from the inside. They then peered through a small opening under the roof. The scene which met their eyes apprised them of the tragedy which had struck the solitary camp. Two corpses lay there, one on the bed, the other on the floor near the door. Horrified, unable to help their friends, and not knowing whether they were in the presence of a contagious disease or a dastardly crime, they decided to proceed immediately to Long Point to announce the calamitous news.

After covering a distance of more than two hundred miles of forest on snowshoes, travelling night and day, they arrived in the evening of the sixth day at St. Jean. As Father Gallant was absent, Nurse Pelletier had the dismal task of breaking the sad news to the poor parents. Doctor E.-E. Binet, the coroner of the district immediately organized a trip to "Lac Croche".

On Palm Sunday, March 21, 1937, an airplane piloted by Lucien Gendron, accompanied by air mechanic Fecteau, carried Doctor Binet, Joseph Collin, the father of the two young men, and Georges Méthot as a guide to the lonely cabin. The body of Willie Collin was stretched out on the bed, wrapped in tent canvas. Edgar's body lay on the floor, curled up against the door, his head resting on his right arm. After saying a prayer, Mr. Collin did not have to look for letters or a diary, which he expected to find, for the day-by-day account lay on the floor in plain sight. Two watches dangled from the wall and a few photographs of relatives and friends peered out from a small shelf. Excepting these articles the cabin was completely destitute. Not a single stick of wood was left. The last survivor had burnt everything, even the last chip of wood he could hack from the wall with his axe.

What attracted the attention of the public to this drama in the forest was the diary, written alternately by the two brothers, from December 24, 1936 to January 26, 1937, while they were undergoing the most frightful moral and physical sufferings in their poor cabin.

This diary was published, at the time, in a few newspapers and moved readers to tears.

Thirty-eight times the two brothers wrote of their hopes, their griefs, their thoughts, which they believed would be of interest to their parents, their brothers and sisters, and their friends back at the village.

Every day, they mentioned the weather and reported their state of health, which grew progressively worse.

On December 31, Willie Collin accidentally gave himself a bad stroke on the leg with the axe and was thus forced to take absolute rest in the camp. Flour and pork were the only provisions left. Moreover, Edgar suddenly became too weak to go out and hunt for wild animals in the forest, the flesh of which would have given him strength and courage.

On January 1, a rabbit was snared near the door of their camp : "Our New Year's Day roast," one of them wrote in the diary. It was to be their last.

From then on, their only thought was of leaving this inhospitable cabin in order to rejoin two comrades encamped some twenty miles to the south. But always Willie's wounded leg, which refused to heal, prevented them from essaying the trip.

Only one hope was left now : the arrival of the Méthots, who had promised to join them for the return journey.

Hereafter, as their diary mentions, the young Collins put their trust in God, praying and mutually bolstering their courage, writing to comfort their parents and expressing their hope of seeing them again.

On the 19th, Willie found sufficient strength to take up his pen and write a few words of farewell : "I could not write yesterday, I was too weak. Edgar is very courageous. He is still able to eat a little, and that gives him enough strength to turn me about in bed. My whole body is racked with pain and feels paralysed. Do not grieve, my dear parents and friends ; if I die, Saint Anne will surely guide me. This may be the last time I address you. Adieu. I shall not forget you in heaven. Willie."

Indeed, after that day, Edgar kept up the diary alone. On January 19, he wrote : "Another day has gone by. Nobody has yet come to help us. Already five months have passed since we left you, my dear father and mother. On the morning of our departure, when I said good-bye to you, dear Mom, you kissed me and tears rolled down your cheeks. Little did I think then that it was to be the last time."

The younger brother was still able to drag himself outside to bring in a few sticks of wood and, another time, a bundle of branches to keep the fire going during the night. After this, he was forced to burn the wooden forms on which trappers stretch their skins.

These are the last words penned by Edgar Collin during the last two days passed by these young men in the Labrador forest.

January 25 : "My dear parents, I was still able to haul in a log for the night. Willie is extremely weak now. I am afraid he won't last the night, he is continually restless. How sad it is to see ourselves so far away from home ! O God, send us help !"

January 26 : "My dear parents and friends : I am very deeply grieved at having to inform you that Willie

A HAPPY MONTAGNAISE

MAIL CARRIER WITH « KOMETIK » AND DOG TEAM

died last night around eleven thirty. I don't know what to do. I can hardly lift the axe to cut the few pieces of wood I find in the camp.

"My dear parents, it will probably be my turn in a few days. Do not grieve too much for us. We have suffered too much not to be saved. I will say goodnight, as I can hardly see. When you can't find any other entry in this note book, it will mean that the Holy Virgin has come after me, too. I am saying my beads and am weeping and shivering from the cold."

January 26 was the last date entered in the Collins' diary.

One can well conclude that Edgar Collin, as he himself leads us to surmise, died a few hours after his brother, not long after he wrote the touching letter of his supreme farewell.

According to Doctor Binet, these two deaths were due to avitaminosis, a deficiency of the foods that furnish the body with the vitamins and salts necessary to life. How many of our trappers would have died in the same way had they not changed their diet on time.

This last month of life of the two Collin brothers was very painful, yet inspiring from the spiritual point of view. What a contrast between the elevated sentiments of these edifying Christians and the sombre, futile thinking of materialists, whose limited horizons are bounded by despair and suicide! These young men exhibited an admirable belief and confidence in God. Their hearts teemed with tender and loving thoughts of their parents, family, and friends. They are staunch models for our contemporary youth, sometimes too forgetful of their duties towards God and neighbour.

CHAPTER SEVEN

THE POSTAL SERVICE

The mail sack on the carrier's back. -- By dog sled. Jos. Hébert. -- The mail carriers. -- The arrival of the first boat in the spring.

ONE of the greatest moral tortures imposed on the North Shore missionaries before the advent of airplane was, without doubt, the privation of daily papers and favourite magazines, which previously they had received regularly. Man does not live by bread alone ! Mind and soul must also have their nourishment. Sometimes, one had to wait very long for the mails in Labrador !

Napoléon-Alexandre Comeau remarks in his book, *Life and Sport on the North Shore*, that in 1859, only one post office was open : in Bersimis. People living east of this Indian village had only one means of corresponding with Quebec, namely, to entrust their letters to coastal boats and to fishing schooners which, at certain times of the year, journeyed towards the capital.

I imagine that letters then were strictly business : "I am sending you seal skins, salted cod, herring. In return please send me the provisions listed herein." Such must have been the letters carried by the benevolent captains of fishing schooners. During the winter, towards mid-January, the Hudson's Bay Company's

THE POSTAL SERVICE

clerk at Mingan used to organize a trip at his Company's expense. Three men would leave the village to return six weeks later, covering some six hundred miles. The Molson Iron Works of Moisie also used to send two hardy couriers with its mail bag of fifteen to twenty pounds of mail, five or six times per season. Salomon Arsenault and Fred Deslauriers travelled between Moisie and Bersimis. Other valiant mail carriers were David Miller, Willie Ferguson, and Fred Bourdage.

Jos. Hébert was the most famous dog teamster of his day. He came from Berthier with another Canadian who became well-known throughout Labrador, Narcisse Blais, the grandfather of the merchant, Louis-T. Blais. He settled at Tête-à-la-Baleine, where he fished or hunted seals. When a somewhat regular postal service was organized between Blanc-Sablon and Esquimaux Point, he became the only mail carrier of this vast district. Twice every winter he would set out with the mail bag on his back and his snowshoes on his feet, when necessary, to cover the 900 miles return trip. As this trip took him over relatively flat terrain around bays and through archipelagos, whose every island and islet were early joined by ice bridges, he was the first one to think of utilizing dogs. He rapidly became expert at this. He would harness eleven dogs to a fourteen-foot sled which carried up to 600 pounds of mail.

It was not astonishing that Jos. Hébert was an individual set apart from others. Short, stocky, with long hair and a thick black beard, he was, as malignant tongues were wont to say, "as hairy as a bear." Dressed in warm and durable garments, utterly foreign to the latest styles, he always had ten pairs of thick wool socks ready "against the surprises of the journey." Nothing could frighten this energetic man. If forced to sleep under the open sky, he set up his nocturnal dwelling in the forest protected from winds when feasible. The dog sled was upturned to keep the mail-bags from the snow. The eleven dog slay down in a circle in the middle of which the master would place himself for the night, having near him the mail for which he was responsible. If he did not always enjoy a profound slumber, he at least got enough rest to resume his journey at the first sign of dawn.

This voyageur par excellence always insisted on giving his dogs a good meal at the end of a day's work. The people of the villages where he was expected at night knew it well and were ever careful to have the food ready.

It is said that Mrs. Bill Foreman of Muskuaro had one day neglected this duty. Jos. Hébert called on her during the evening : "Ah, Madame," he exclaimed, "an unfortunate thing has happened. I shall have to kill my dogs, as they are becoming too troublesome. They have just eaten ten of your beautiful bustards." "Don't do that, Mr. Hébert," remonstrated Mrs. Foreman, "my birds are not as important as your dogs." Who could have opened the door to the hen coop and brought about this slaughter? Public opinion did not err in this matter. Jos. Hébert also had the reputation of being very clever, as when he would sing the praises of an inferior dog which he wanted to get rid of so as to buy a better animal seen along the way.

The mail carriers had a particularly difficult task in the Bersimis – Pointe-des-Monts section. In this area, besides the long treks on foot or on snowshoes, they had

THE POSTAL SERVICE 105

to do some canoeing through the ice floes of the Gulf. When the regular service was instituted, this vast territory was divided into four sections: Bersimis to Pointe-des-Monts, Pointe-des-Monts to Moisie, Moisie to Esquimaux Point, Esquimaux Point to Blanc-Sablon. Some of the regular mail carriers in the section of Esquimaux Point to Moisie were Philippe Dupuis, Pierre Prévereau, and Jos. Cormier dit Cabot. These pioneers had to be rugged men. If the shore was inaccessible, or if sheer weariness prevented them from climbing the rocky ranges all along the coast, they made their way through the forest. Very rarely would they hire a guide, for they had very few funds to pay a salary. They had to depend solely on their experience, on their compass, and on the sun, when it shone. They invariably hastened their steps, eager to reach the first hamlet on the way before nightfall.

If, in spite of the precautions taken, they were forced to sleep in the open, they chose a protected clearing in the forest and lit a campfire, which was kept burning all night. While one of them slept on a bed of fir branches, the other stood on guard over their precious burden. This burden was not very heavy but became rather so on the carrier's back in the course of a journey along a rough and uneven route. The maximum weight for each man to carry was set at 50 pounds. No fixed rate of payment was set for the errands which they accepted along the way. In the beginning, twenty five cents per letter had been talked of, but the mail men were very charitable and seldom asked for any return. Out of pity for their isolated compatriots they always found place in their mail bags for much-needed medicines or for postal matter which people entrusted to them along the way. Yet, the government did not overpay them ; it assured each carrier of $50 per trip, a journey often lasting a whole month ! Three such trips were made every winter.

The mails became more and more considerable as the telegraph line, begun in 1880, lengthened by some 40 miles each season, thus opening a narrow trail to the travellers. Dog sleds, now necessary, travelled over this miserable trail. So as not to carry too far the cedar poles brought from the upper country and deposited along the shore, the crews disregarded the obstacles in their way, thus subjecting the mail carriers to very rough terrain.

One of these precipices between Manitou and Pigou, familiar to travellers on the North Shore, is known as the Great Coulee. There were thirteen telegraph poles on one side, six on the other, a declivity of about 4,000 feet, practically at a ninety degree angle. It was said that, after an abundant snowfall, mail carriers sometimes took four hours to emerge from this pit, which, moreover, was not the only one along the coast.

The communications of the first inhabitants of the North Shore with the exterior were thus very restricted. In 1903, at the arrival of the Eudist Fathers, they were still far from perfect. At Natashquan the missionaries learned that their first winter mail, which left Quebec at the beginning of November, reached them only late in January. In a letter dated Jan. 25, 1918, a missionary wrote these desolate words : "Our beautiful country now lies buried under its white veil, but still the weather is much too mild. The bays and rivers are still not frozen. The mails, which left Quebec on November 24, 1917, still haven't shown up around

THE POSTAL SERVICE 107

here. No letters ! No newspapers ! Nothing to read, not even the church calenders (*ordos*) to guide us in reciting the breviary and in saying Mass."

The missionaries, both witnesses and victims of these miseries, could not remain indifferent. Very naturally they could not but sympathize with civil employees forced to do such hard labour for a salary of seventy five cents a day. It was absolutely imperative that something be done to better the lot of these poor fellows, a task which should not prove too difficult if the Government would only show some good will.

The first thing to do was to reduce the length of the carriers' run, which meant increasing the number of post-offices and postmen. Some valleys were too low and narrow ; the dogs could not pull any load in them and even had difficulty pulling themselves out. This obstacle could be obviated by cutting around the valleys, through forest trails which might be longer but easier to travel on. On the longer runs, camps were to be erected as hospitable refuges for the night against storms and other hazards. A reasonable salary was to be given to these courageous Labrador mailmen, who were serving the country so well. Finally these valiant Canadian and Acadian pioneers, who had settled on a land of such inhospitable appearance, were to be helped and their relations with the outside world facilitated by a more frequent postal service.

These ideas were submitted by the missionaries to the members of the Legislative Assembly, to the Ministry of Postal Service, or to the Deputy Ministers. Negotiations were pursued, and letters were exchanged, insisting, demanding, until the point was gained.

Father Joseph Gallix, looking one day through a note book wherein a colleague used to list the letters sent by each mail, teased his friends about the number of these letters which, to him, appeared enormous. Really, there was nothing excessive in this number. In Labrador, from 1910 to 1918 and even later, one could not undertake a trip to Quebec City every day. If such a voyage was made during the summer, and if it lasted fifteen days, only three of them could be spent in the city. Only through correspondence could the bulk of the people communicate with those outside and obtain some results. Mail contracts, more numerous and better remunerated, were, in fact, given to hardy and honest men. Unfortunately, it was the Government's policy to grant such contracts to the lowest tender. As a result a curious jealousy or senseless rivalry often proved prejudicial to the whole population : men with little experience or lacking the physical requirements imperfectly discharged a function little suited to them.

The Eudist Fathers owe a debt of gratitude to the mail carriers. How often did not these stalwart men give them a lift on their dogsleds or precede them to show the way or beat a path, thus adding to their fatigue ! Among them, the names of Georges Flowers and Uriel Cormier from Esquimaux Point, Xavier Arsenault from Rivière-au-Tonnerre, Jos. Hébert from Blanc-Sablon, Philip Blaney, Néris Richard, and Xavier LeBlanc are particularly remembered. At Natashquan, Dominique Landry and Alphonse Collard rendered untold service to their fellow citizens. Both of them saved the life of their missionary on two memorable occasions.

Father Charles Decq, well known all over the North Shore for his great piety, has related "his first trip to Baie Johan Beetz" in the *Revue des Saints Cœurs*. A long journey it was for one inexperienced in travelling, from Havre Saint-Pierre to the next village to the east. The Father stopped for two days with a family living at Bethchuan both going and returning.

"After leaving Bethchuan," he wrote, "we arrived at Baie-à-Victor, acknowledged as one of the most dangerous bays on the North Shore. At first glance, it appeared solidly frozen. In reality a storm had completely broken it up a few days before. It was a shambles of blocks of ice, some frozen together, some separated by an invisible crevice, snow having fallen into these spaces and covered the thin coating of ice made by the low temperature of the preceding night. Apparently, it presented a beautiful, smooth surface, but of which many would have been wary. Our guide did not hesitate. He drove straight on towards the middle. The others, who had been retarded and had fallen behind, were too far to warn him of his imprudence. And so what was bound to happen actually did. As I was but little accustomed to travel over bays and had full confidence in my guide, I followed him. To lighten the load for the dogs, I soon got off the sled and walked behind it. Suddenly, I fell through. My clothes, which were caught in the slush and frozen stiff by the cold, prevented me from moving about. Fortunately, I had time to catch hold of a piece of ice. Meanwhile, the dogsled kept on going at a rapid pace. My distracted and confident guide did not look behind, nor did he hear my calls for help. The dogs, luckily, had keener ears. They looked around and attracted the guide's attention to my predicament... I was saved!... No, not yet!! The other dog sleds had caught up with us by this time. Uriel Cormier, one of the most expert mail carriers, was, thank God, in the shelter of a nearby thicket. The missionary, perplexed, surprised, and hesitant, was pressed into removing his garments and was helped in the arduous task. A roaring fire quickly warmed him, and his trousers were given back to him completely dried, after having been wrung by vigorous hands."

Presently, the party was able to resume its journey after an incident which could have become another tragedy of the Labrador ice.

If the postal service has never been either regular or frequent during the cold season, the great distance stretching between Labrador and Quebec, the starting point, will long prevent it from being perfect. Of course, man can always adapt himself to any circumstances, but he cannot prevent his nature from protesting now and then. One can read in a letter written on the North Shore and dated February 15, 1918 : "Life is monotonous this winter. Our time is divided among the ordinary occupations of the ministry, some reading, spiritual exercises, visiting the parishioners, and heating the house. Soon, everybody will be asking the same question : 'When will the boat leave Quebec?'" One day in the spring of 1912, Father Leventoux, the future Vicar Apostolic of the Gulf St. Lawrence, felt more keenly than usual nostalgia for his native land, of which each mail brought some small part. At Baie Sainte-Claire on Anticosti Island, where the Father was pastor, the arrival of the icebreaker *Montcalm* was finally announced... It is drawing near... The

THE POSTAL SERVICE

Father promptly came out of his rectory and climbed the ladder along the wall up to the top of the roof ... It was true, smoke could be seen about two miles off shore, beyond the white blanket which surrounded the island. As he entered the rectory, Father Leventoux remarked with melancholy : "That is about as much as we'll see of the boat," and went on to read his breviary.

"Yet", wrote Father Laizé in the *Écho du Labrador*, navigation has begun. A boat was promised us for Easter week. Since then, however, winds and ice have delayed it, to the great disappointment of our lumbermen, who are now forced to inactivity and boredom. There is no work for them, for the man in charge of the wood cutting has not arrived from Quebec ! On April 12, the steamer *King Edward* appeared at last within sight of our town of Pentecost, but without being able to let off either passengers or the eagerly awaited mail. It pursued its course towards Seven Islands and Esquimaux Point, and, upon its return on the seventeenth, a favourable wind having blown away the obstructing ice, was finally able to give us an abundant and ardently desired mail."

On the other hand, besides these wistful comments, which were often uttered, now with regard to one hamlet, now with regard to another, even during the summer, here is a more cheerful picture, often reproduced along the Labradorian shores : "For five months now, the ruthless winter has reigned supreme on the North Shore. April is nearly over, and still no bird has appeared as a harbinger of spring. When, oh when will this imprisoning circle of ice disappear ? Soon, they say, because a rumour is going around that the steamer *King Edward* left Quebec Friday, three days ago, and will arrive tomorrow, bringing the mail. More precise information has come that it will arrive tonight... To spot it sooner, I shall walk towards the ramparts of ice formed along the shore. It is a beautiful day ; the sun has deigned to temper the icy winds, and my snowshoes sink in the melting snow. As I walk slowly, I contemplate the rime, which falls with tinkling sounds from the boughs. Often my eyes turn towards the sea to the group of "Carasol" (eroded cliffs) covered with snow and presenting such beautiful mirages on certain days. 'Here it is !' I exclaim suddenly, 'this dark smoke isn't a cloud !' It is the steamer, indeed. It sails around the island and heads for the portion of sea cleared by the south wind. It enters the bay ! I hurry to the village and jump on a dogsled in a race to meet it. The small boats are not yet in season to go out and approach it. What a nice spectacle it is to see all these sleds converging on the same spot, racing as they draw nearer. Here we are ! Nearly all Seven Islands is represented. What enthusiastic cries issue from 180 throats as an answer to our welcome, while, back in the village, flags are flown from the houses. The vessel then comes to a stop, and everybody is eagerly scanning the passengers leaning over the rail for relatives or acquaintances. Happy greetings are exchanged. The *King Edward* is right near us, and we reach it by a floating pier of 24 inches of ice. The passengers are all so happy to return home after a five-month spell in the lumber camps further up the river. Suddenly a strange clamour arises, made of laughs, howls, and moans. It is the canine population in full revolution. The harnessed dogs have seen

THE POSTAL SERVICE

other dogs at liberty. 'Look,' they say in dog language, 'police dogs, without doubt. Let's tear them to pieces.' Soon the battle is on, with all the teams joining in, and the intruding dogs get the worst of it until an energetic wielding of the stick restores peace, which lasts until the departure of the first sled. Then, another scene : all the teams want to follow, to race, in spite of overturned sleds. I nearly missed my conveyance and barely waved good-bye to the *King Edward*.

"In the evening, we had plenty of mail from which everybody found cures in the almanachs for all their ills and, in the seed catalogues, the assurance that spring was here. Today, our floating pier of ice has disappeared. The sound of waves lapping the shore has returned, and for the first time, the rays of the setting sun gild the calm waters."

CHAPTER EIGHT

TRAVEL ON THE NORTH SHORE

**The *kometik*. — Its advantages. — Its dangers.
Father Conan. — Father Pétel. — Nights in the open.
The narrow escape of Father Le Strat
and Mr. Grogan.**

TRAVEL on foot was, for a long time, the only means of getting about on the North Shore, even for the transportation of mail.

One would receive letters two or three times during the winter and letters only, for the strong and energetic mail carriers could not carry more.

How full of hardships these trips must have been when one had to follow the shore as it was then : now abrupt cliffs, which plunged into the Gulf leaving no passage for the pedestrian, even at low tide, now a thick forest of young spruces extending to the sea. How could one overcome such obstacles?

The rivers very often offered firm and safe estuaries to the travellers, but, on the morrow, through the influence of winds and tides, they presented vast and unfordable areas of water. One can easily understand, then, the detours which had to be made, the unforeseen delays imposed upon the inexperienced traveller in particular.

TRAVEL ON THE NORTH SHORE

The missionaries of the first years, from 1857 on, often had to undertake such trips. With snowshoes, an axe, and the Holy Viaticum kit on his arm or slung over his back, the missionary would leave at the first call. He was wise if he had himself accompanied by one or more guides, as needed.

Those who travel much nowadays must rejoice at not having to use the *kometik* and in being able to get around in a modern plane. An hour through space would mean two or three days by dog sled.

In the same way, great must have been the joy of the first Labradorian to inaugurate the use of the dog sled. The *kometik*, or dog sled, is a light sled, well adapted to the nature of the terrain to be covered. Two boards, curved up in the front, are held together by transversal bars fastened with leather thongs or nails. This vehicle must be light, if it is to slide easily over the surface of the frozen lakes and rivers or over the frozen areas of the Gulf. It must also be narrow in order to pass through the little meandering paths of the woodland or to follow the trail of the telegraph line, a then recent and long hoped-for improvement. Soon, the *kometik* became the general mode of travel.

It was used in the villages to haul wood for fuel. The children used smaller ones to slide down snowy slopes, delighted to find a physical exercise necessary to their young years. Every day now, all along the North Shore, there were travellers : trappers going to or returning from their hunting grounds, fur buyers, lumbermen, mail carriers, and friends, happy to visit isolated neighbours while on their way to procure necessary provisions from the more important villages. At the entrance to a village, one could see a long file of dogs. The arrival of a *kometik* always caused excitement among the villagers. The telegraph would report it all along the coast. It was looked forward to, especially if it brought His Majesty's mail or a fur buyer.

"Have the mail carriers arrived yet? How late they are! Do they have a heavy mail? How many pounds per *kometik*? How many pounds did the last telegraph office report?" Mail interested every inhabitant of the North Shore, and its arrival was a great event. Women, children, any man who happened to be free at the moment hastened to the post office to read the newspapers and, especially, letters from relatives or friends.

One must count the missionary among the greatest amateurs of dog sled travel. In front of every rectory, six, seven, or eight dogs, already harnessed, lay before the gate impatiently awaiting the signal of departure. The sled was there, carrying at the back a box or chest of as varied a form as the tastes of the owners. The seat of the missionary and of his guide, if he had one, was towards the front; to it was attached the bag containing the dogs' pittance and the men's baggage. The missionary took particular care to fill his bag with all things indispensable. Woe to him if he made an important omission.

He was hardly recognizable in the picturesque garments which he donned in order to protect himself against the bitter cold. Yet they were sufficiently light for the strenuous exercise which such a trip involved. A last look into his bag to see that it contained his breviary, the Holy Viaticum, wine for the mass, wafers, altar cloths, bread and cheese for a lunch

ARRIVAL OF THE FIRST BOAT IN THE SPRING (THE S. S. SABLE ISLAND)

on the way, and he was off. As soon as the rope, which tied the sled to a post was undone, the dogs shot out at top speed in the indicated direction, but soon slowed down to a regular, steady trot. From time to time the driver yelled : hec-hec-hec, meaning to the right, or ra-ra-ra, to the left, or ha-ha-ha : stop. This language was usually well understood by the team. If the driver had his dogs well in hand, they did their work very well, giving all they had of strength and endurance, from morning till night, and if necessary, even all night.

Axe in hand, the prudent guide walked in front of the dogs for all crossings of bodies of water and tested the ice. Alexandre Comeau held that salt-water ice must be at least three inches thick to carry a man of average weight, and that, should the weather be mild, four inches may not be safe. Fresh water forms a more solid ice, offering the same advantages with half the thickness.

The *kometik* has been indeed very useful on the North Shore. Many have enjoyed this mode of travel. In the spring, for example, when the sun has softened the snow, hardened by the cold of the previous night, travelling by dog sled is relatively easy ; the dogs pull their burden with facility then over the plains and frozen bays. Some missionaries have made magnificent excursions in this way. One, in particular, has remained famous.

On March 1, 1933, the former pastor of Baie Comeau received a telegram from Bishop Leventoux summoning him to accompany the bishop to Rome to attend the ceremonies of the beatification of Sister Marie-Euphrasie Pelletier. As Father Gagné was then stationed at

Blanc-Sablon, he did not believe he could cover the 400 miles which stretched from Blanc-Sablon to Havre Saint-Pierre in less than 15 to 20 days. But with the help of the wind, which blew continually from behind the traveller, and with the sleet-covered ground offering little resistance to the runners of the sled, he averaged nearly 100 miles a day. Bishop Leventoux was startled to see his missionary arrive in the evening of March 8. A newspaper later reported the " sensaional journey " accomplished by the missionary of Blanc-Sablon.

The missionary of Rivière-au-Tonnerre recalls leaving his rectory after Mass at least twice and reaching Pigou, his furthermost mission, 50 miles away, around 5 o'clock in the late afternoon. During the evening he recited his breviary and, after a long conversation with his amiable hosts, the evening prayers and the beads were said. The following day, early in the morning he heard confessions, said Mass, and distributed communion. In the evening, the missionary was back in his rectory before nightfall without being too tired to read his breviary and say the evening prayers. A hundred miles in two days ! That wasn't too bad !

Somebody has described a real dog race as a witness of one in 1925.

"As if to help us forget the rough weather of the cold season, February has been surprisingly mild, allowing the dogs of Labrador to beat a hard path and thus form a highway. There was great movement all along the coast. The fur traders appeared : Messrs. Jos. Gagnon from Bersimis, George Maloney from Mingan, his brother Patrick from Seven Islands, and Mercier from Quebec. They all passed by, clipping along at

10 to 12 miles per hour in a race to obtain the coveted furs of the North."

One of the dangers of travelling by *kometik* was that of having to spend the night in the open. Such an adventure has happened to many missionaries. Father Louis-Philippe Gagné, for instance, was forced to camp on the bare rocks of Blanc-Sablon. To combat the cold and save four lives he had to cut down a few telegraph poles. Two *kometiks* composed the party. A crime against the law ? No, a case of extreme necessity.

One day, the missionary of Natashquan was called upon to assist a dying person at Johan-Beetz. It was noon, too late to leave for the village sixty miles away and difficult of access, for one had to follow the detours formed by the bays and rivers. How often has not this trip taken three complete days? Nevertheless, with a good guide and six good dogs, the party got under way. At two o'clock, they arrived in Aguanish. Without stopping, the two men pushed on in an effort to make the camp of John Rochette at Pachachibou, where they expected to meet somebody sent from Baie Johan-Beetz. Alas ! a great storm suddenly arose. A violent gale from the west blew the snow in our faces, completely blinding us. It was impossible to look ahead or effectively direct the leader, whom we could barely distinguish. The wind slowed the dogs, who were trying to make their way through the snow, each on his own, over a beach strewn with pieces of ice. This rough, uneven surface, was most uncomfortable for the occupants of the sled. As a result of these obstacles, moreover, the harnesses became hopelessly entangled, and the dogs could no longer pull anymore. A halt was called to unfasten the harnesses and free the dogs, a task which required a quarter of an hour, really too long.

Meanwhile, darkness had nearly overtaken us, and the leading dog, the guide on whom we depended, had lost his way. Fortunately, we noticed it in time. It seemed to us that we were travelling on a frozen bay and that we were heading towards the open sea. On either side we could vaguely perceive the sombre masses of the trees of the forest. There was no time to lose! We did not want to risk reaching the edge of the ice in this dark, stormy night. We turned in the direction of the forest. Luckily, we happened on a protected opening. As we were forced to spend a cold February night in the open, we had to organize ourselves accordingly. We built a quick fire. As we had no tea, we simply warmed some water. We had nothing to eat! Equipped with an axe, without which no traveller should dare set out, we searched for dried spruce to keep our fire alive. We found nine, which we straightway chopped down and hacked into pieces. We dried our clothes by the heat of the blaze and settled around the salutary fire to spend twelve long hours in an unknown corner of the forest. The cold was bitter, and the snow still fell... One's morale has to be good in these situations. On the following day, my companion, Dominique Landry, confessed that only our common cheerfulness and high spirits had kept up his courage during this long vigil. We spent our time keeping up the fire, saying the beads, and discussing the probable location of our improvised camp.

When, around six o'clock in the morning, a grey light seeped through the darkness, we recognized the surroundings. Providence had been kind to us. We were on an island, and the camp, which we had failed to reach the evening before, was but a few steps away from the spot where we had spent the night. A white smoke rose from its chimney, and Delias Tanguay was waiting for us there, very much worried about our fate. Tea was ready, as also some warm, appetizing meat pies. Soon, we resumed our journey.

After such a long fast, my stomach was somewhat upset all through the day. My companions must have found me less agile than usual when I had to get up and run in the snow.

Father Hesry should have left us more details about the 56 hours which he spent on a Labrador bay : two nights and a whole day without seeing land or sky, without being able to budge from the spot, with the snow falling thickly and complete darkness surrounding the travellers. It has been said that the good Father Hesry, seeing the provisions running low, gave most of his share to the driver so that he would have enough strength to resume the journey as soon as a glimmer of light would permit them to find their way.

An ailment, hitherto unknown, has often overcome the missionaries while on a journey. Here is an example. It was a bad day. The weather had become milder, the snow stuck to the *kometik*, and the dogs were unable to pull the load. To lighten their burden, the missionary rose and put on his snowshoes. Strangely, he found himself incapable of taking a step. A sudden violent hunger deprived him of all strength and incapacitated him. Without doubt, it was this strange affliction which struck Father Louis Héry, who was then pastor of Rivière-au-Tonnerre, half-way between Sheldrake and La Chaloupe, two of his missions. The inhabitants of La Chaloupe noticed that he was quite late in arriving. Some young men put on their snowshoes and went out to find him. Six miles from the village they came upon him sitting in his sled, conscious, but unable to make any movement. His dogs lay all around him.

Some time after this adventure, Father Héry, whom his colleagues had considered as the most vigorous of the "Old Guard", had to leave his parish. The unknown sickness paralysed first one foot, then the other, and later, his two legs, thus condemning the poor Father to complete inaction until his death at Bathurst College one year after his first attack.

The deed of the young men from La Chaloupe brings back the memory of many instances of devotion shown by the Labradorians to their missionaries. It would be too long to enumerate the names of all the charitable persons, of all the families, whose good will and cordial hospitality helped them to forget the painful side of their apostolic travels.

How many instances there are, alas ! of dangers even graver than nights spent in the open or of weakness caused by sudden hunger.

Father Villeneuve has stated that, during his eight years on the North Shore, he had often found himself on the threshold of death. One day, he had to visit a sick person in Moisie. He sent a telegram requesting that someone be sent to meet him and then left with his *kometik*.

" As we approached Pointe-de-l'Îlet," he wrote, " I began to worry about going around the point. Was the ice strong enough ? As I was asking myself this question, I saw the dogs fall in slush-like snow through which the water was rising. About ten feet in front of us I could see a huge block of ice, which was separated from the land by a narrow margin.

" 'Hang on to the sled,' I yelled to my companion, 'and jump after me.' I jumped but did not quite reach the ice. Nevertheless, I was able to seize the edge with both hands and drag myself out with one boot full of water. The dogs imitated me and managed to scramble out, dragging the sled and my companion, who was still hanging on to it." Cool-headed thinking and a prompt decision had saved two lives.

In the last days of January, 1908, Father Conan, missionary at Clarke City, did not meet with the same luck. "The weather was clear but very cold," wrote Father Divet, who later became pastor of Seven Islands. "The dear Father arrived, on the eve of the fatal day, alone with his two dogs. He left with three, as I had lent him one of mine. The day before, he had bought a heavy suit of sealskin at the store. After his departure, I took a walk down the forest road. Two hours later, upon returning to the rectory, I was surprised to see the three dogs at the door. Just then, a half-breed came by, looked at the dogs, and remarked that they were wet.

"As we realized the portent of this fact, we immediately organized a searching party and began following the tracks of the Father's sled. Alas ! we soon agreed that it was too late that day for further searching. On the following day, we returned to the scene of the tragedy, chopped the ice, and probed about, but without any success. The dogs had managed to escape by clawing the ice and getting rid of their harness. The poor Father had evidently been paralysed by the cold and hindered by his cumbersome garments."

This loss was an occasion of great mourning for Bishop Blanche and all the missionaries, who held their elder colleague in high esteem.

Eight years later, on the Bersimis River, tragedy struck again. On Christmas Eve, 1916, Father Pétel, missionary of the Montagnais, left to celebrate Midnight Mass at Pointe-aux-Outardes. It was a ten or fifteen-mile trip, according to the route chosen, over the large bay which penetrated far inland between the mouths of the Bersimis and Outardes River.

The departure was set for the early morning so as to take advantage of the tide and reach the opposite shore. At seven o'clock the *kometik* of 16-year-old Robert Malouin left the shore and started over the ice of the bay. To save time, two hours perhaps, they travelled in a straight line, over the habitual route of the mail carriers, Jos. Miller and David Malouin.

"I was following the sled on foot," related Robert Malouin. "The Father, seated in the *kometik*, was driving the dogs. We had hardly gone over a few feet when I felt the ice giving way. 'Father!' I yelled, 'we had better hurry back ashore!'"

Immediately, the sled was turned around, and an attempt was made to retrace their steps. Unfortunately, the Father broke through the ice with the *kometik*. His clothes became soaked with the icy water, and he found himself immobilized. His courageous companion lay full length on the ice, crawled over it, in the manner of seals, as he expressed himself, and asked the Father to take hold of his foot. Father

Pétel was thus dragged for some distance, until he was safe on a piece of thick ice which had drifted there.

The two travellers believed themselves lost. The Father gave absolution to his companion and lay down, saying he could not see very clearly any more. Robert Malouin then set out to cover, as fast as possible, the four miles to the rectory. Two hours elapsed before the rescue party, comprising Jos. Miller, Alexandre Boulianne, and David Malouin reached the Father, whom they found lifeless, with half his head in the water. The body was carried back on the fatal sled, which the men had hauled out of the water.

A hundred other similar instances could be recalled. Those we have set down here suffice to bring out the dangers of dog sled travel and to record for posterity the names of two Eudist missionaries who lost their lives in the honourable discharge of their duty amidst the ice and snow of Labrador, the two valiant sons of Brittany, Fathers Conan and Pétel.

This chapter was already written when the author had the pleasure of hearing from Father Joseph Le Strat, one of the veterans of the Eudist apostolate on the North Shore, an adventure so typical of this region and of such an absorbing interest that he felt it imperative to include it here. The story follows in Father Le Strat's own words :

"It was during the winter of 1909. I was then missionary at Rivière-Pentecôte with Father J.-M. Leventoux. It was part of our parochial task to take care of a post at the May Islands, east of Pentecost, where Mr. McDougal operated a sawmill. The ice-breaker *Montcalm* was making her first trip that winter on the North Shore. While it was at anchor in our bay, Mr. Grogan, the manager of the company of Pentecost, and I decided to go aboard, bringing with us five good dogs and a sled. I looked forward to visiting Bishop Blanche at Seven Islands, and Mr. Grogan desired to see his father, who was then manager at Clarke City. We had planned to return by land.

"Everything went off smoothly till after our arrival at Clarke City. We left this small town Sunday after Mass. We halted at noon in Jambon for a hasty lunch, eaten standing up in the bitter January cold. Darkness fell just as we reached Portage-des-Mousses, near the site of the actual town of Shelter Bay. Three Indian tents stood there, one of which contained two caribou lying in a pool of blood on the floor. Here was an excellent occasion to taste of this exquisite game, which had been graciously offered to us. As the sky was clear and starry, however, and as moonlight flooded the land, and the Indian camps were not too attractive, we decided to pursue our journey.

"We travelled three miles over ice which seemed really solid. Then, as an abrupt cliff full of obstacles confronted us, we decided to go around it. Suddenly our *kometik* began sinking and settled on an accumulation of pieces of ice having no consistency. Thinking that the dogs would be able to pull us out of this hole and believing that the ice was thicker towards the sea, we left the *kometik* but had hardly taken a step when we both sank up to our armpits in slush. Without losing a moment, we seized our snowshoes, which we placed one before the other on the opposite side of the sled, crawled over the sled and over our snowshoe bridge, and hus managed to reach a spot where we could safely stand. As the ice did not crack beneath us, we believed ourselves nearly saved. We called the leader of the long file of dogs and dragged the sled out with the traces. With great difficulty we then scaled the rock by clinging to whatever afforded a grip. All this was done promptly, without hesitation, in full accord. This time we were safe. We both thanked God and the Virgin Mary for having spared us a horrible drowning.

"Nevertheless, our situation was not ideal. The intense cold of the night, the bitter north wind, the weight of our damp clothes left us feeling miserable. Should we leave the sled behind and try to warm up by walking briskly on our way? This was my idea, as we did not have even an axe to make a fire that would dry our clothes. But, as Mr. Grogan felt too exhausted to walk with snowshoes, he insisted on trying to reach the village with the dogs. I went ahead with my snowshoes and looked back now and then. Mr. Grogan was sitting on the sled, which followed me quite closely. As we were going down a steep incline, I saw Mr. Grogan fall off the sled and roll in the snow while the dogs continued on to where I was standing. I rushed to my companion, whom I found stretched on the ground, unable to move. 'What is wrong, Mr. Grogan,' I asked, 'do you feel ill?' Numbed with cold, he could hardly answer me. He spoke like an inebriated man, hardly able to pronounce his words.

"I became very much worried. I soon understood, however, that the only way to save his life was to make a fire. All sleds carry a box in the rear, which is used both as a seat for travellers and as a container for indispensable supplies. Luckily, it contained a waterproof box of matches. By the moonlight I could distinguish a clump of alders and a few slim birches. With my pocket knife I succeeded in pulling off some birch bark and in picking some dry branches from the alders. I then lit a fire near my companion. As soon as he saw the flame, he stretched himself on his back and placed his two feet, which had turned into two blocks of ice, smack in the middle of the blaze. Little by little, the heat produced its effect. Mr. Grogan spoke more distinctly and was even able to stand by the fire. One of his feet, more affected by the cold than the other, caused him a deal of pain. He asked me to take his boots off. Fortunately, I found a pair of stockings in the box of the sled, put both of them on the frozen foot and added others that were half dried by the fire. I found a can of beans, also, and a loaf of bread, on which the crust was frozen solid. The weakness of my friend then struck me ; he could hardly pull his knife out of his pocket, and I had to open the can for him. While he was trying to swallow some food, I banked the fire with all the dry branches I could find. My friend became more and more like himself. I then proposed that he stay near the fire and keep it burning while I would speed the dogs on for some help. But he maintained that he was strong enough now and insisted that we leave together.

"At first, all went well. But, hardly had ten minutes elapsed when the cold began to affect him again as before, rendering him unable to walk or even sit in the sled. As we were getting on at quite a fast pace over a smooth surface, I knelt down and held him with my arms so as to prevent him from falling off the sled at every jar. Once the bay was crossed, we came to an abrupt hill, which constituted an annoying, unexpected obstacle. Like many other hills in that region, it forced travellers to climb as best they could on hands and knees. Knowing that the dogs would be incapable of pulling any load up such a trail, I said to my companion : 'Try to hold on to the seat, and I shall go pull with the dogs.' 'It is impossible, Father,' he replied, 'leave me here and go for some help.' These words, which appeared sensible in themselves, were said, however, in a voice so weak as to be almost a whisper. Could I leave my friend in this state? But, as I knew that the village of the May Islands was quite near, I decided to cut short all deliberation and take the only possible issue : 'All right, Mr. Grogan,' I agreed, 'I shall go, but upon one condition. You must promise me to move about all you can during my absence. Do you promise?' 'Yes, Father, I swear to keep moving continually.'

"In a few minutes the dogs bounded over an ideal trail, and I reached the houses of Gustave Poulin, the keeper of the May Islands' lighthouse, and of his son-in-law, Jos. Corby. At this hour, all the villagers were asleep. I had to knock loudly at the first door, calling for help and explaining Mr. Grogan's plight. In a minute, everybody, men, women, and children were up, ready to follow my orders, which I issued without pausing to remove my snowshoes, thinking only of the predicament of my unfortunate friend.

"When the rescue party finally went on its way, I entered Gustave Poulin's dwelling and sat by the freshly-fired stove. With difficulty I removed my ice-coated boots and put my feet near the heat. I immediately felt a sharp pain in both feet, a burning sensation similar to that felt when a spark falls on the bare skin. My feet were frozen! Instinctively, I drew away from the stove and asked for a basin full of cold water and snow to put my feet in, an excellent way to produce a rapid thawing. At that moment, Mr. Grogan was brought in. He had kept his promise faithfully. He was found kneeling in the snow halfway up the hill, dragging himself slowly up with whatever strength and energy he could muster. My own experience had just taught me how to help him. With a knife, we quickly broke the mass of ice that had formed around his boots and stockings and put his feet in the beneficent foot-bath. Needless to say, we felt sharp pains for the rest of the night and were unable to sleep or rest. Yet, the following morning, I felt well enough to say Mass, conduct the mission, and the day after this unforgettable adventure, resume our journey towards Pentecost. A few days later, the skin of our frozen feet began to peel, and the swelling gradually subsided."

How often, subsequently, did not Mr. Grogan repeat to the resourceful and energetic missionary: "If it had not been for you, Father, I would not be in this world."

CHAPTER NINE

ATTEMPTS AT PROGRESS

ALL the Eudist Fathers have had to look after certain material undertakings, which they deemed indispensable. At Natashquan, the church and the rectory had been built on a sandy point bearing only a few stunted spruces. The sea, repeatedly crashing against this weak rampart, little by little undermined the very foundations of the two main buildings of the village. After several futile attempts to stem the action of the sea by means of posts driven in the sand, it was decided to build piers or box-like constructions filled with rocks. All the men generously cooperated in this project and gave of their time and work without any remuneration. For the first time in this region, a minister, the Honourable Mr. Devlin, contributed the sizable sum of $700 for this work at Natashquan.

The new breakwater stood up against the fury of the waves this time and saved the church and the rectory from certain destruction.

Elated by this success, the missionaries turned their attention to another problem. The village is divided into two parts by a river, whose estuary swells and widens with each rising tide. This division then occasioned a daily hindrance to the inhabitants.

The missionaries, who were also victims of this state of affairs, conceived the bold project of building a bridge. It was resolved to appeal to the generous minister who had already helped us in the matter of the breakwater.

For this purpose, one of the missionaries was to undertake the trip to Quebec by the first boat. As I was the older of the two, I left, confident in the success of the entreprise. I had the honour of being received by the Honourable Mr. Devlin, who was then, in our opinion, the most sympathetic of men to the woes of mankind. A good friend of mine, Father Robin, who was highly interested in this daring interview, accompanied me. We both felt very humble in the ministerial office, which appeared to us elaborate and immense.

The Minister asked routine questions with which I was unfamiliar in 1910 and which I did not at all foresee. One of them was rather embarrassing and nearly ruined our chances by drawing a loud laugh from Father Robin, whose voice, according to Father Dagnaud, frightened children who heard it for the first time. My companion told me after the interview that he could not help but wonder what I would answer. "How many horses are there in your parish, Father?" the Minister had inquired. After a moment of reflection I replied : "We have only one horse at the moment, sir, but if we had a bridge, who knows?"

After a while, the Honourable Mr. Devlin arose, shook my hand, and said sympathetically : " If the cost of the bridge did not exceed $1,400, I should have very willingly consented." Unfortunately, the engineer, Mr. Gastonguay, had listened to our description of the place and estimated the cost of such a bridge at a minimum of $4,000. Our visit thus ended in frustra-

ATTEMPTS AT PROGRESS 133

tion. I returned to Natashquan disappointed, but not discouraged.

I wrote a host of letters to the Minister and to his engineer thereafter, insisting that they send an expert to visit the village and realize our need for this project. Finally, Mr. Gastonguay came. The bridge was granted and built during the summer of 1912.

What worries did it not occasion later to the promoters of the project ! Ice adhering to the piles and understructure of the bridge would lift it with the rising tides. Thus, the structure of the bridge was nearly ruined and retained, in spite of urgent repairs made periodically, a dilapidated appearance up till 1948. It was then replaced by a modern bridge, which cost $80,000 ! Things are done on a grander scale nowadays !

During the summer of 1912 a great celebration was held at Natashquan. People flocked in from the neighbouring missions and from as far as Havre Saint-Pierre to attend the blessing of the bridge and of a wharf that had recently been built in the harbour.

This wharf, one of the first on the North Shore with the exception of those at Havre Saint-Pierre and Seven Islands, has its own interesting history.

Mr. Joseph Girard, Federal Member of Parliament for the county of Chicoutimi, once visited his furthermost constituents. He saw the little boats of the fishermen draw near the steamer at anchor at quite a distance from the shore and return with their load of merchandise and provisions. He realized that this transportation of all the supplies for Natashquan and the neighbouring posts by rowboat or sailboat was not a simple affair, especially when the sea was agitated by the southwest winds.

The barges were held close to the steamer by means of ropes. In the fearful swelling of the rolling sea they awaited their turn to receive their share of the merchandise from Quebec City. They had to navigate, then, through the breakers at the entrance of the harbour, towering waves, frightening even to the boldest pilots.

What frightful memories have not these encounters with steamers in the open sea left in the minds of those who took part in them : broken hawsers, damaged masts, sudden leaks produced by unforeseen clashes with neighbouring barges, long waits on the water for the delayed steamer, getting caught by sudden storms and forced to return ashore with no cargo !

All this our M. P. had seen, and he understood our difficulties. We asked him to obtain a government grant for a wharf. Mr. Girard made a memorable speech and gave a formal promise : "If the inhabitants of Natashquan will not forget me at the next election, you will get a wharf for your beautiful harbour." It is not customary for missionaries to meddle in politics. Did they, in this unusual circumstance, permit themselves to make a few suggestions ? The villagers all voted for this devoted man. During his term Mr. Girard valiantly tried to help this vast country, whose needs he knew so well. This time, in spite of his lifelong allegiance, he even changed party in order to have his share of the budget and keep the promises he had made.

After this visit, and later on, I wrote often, very often, to our good representative until he must have become tired of my prose. We even thought it would

ATTEMPTS AT PROGRESS

be necessary to have recourse to the Rt. Hon. Prime Minister.

As a result of all this, however, the large sum of $50,000 was voted at the next session. But Natashquan was situated 600 miles from Quebec City. How were we to obtain the necessary wood for this construction which appeared, to us, colossal?

A group of courageous men resolved to go after some logs along the great Natashquan River and float them down to the site of the wharf. This meant a drive of one hundred miles on the river and five on the sea along the shore.

All this appeared new and stupendous to us then, and all conversations revolved around this project.

Unfortunately, our lumbermen and log drivers had not yet been in contact with the big lumber camps and lacked experience. One day, three of them embarked in a canoe in order to break a jam of logs, which had formed on a reef above a high waterfall. A strong rope tied to a tree and held by strong arms should, it seemed to them, provide sufficent security for this operation. But the current was too strong. By some miracle, one of the occupants, Dominique Landry, father of 12 children, saw the danger. Nimbly, he untied the rope which held him to the canoe, jumped overboard, and clung to the nearest logs. The other two, Wilfrid and Odilon Landry disappeared in the abyss. Tragedies such as these, when they happen in a small village, where many of the inhabitants are closely related or intimate friends, assume unheard-of proportions, causing wide grief and engulfing the village in a pall of gloom. I can still see the organizer of the enterprise, William Landry, on the day of this tragic accident. He had straightway run from the distant and fatal waterfall to tell the missionaries and have them break the news to the bereaved mothers. A year later, the body of Wilfrid Landry was found. His scapular, having become entangled in some alders along the shore, served as a clue.

We still had to carry on some persistent negotiations and even authorize a 24-hour strike so as to give the wharf at Natashquan the only useful direction in accord with the topography of the place. It still stands strongly and has rendered untold services to the inhabitants of the locality.

About this time an engineer arrived from Ottawa. He had come to make assay borings on the sandy dunes on the east side of the large estuary of the Natashquan River. Twenty men were kept busy for three consecutive summers by these operations.

Our aim was to find work for our parishioners. Moreover, we would have liked to know the real value of the black sand (ilmenite) which covers the shore for a long distance.

Have the experts said the final word on the minerals of Natashquan? Thousands of samples of ilmenite have gone to Toronto, Montreal, and the United States to be analysed. It is now known that it contains the same minerals as are found in the rocks of the now famous Lake Allard.

In June, 1918, His Excellency Bishop P.-A. Chiasson requested me to leave Natashquan for Rivière-au-Tonnerre. No sooner had I taken charge of this mission than I began to dream of obtaining a wharf for the inhabitants, who stood in need of one as did my former parishioners.

It would be too long to give an account of all the negotiations which were made for this purpose and the setbacks which were suffered in the process.

For seven years the possibility of erecting a wharf in the harbour or at its entrance was studied. Then the project was temporarily abandoned. Later, however, another site discovered by the missionary seemed to him ideal. Triumphantly he announced his discovery, but upon hearing of it, his audience believed he had lost his mind.

Pierre Casgrain, our Member of Parliament answered quite amiably to the letters which he received for two years from Rivière-au-Tonnerre. Finally, he wrote : "Father, I cannot demand a wharf just for you. The project would cost $100,000. Think of it ! If, at least, you had a real municipality."

We now had to organize a new municipality. Two years of hard work and delay passed when, one day, Father Hesry arrived from Ottawa and happily announced to everyone he met that construction was to begin on a wharf for his parish of Bras-d'Or. Not a word about ours. Yet, I had so often requested this great friend of mine to put in a word for his former parishioners of Rivière-au-Tonnerre. We all depended on him. He was renowned for his kindness and his unequalled charity. Our case was, in reality, more urgent than his. This occasioned a great deception and some jealousy which, however, was soon forgotten.

The following year, after a visit of the engineer, Bourgoin, a favourable vote was taken in the House of Commons. We would have our wharf. The estimates rose to $127,000. Work was begun the very next spring (1930).

In the course of construction, a furious storm, very similar to a tidal wave, washed away the machinery, rails, cars, and other important materials. Two piles, partially completed and erected in the harbour, were carried off by the wind and left on the sand of the beach from which it was impossible to recover them.

The situation now looked hopeless to the missionary. Once again he had to renew negotiations, which had already lasted ten years. Our perseverance persuaded the Minister of Public Works to send us one of his most experienced engineers from Ottawa. This man directed the construction with perfection and brought the project to completion.

In that part of the North Shore, the villages are relatively close to one another, five, six, eight, ten, or at the most twenty miles apart. The traveller who follows the shore by boat will now and then see a more or less important group of dwellings clustered around a chapel or a neat-looking, well-centered church. These hamlets are Rivière-aux-Graines, La Chaloupe, Sheldrake, Rivière-au-Tonnerre, Magpie, Saint-Jean, Long Point, Mingan, and Havre Saint-Pierre. Although only a short distance apart, in 1918 these villages had no means of communication other than by boat or by a road in an embryonic stage, which permitted travel on foot from one village to another but with great difficulty.

I shall never forget a certain November evening in 1918. Influenza was then rampant in my missions, attacking all the families simultaneously. It was terrible. The missionary kept travelling from one place to another, caring for bodies and souls, unable to suffice at the task. One evening, I was called to a lonely settlement called La Couture in memory of a

ATTEMPTS AT PROGRESS 139

Montmagny fisherman. There were three houses in this hamlet. I visited all three, consoling the bereaved, administering the last rites to the dangerously ill, and then I attempted, in the pitch-black night, to pick my way back with only a miserable lantern to light the way. Nobody had been able to show me any road or path. A great foreboding began to seize me. What if, by some fall or accident, I broke my lantern? What if I lost my way or deviated from this tiny path through which a pedestrian can barely pass? All these sombre thoughts kept haunting me on the way back, some two hours, which seemed longer than an entire day. I regained my composure only when, upon nearing Rivière-au-Tonnerre, the wide road assured me I was safe.

Were we able to dream then of obtaining better means of communication in such a wild and destitute region?

In 1919, I resolved to make the acquaintance of the new Minister of Colonization. I considered it my duty to tell him what I had seen and what I deemed as necessary undertakings that would change and better conditions of life for the valiant Canadians who had settled in this corner.

It was in that frame of mind that, early in the spring, I set out for Quebec. I immediately tried to obtain an interview with the Minister. I presented myself to his secretary, who told me: "Come back tomorrow, Father, at one in the afternoon." The following day, at one o'clock sharp, I was in the anteroom of the Minister's office. Then, as the Minister delayed in coming, I went to his office where Engineer Castonguay was also waiting for his chief. Two o'clock, three o'clock, four o'clock, five o'clock struck and still no

Minister. Suddenly, twenty to thirty young men, who had been invited by the Minister to discuss certain questions of colonization, came into the office where I was still wearily waiting. The Honourable J.-E. Perrault entered, greeted everyone except me, and sat in the presiding officer's chair. What was I to do? Unobtrusively find my way out and return home the next day without speaking to the Minister?

Mustering up my courage, I approached his desk and politely reminded him of the interview which I had been promised the preceding day. "Oh, is it you, Father? Tomorrow, at nine o'clock! I will see you first." At the stipulated hour I was in the anteroom and was immediately shown in.

I seized the opportunity to plead all the causes which had brought me from so far away. Was I not addressing the Minister of Colonization, the future Minister of Fisheries, our own Minister?

From then on, this Minister honoured several missionaries with his friendship. He often received them in his office, introduced them himself to his colleagues, and lent his support to their requests, whenever it was needed. He can indeed be regarded as one of the greatest benefactors of the North Shore.

This time, my desire was to link some of the villages one to the other. The Honourable Mr. Perrault sent his Chief Engineer, Mr. Émile Normandeau, to inspect these places. He stopped successively at Pentecost with Father Regnault, at Seven Islands with Father Divet, at Rivière-au-Tonnerre, and at Rivière-Saint-Jean with Father Le Strat. Thanks to him, sizable sums were entrusted to the missionaries to open roads and build sorely-needed bridges.

ATTEMPTS AT PROGRESS 141

Work was begun immediately. Gangs of men set to work in October, after the fishing season, and kept at it until the hard frozen ground would not yield to the pick and shovel. Thus, those of our parishioners who wanted to were able to earn a few dollars before the long cold season.

Were the works always directed with the necessary competence and briskness? One day, a missionary was walking towards a new section of road being built. From afar he could perceive that the men were all sitting down on the side of the road... Very likely a few minutes of rest granted by the foreman. Suddenly, he heard the foreman saying: "The tide is rising." In their code this meant: "Better get back to work, boys, here comes the Father." In the future, thought the missionary on his way back to the rectory, it may be wise to have the tide rise more often.

Nonetheless, very useful work was accomplished. An engineer, Thomas Normandeau, the brother of Émile Normandeau, directed the construction of the important bridges of Rivière-au-Tonnerre and Magpie. At the same time, he taught the best workmen of the region who, from then on, were able to undertake such tasks by themselves.

Roads, quite rudimentary, it is true, were opened in the missions of Pentecost, due to the efforts of Father Étienne Régnault. Pointe-des-Monts, Trinité, Îlets-à-Caribou, Pointe-aux-Anglais, and Pentecost were joined by trails which, during the depression, were easily converted into suitable roads.

At Clarke City, Father Robitaille ingeniously improved communications between this important centre and Sainte-Marguerite, as well as the villages along the Bay of Seven Islands.

If it is possible now to motor from Clarke City to Seven Islands, Moisie and Pentecost to Pointe-aux-Anglais, this progress is due to the bold initiative of some missionaries.

East of Seven Islands, roads that used to be travelled over during the winter for the delivery of the mail were straightened, improved, and well marked. For a distance of 40 miles it was possible to use a wagon or carriage drawn by horses or oxen, starting from Sheldrake.

At Blanc-Sablon, Father Gagné, through the courtesy of Mr. Gibault, superintendent of Maritime Fisheries, obtained the sum of $500 for the construction of a bridge which joins the two villages of Our Lady of Lourdes and Blanc-Sablon at the very extremity of the Vicariate.

All these enterprises brought a little money and ease to some poor households, though they imposed a considerable amount of work upon the missionaries during the months of October and November. They were responsible for the division of work in each village and in each sector, for the preparation of the pay rolls, and for the distribution of the wages to each worker when the allotted sum was deposited in the bank by the Chief Accountant of the Department of Colonization.

This preliminary work, done by the missionary of Rivière-au-Tonnerre and his neighbour, Father Le Strat, bore excellent results.

During the winter of 1938, a delegation flew to Quebec to present a request that these all too modest roads be transformed into a good coastal road from

Havre Saint-Pierre to Seven Islands. In June of the same year, powerful machinery was unloaded on the wharf of Rivière-au-Tonnerre. The land was levelled by up-to-date caterpillar tractors, and the rocks were blasted and crushed according to needs. Forty miles of highway were then made, offering a reasonably good route for vehicles of all kinds. Our Member of the Legislative Assembly, Mr. Arthur Leclerc, who headed the delegation sent out in 1938, had promised to obtain this road for us. His successor, Mr. Pierre Ouellette, will, we are sure, continue the good work of his predecessor and of the missionaries. To him will accrue the honour of endowing the North Shore with the long awaited national highway.

The missionaries frequently had recourse to the governments both of Ottawa and Quebec. When one is living completely isolated, far from the more populous areas, there is little to distract the mind, and one's thought naturally turns to persons and things with which one is in daily contact. Thus, events and things assume proportions which a passerby would very likely not even suspect. This applies, also, to all the Eudist missionaries ever since they came in contact with the North Shore in 1903. The long distances prevented them from travelling far from their residences. They were, consequently, particularly exposed to hearing the grievances of their parishioners and to discovering some hidden misery. Could they witness these hardships without seeking to alleviate them? In fact, their intervention was absolutely necessary, and one can truly affirm that nothing accomplished in any domain at that time could have been done without them. Is it not where the activity of the clergy is most efficacious that one finds the best economic, social, and religious stability?

One will see, in the following chapters, how these humble beginnings were outstripped by the progress brought by the pulp factories and the lumber camps of the North Shore.

CHAPTER TEN

PROGRESS

I

*The pulp mills : Clarke City, Baie Comeau.
The lumber camps. — Tragedy at the Lac des Quinze Milles.
Father Tortelier.*

THE first centre in the remarkable development of industry on the North Shore was Clarke City. Its pioneers were the four Clarke brothers, William, James, John, and George, who decided to build there the second pulp mill of the Province of Quebec (Chicoutimi had operated the first one.)

"In 1898, a yacht entered the harbour of Seven Islands. It carried two brothers, William and James Clarke. From this little boat, the two men viewed the entrancing scene presented by the thickly-wooded hills, which ranged all around the vast bay. On that day, a daring plan began to take shape in their minds : that of building a town in the heart of the forest, making a dam, constructing an electrical plant on the Sainte-Marguerite River, and setting up a modern pulp establishment." (EDMOND CHASSÉ). It was a tremendous undertaking at the time, one which, in the minds of the inhabitants of the North Shore, took on stupendous proportions. Everywhere, from the camps of Manicouagan to those of Pentecost, in all the homes, everyone talked about this herculean enterprise !

Nearly fifty years have since gone by ... Clarke City is still a neat little town built around the house of William Clarke on the plateau which dominates the falls of the Sainte-Marguerite River. It has a church, rectory, convent, schools, a hospital, hotels, etc.

For over forty years now, Clarke City has provided means of livelihood for a great number of workers from the Magdalen Islands and the North Shore, particularly from Seven Islands and vicinity. Its founders well deserve our gratitude.

The little town was, for a long time, managed by a man whose name is still uttered with respect. A tireless worker, a righteous man, one who stood for law and order, an exemplary Christian, who could be seen every morning walking to church to invoke God's help in his daily tasks, James Hanrahan can also be considered as one of the benefactors of the North Shore. He was responsible for the arrival of the Little Franciscan Nuns of Mary, who are so greatly appreciated and admired in the town. On all occasions, he has shown the greatest generosity in his help to the missionaries for all their enterprises.

With his name we must also associate that of Philippe Gallienne, "everybody's father", as the townspeople were wont to refer to him. This man was the embodiment of loyalty to his employers, of charity to his fellow workers, and was a Christian of very deep faith.

Before 1900, only the saw-mills had promoted manual labour. In 1883, capitalists had built an important saw-mill and harbour at Pentecost. Their aim was to export wood to England and elsewhere. Then, other saw-mills were built at the mouths of the Manicouagan,

Godbout, and Sainte-Marguerite Rivers, and at the May Islands.

From 1900 on occurred the great revolution of pulp and paper. The little businesses were bought by larger enterprises, and the old saw-mills were abandoned or converted into barkers. In 1908, the pulp mill of Clarke City began to operate. In 1918, another one opened at Franquelin ; in 1919, at Shelter Bay ; in 1923, at Godbout ; in 1928, at Trinity. The 1928-1932 depression closed all the mills of the North Shore except those of Franquelin, Godbout, Shelter Bay, and Clarke City. Providentially, the North Shore Paper Company had begun to open Baie Comeau at that time.

The North Shore, evidently, has now become industrialized, open to engineers, electricians, mechanics, carpenters, masons, workers of all kinds, timber contractors, and lumbermen. The tiny hamlets of yore have now assumed the aspect of modern towns, wherein automobiles of the latest model, trucks of all dimensions, and powerful tractors circulate.

Young missionaries, namely, Fathers A. Régnault, L.-P. Gagné, J. Bourque, L. Lebel, A. Poulin and J. Lapointe are now at these posts, welcoming the newcomers, opening their churches and rectories to them, and giving them advice and encouragement, ever so helpful to these men uprooted from their families and transported to unfamiliar surroundings.

A Eudist Father residing at the little port of Manicouagan several years ago then dared to prophesy a brilliant future for this region. In 1905, he wrote in the *Écho du Labrador* : "The wealth of forests covered with spruce of all kinds and sizes, with occasional clumps of slim birch, watered by innumerable rivers and immense lakes, the wealth of water power, moreover, which Providence seems to have designedly disposed there, will, sooner or later, tempt the capital of the old or the new continent."

Forty years later, a young pupil of the Sisters of the Holy Cross, Miss Gabrielle Gallienne pointed out the realization of this insight in our future : "When one visits the electrical plant of Baie Comeau," she wrote in an essay, "one's attention is drawn to a painting on the wall. The painter has represented Colonel McCormick standing by a tiny river and contemplating its flow. By his expression one can read a determination to accomplish a project of magnitude. Without any doubt on his part, these little cascades will become powerful falls from which will rise the mainspring of the industry he plans to build."

In 1936, the dream became a reality. In the spring of the same year, groups of workers of all trades began operations under the direction of experienced foremen. The little river, held back by enormous dams, swelled and became powerful enough to turn huge machinery producing an electrical force of 75,000 h.p.

At the same time, around Baie Comeau, other gangs of lumbermen, miners, and carpenters, who were housed in little log cabins, pushed back the forest and removed rocks to make space for the huge buildings of the new mill, where hundreds of employees were to work night and day and which was to produce four hundred and twenty five tons of paper every day of the week. Soon, around this isolated fjord of the North Shore, visited previously only by a few hunters, the renowned Napoléon Comeau in particular, there appeared, as by enchantment, a picturesque little town with wide

BAIE COMEAU ... INDUSTRIAL QUARTER

BAIE COMEAU... CHURCH, CONVENT AND RECTORY

streets lined with hotels, stores, warehouses, a community centre, library, hospital, churches, and schools. From its very beginning, Baie Comeau bore the aspect of a modern city, endowed with all the services and advantages of other much more ancient and more populous towns. It is true that, to give birth to this town and make it develop, the Quebec North Shore Paper Company spent liberally indeed. The mill, the wharf, the electric plant, the roads linking all the essential services, the aqueduct, and the lighting system have reputedly cost a cool eighteen million.

For the great number of men who flocked from all parts of the country to benefit by the excellent salaries paid in Baie Comeau, a religious organization was necessary. In 1935, Father Louis-Philippe Gagné was authorized to direct it and to build a rectory and a church. This beautiful church of Baie Comeau, a temple of a Dom Bellot style ot architecture, admired by everybody, enriched by remarkable frescoes, is the work of the celebrated artist, Guido Nincheri.

Here, therefore, one finds nothing of the old North Shore. Without seeking it, without planning for it, but uniquely by allowing himself to be carried by the current of multiple activities and constant progress, of which he was a witness, Father Gagné built his church, adorned it, and endowed it with the bells imported from France, a Way of the Cross from Italy, and, on August 11, 1946, he was able to offer to His Excellency, Bishop N.-A. Labrie, a cathedral truly worthy of the first Bishop of the Gulf of St. Lawrence.

Sixty-five miles west of Baie Comeau, a rival town, well situated on the shore of the St. Lawrence, was built by the Anglo Pulp Company. It grew progressively, providing work to thousands of labourers and lumbermen. There, also, a task of organization awaited the missionary both in the lumber camps and in and around the new town. Reverend Father Luc Sirois, already well known in the region, having been for eleven years a missionary among the Indians at Bersimis and all along the Shore, displayed remarkable talent and interest. Soon, one witnessed in that locality, where numerous families of colonists settled, a religious organization complete with church, rectory, convent, and schools.

The lumber camps, it can be affirmed, began their activity at a most providential hour. What would have become of the disastrously impoverished population of the North Shore as a result of the depression of 1927-1935? No more fishing, no work to be found anywhere.

It is only since the opening of these lumber camps that it has become possible for these people to breathe more freely, to see in these regions a revival of the old spirit. The forest industry of the North Shore has certainly been a boon to the young unemployed men of the Gaspé peninsula, of the Magdalen Islands, of the counties of the Lower St. Lawrence, and elsewhere.

In 1903, two lumber camps opened at Manicouagan and Pentecost for the purpose of furnishing lumber to the saw-mills, About five hundred men from localities all over the Shore worked there for a salary of fifteen to twenty-five dollars a month. When they arrived in these two villages, they scattered to rustic log camps built at ten, fifteen, and twenty miles from the village. The farthermost was sixty miles away, at the "Fork," where the Manicouagan River branches out in two directions. There, a hundred men used to cut the finest logs.

Every week, horse-drawn sleds carried provisions to all these men. The missionary usually formed part of these convoys. He rode up, seated on sacks of flour or oats, and returned on the same sled, this time occupying a nondescript seat. The weariness of both men and horses on the way over obliged the party to come to a halt early in the day. Twenty miles was sufficient for the first day. Night was spent in miserable huts, where the food was none too good and sleeping conditions even worse, as the shelter had to be shared with the horses.

The third day, at last, our destination was reached: four camps, which served as dwellings for the lumbermen. Very poor dwellings they were at that time, low and poorly lighted. How very far removed from the modern camps of today!

The camp cooks, then as now, did their best to prepare the most palatable food for their companions and hosts. Their efforts were limited by the materials brought from far with the utmost difficulty and consisting mostly of flour, lard, beans, peas, syrup, beef, and salt pork.

Needless to say, the missionaries returned from these excursions, weary and very glad to find themselves back in their humble rectory.

Soon, the Clarke City Pulp Company opened other camps on the Sainte-Marguerite River. Housing and food for the lumbermen gradually improved.

A letter dated February 21, 1921, and addressed by a missionary to his brother in France gave a few details concerning the lumber camps set up by the same company east of Seven Islands, on the Manitou and Pigou Rivers. "I cannot help dreading the fact that soon I shall have to travel to the lumber camps to celebrate Mass some fifty times and put up with certain inconveniences always disagreeable to a man too fond of comfort and too solicitous of his health. Although I keep before me the motto : 'Expect the worst, hope for the best, accept what comes,' everything seems frightening after I have enjoyed for a few days the kindly heat of the stove and the comforts of 'home, sweet home.' "

The prospect of these forest missions was, therefore, far from inviting. The missionary, indeed, had to travel for fifty miles by *kometik* to reach the farthest camps. He had to cross the great Manitou Lake, follow the snow-covered rivers, run from camp to camp, hear the men's confessions, preach, say Mass, and, if possible, be back at the village for Sunday Mass.

Fifty Masses in the woods looks like a record. However, during the winter of 1930-31, Father Lucien Bourque conducted a total of fifty two missions in the camps of Godbout, Saint-Nicholas, and Franquelin, an area of approximately 300 miles.

All the Eudist Fathers who are still exercising the holy ministry in the diocese of the Gulf of St. Lawrence have had to make the rounds of the lumber camps within their territory at some time or other. Each can recall some incident of travel that was annoying and even dangerous because of snow, storms, or some other unexpected contingency.

Whenever possible, all the directors and managers of the companies, as well as the contractors, did all in their power to make it easier for the missionaries to travel to the lumber camps.

In 1935, a great improvement gradually spread over the North Shore : automobiles and trucks superseded horses and dogs so that in certain camps the hauling of logs was done almost entirely by trucks over ice roads. Ten years later, an even greater boon was brought to the region with the arrival of the snowmobile, which completely revolutionized communications with the great woods. This conveyance, rapid and even heated, can transport a dozèn lumbermen to faraway camps within a few hours. Furthermore, during the winter of 1948-49, successful experiments were carried out which point the way to the advantageous use of the snowmobile to haul wood instead of horses. One such vehicle on favourable terrain would accomplish the work of eight horses. How often, in these last years, have not the missionaries made capital of this mode of travel to visit, rapidly and agreeably, all the lumber camps.

The lumbermen of 1903 would have much to say on the differences between their mode of living and that of their successors of 1949. Now, their dwellings are spacious, well lighted, evenly heated, and attractive. The radio plays all day long. A delco provides electricity. The men have dryers for their clothes, running water, and bathrooms : a veritable palace compared witht he uncomfortable and dark hovels of days gone by.

Cheerful cooks, responsible for the good humour that usually goes with a civilly-treated stomach, bake bread, pies, cakes, meat and vegetables, beans also, but only occasionally ... a fare as good as in some of the best hotels.

Let us add that, in the co-operative lumber camps, experienced and zealous apostles are at work creating for our young lumbermen an atmosphere of Christian charity, of wholesome recreation, and of economy. All co-operative camps have become centres of study, of cooperation, of mutual help, where the worker toils and relaxes in a family atmosphere under the protection of Christ to whom they address their prayers together morning and night, before and after meals. The sight of the peace, gayety, and friendly emulation, which reign in these camps, makes one realize the extent of the good accomplished by a relatively young organization of Catholic Action.

It has uplifted and ennobled a type of work, a way of life which, not so long ago, was detestable. The craft of lumberman thus understood has become moral, remunerative, and, to quote Father Alexandre Dugré, S.J., after a visit to the Baie Comeau Co-operative Camps in January 1949, a type of work that is "not ruinous for the body, not enslaving, not stultifying for the mind."

The missionaries always experience a particular warmth from their very first meeting with these valiant woodsmen, who have travelled far from their homes to earn by dint of hard work a living for their families. The priest is always welcome among them. He feels at ease with these good men, especially if he is used to ministry in the wood camps. He associates himself with their way of life for a few hours, prays with them, encourages them, and brings them the moral strength which our religion brings to men of good will. The evening is spent in serious pursuits but is not wholly devoid of merriment. After the meal taken in common and shared by their beloved visitor, they chat, laugh, discuss various questions, sing, and play a few pranks on unsuspecting comrades. Then comes the hour of prayer, and, as all are eager to hear the Word of God after having been deprived of it for so long, the missionary makes a short sermon. The sermon in the wood camp ! It is more an intimate talk in which the orator is less preoccupied with rhetoric and more with getting across eternal truths in a simple, paternal manner. The message he wishes to convey is that of the happiness of the soul at peace with God and with his fellowmen. His aim is to give to each one the opportunity of intensifying or recapturing union with God by sanctifying grace. For this purpose, the priest retires to the most discreet part of the camp to receive the penitents one by one in the absolute secrecy of confession. All missionaries leaving this improvised confessional where they have blessed, encouraged, consoled, and given absolution have experienced some of the purest joys of their ministry.

On the following day, the presence of the priest still sheds a religious character on the daily routine of camp life. On a rustic table around which the men ordinarily assemble for meals and the clatter of plates and forks is heard, a snowy tablecloth is spread. On it the priest arranges all that comprises the portable altar. Everyone dresses with more than usual care, and, at the time set by the foreman, all congregate to hear Mass, which the priest says early enough so as not to overlap on the men's hours of work. Often, during the Mass, very beautiful, resonant voices intone liturgical chants to the accompaniment of wind blowing through the tall trees. All receive Holy Communion. After breakfast, the men scatter to resume their daily tasks.

"Goody-bye, Father, we would like to be able to keep you longer, to see you more often. Thank you and come back soon!" The missionary who shakes hands with his boys in the camp for the last time feels a certain nostalgia for the camp ministry, which later causes him to repeat often : "How I liked visiting the wood camps ! One was able to do so much good to our men."

These apostolic visits to the wood camps, of which the Eudist Fathers have kept such good memories, were once, unfortunately, the scene of the unforgettable tragedy of the Lac-des-Quinze. It would be unthinkable to omit this drama which cost the life of a young missionary whose heart was full of the desire to do good, Father Augustin Tortelier, an expert in the Montagnais tongue. He was beloved by the Indian roamers of the great woods, who used to call him "the Father who speaks like us." Father Tortelier was to spend the winter of 1922 with Father Étienne Régnault. These two Fathers were in charge of the missions of Franquelin, Godbout, and Shelter Bay. A considerable group of people had organized themselves some thirty miles from the sea, at the far end of Quinze Lake, for the purpose of cutting pulpwood. There were 550 persons in that settlement, 121 of whom were children and 95 women, a real parish in the woods.

Messrs. Bouchard and Rouleau, the foremen of the camp, had begun the building of a little chapel for the priest, whom their employees and they themselves were eager to have come. A lake, the "Lake of the Fifteen Miles," was a serious obstacle to travelling between Shelter Bay and the wood camp. From November to mid-January the ice was not safe and navigation impossible. No route had yet been made between these two points. It was therefore resolved that Father Tortelier would spend at least two months with this group while Father Régnault would take charge of the ordinary missions scattered along the shore along a distance of 115 miles between Franquelin and Shelter Bay.

Did Father Tortelier have some premonition of his death before his departure? It was found that he burnt all his correspondence, and the only thing that remained in the drawers of his desk was a brief testament which read : "I have had my way too much in life to leave some request at the hour of my death. I would only ask those who have known me to pray that my soul may escape the flames of purgatory as soon as possible. Signed : Augustin Tortelier, Eudist Father and unworthy missionary." After such an admirable act of faith and of humility, the details of his death matter but little. Let us, however, note these words of his reported by Father Régnault : "I will not let myself be drowned like the Fathers of Bersimis. If I should drown, it will be because of my guides."

Towards 4 o'clock on a Sunday afternoon, the party left Shelter Bay by dog sled. At five o'clock it reached the camp where it was to take a small boat named *La Vitesse*. The wind blew furiously, however, and a discussion was held as to whether the members of the party should leave that evening or not.

Father Tortelier opposed leaving. The mechanic, Therrien, however, had received a telegram from his wife, who was ill at Tadoussac, and he expressed his desire to make the trip without further delay so as not to miss the boat of the Clarke Steamships, soon due at Shelter Bay. Finally, the opinion of Doctor Vézina, whom patients were expecting at the camp of Messrs. Bouchard and Rouleau, prevailed. Besides those already mentioned, seven other persons were in the party : Georges Rousseau from Escoumains and his wife, Anne-Marie Lapointe, the blacksmith, Tremblay, from Baie Saint-Paul ; young Maher, son of the head foreman of Shelter Bay ; Mr. Therriault, assistant wood-scaler ; another scaler, and Mr. Morin from Sacré-Cœur, ten in all.

They left, accordingly, around six o'clock, in complete darkness. They stopped at Louis Bernier's camp where Doctor Vézina wanted to visit a few patients. It was half past six when they left this camp. Half an hour later, the men of Pit Gémus' camp heard outbursts of laughter and songs ... then, nothing. A barge named *La Sauvagesse*, which had left from the same point of departure as *La Vitesse*, and drawing a load of fresh beef for the camps at the upper end of the lake, arrived there at midnight. Albini Bouchard, who subsequently reported the details of the tragedy, headed the enterprise. He inquired whether they had seen *La Vitesse*. Mr. Isabelle, captain of *La Sauvagesse* pointed out to Mr. Bouchard that there was ice in the strait uniting the two lakes. Immediately, Mr. Bouchard had some inkling of what had happened : upon meeting with the ice of the strait, the *Vitesse* must have sunk ! What had happened to the ten passengers ? "Bring a canoe," ordered Albini Bouchard to one of his employees. "Hurry, let's try to find them !" The two men sped to the scene and, seeing nothing along the way, they went to Gémus' and Bernier's camps for some possible information, but there was none beyond that of the sound of laughter and songs heard around half past six.

There was no doubt possible. A horrible tragedy had just made the strait now called *La Passe des noyés* ("Drowned Men's Pass") sadly renowned. Albini Bouchard nicked the trees of the shore opposite the spot with his axe and stuck a pole in the ice so as to be able to find it on the following day. It took three days to recover the bodies from the water, which was 50 feet deep in that place. Donat Therrien had remained in the boat in a futile effort to stop a leak in the hull with twisted blankets. The opening was at least three feet long and six inches wide.

When, at Christmas, the boat was brought to the surface, the body of Therrien fell through and disappeared in the water, which had to be dragged anew. The twisted blankets still adhered to the opening in the boat.

Needless to say, grief and consternation spread over the village of Shelter Bay, when the bodies arrived, and in each of the parished of the deceased to which the Company promptly had the bodies transported. The body of Father Tortelier was laid to rest in the cemetery of Havre Saint-Pierre. A great number of people who had known the piety and virtue of this missionary demanded parts of his cassock to keep as precious relics. No doubt, Father Tortelier is now one of the most powerful protectors in heaven of the Labrador Missions.

CHAPTER ELEVEN

PROGRESS

II

Navigation and commerce. — Humble beginnings. The Holliday brothers. — Shipwrecks. The Clarke Steamship Company.

THE arrival of the boat has always been a great event in the Labradorian villages. For a long time yet there will be, on such an occasion, the same gatherings, the same exuberant joy of meeting one another, and the same flocking around the boxes and bales coming out of the boat's hold. All this can be explained by the fact that the boat is the only conveyance to bring us our food for both body and mind.

We have already seen how the schooners of the seal hunters of Esquimaux Point and Natashquan used to sail to Quebec and fetch provisions for the North Shore. Narcisse Blais was the first person to become familiar with navigation on the Gulf as far as Blanc-Sablon. While still very young, he left his village of Berthier in the spring of 1866 and, with a few companions, sailed aboard a schooner in the direction of Blanc-Sablon. This schooner was loaded with merchandise which it was to exchange for salmon, salted herring, and especially for the skins and oil of seals, already much in demand in Quebec City.

At that time there was a seal-hunting post at Brador Bay operated by the Jones family. The Robertson family had a similar one at Tabatière, the Gallichon brothers at Old Fort, and the Monger family at Tête-à-la-Baleine. These hunters were looked upon as the kings of the region.

Narcisse Blais put himself at the service of the Robertsons and drew a fair salary. In the spring of 1848 the boat destined to carry the seal-skins and seal-oil was lost at sea. Young Blais, who was then 18 years old, associated himself with three companions. They left Tabatière in a small boat and stopped at Esquimaux Point, four hundred miles to the west, after having made alternate use of both sails and oars. From Esquimaux Point to Quebec they navigated in a sailing schooner of slightly larger dimensions. To accomplish such a trip of more than 700 miles by means of sails and oars along wild shores, which they examined most carefully for danger points as well as for safe harbours, was an excellent apprenticeship in their calling as sailors.

The ambition of these daring navigators was out of the ordinary. They wanted to buy a schooner, fill it with merchandise which they knew was indispensable in the Blanc-Sablon region, and barter these goods for riches unknown to urban dwellers. At first glance it seemed too daring a project. The intrepid young men did not hesitate, however. They found the desired schooner, bought it at a fair price, and undertook the long and perilous journey. A few years later, Narcisse Blais became sole owner of the schooner and subsequently acquired two others.

In 1896, Narcisse Blais ceded his commercial enterprise to his son, Joseph, who carried on with it until

1921, an unlucky year in which Captain Jos. Blais lost his last schooner at Brador Bay. The Messrs. Blais, whose name is still so honourably borne by the well-known merchant, Louis-T. Blais of Quebec, have rendered remarkable service to the population between Natashquan and Blanc-Sablon. The name of Alfred Mercier should also be cited here. After having navigated for more than twenty years in these very waters, he lost his life in a wreck in the harbour of Natashquan.

After several landings of Canadians and Acadians ever more and more numerous at Natashquan, Esquimaux Point, and other posts to the west, navigation by steamer became imperative. For a long time it encountered a thousand unsuspected dangers and difficulties. This immense gulf harbours countless hidden and widely scattered rocks, countless reefs stretching from shore to open sea, several all too narrow straits and innumerable islands around which to sail against the fury of waves and winds. Even so, this north country has many men, many fearless mariners who do not shy away from danger.

In 1885, the Holliday and Fraser Company launched the *Otter*. This steamer plied the waves for thirteen years. On November 18, 1898, it was wrecked on Blanche Island above Rivière-du-Loup. It was replaced by the *St. Olaf*, which was owned by the three Holliday brothers, James, Willie, and Malcolm. On November 21, 1901, Captain Lemaître was caught in a storm around five o'clock off the coast of Sheldrake. In the opaqueness of the night, the *St. Olaf* was thrown on Boule Island as it was entering Seven Islands. It was only on the 24th that Mr. Ross could dispatch

Dan Smith, Clovis Vigneault, Alfred Vallée, and Jos. Gamache, the grandson of the Anticosti sorcerer, to the scene of the disaster. All the members of the crew, including the two passengers, had perished. One body, that of Marie Pagé of Rivière-au-Tonnerre, was washed ashore opposite the site of the tragedy. Of the steamer, all that was left was the watch tower. The clock that hung on the wall indicated 12.30, the exact hour of the disaster.

In 1903 another shipwreck occurred, which was reported in the *Écho du Labrador* under the caption: *A Vessel in Distress.*

"On October 9, 1903, a rumour began to circulate in the village of Pentecost : the *Saint-Laurent* is grounded at Pointe-aux-Anglais. Inquiries were made and everyone scanned the sea in that direction. In the distance, at the extremity of the point, which stretches nine miles towards the open sea from Pentecost, one could indeed see the vessel caught amongst huge rocks already tragically famous and against which the waves seemed ready to cast it at any moment. The *Saint-Laurent* was the mail boat of the North Shore. It had left Pentecost the preceding day at 11 o'clock in the evening and, because of a telegram received from Pointe-aux-Anglais, the captain had directed his vessel towards that locality, which was not one of his regular ports of call. He wished to facilitate the loading of six barrels of cod for two fishermen and tried to get as near the shore as possible. Suddenly, the boat struck the extremity of the rock and smashed its rudder and three blades of the propeller, thus becoming helpless. Only fifteen feet out and the boat would have been safe. Many were the passengers on board, among them

Father Brézel, who was returning to Manicouagan, as the retreat which he was to attend at Esquimaux Point had been cancelled. They were rescued and very hospitably sheltered in the homes of the locality until they were all able to proceed on the steamer *Aberdeen*. But the cargo of the *Saint-Laurent*, comprising some six hundred barrels of cod, was nearly entirely lost, to the great detriment of the Lower St. Lawrence fishermen, who were thus faced with great hardship and penury for the coming winter."

In 1910, more bad news rapidly spread about. In the night of July 10, the *Aranmore* and the *Wolfe* collided opposite La Malbaie. The *Wolfe* sank perpendicularly. The passengers, some of whom had jumped in the water, were all rescued, but the *Wolfe* was a total loss to the Holliday Company.

Although, after this date, shipwrecks became less numerous, we must nevertheless mention that of the *Guide* on October 15, 1926, off Pointe-des-Monts. The preceding evening, Captain Jos. Mathias Caron, Mechanic Jean-Marie Guinard, and Civil Engineer Joseph Laflamme, great friend of the missionaries and brother of Mgr. Eugène Laflamme, then pastor of the Cathedral of Quebec, had visited the rectory of Rivière-au-Tonnerre and, with the missionary, had discussed the project of building a local industry : that of manufacturing commercial fertilizer with fish waste. The following day, the *Guide* left for Seven Islands. Around nine o'clock in the evening, in a rough sea, it suddenly tilted and sank. Five men, who had been thrown in the sea by the movement of the boat, clung to drifting wood until they were rescued at five in the morning by a pulp barge from Matane. Among the

LUMBER CAMP NEAR BAIE COMEAU

Photo Paul Provancher

Photo Paul Provancher

LOUIS-PHILIPPE GAGNÉ, C.J.M.

dead, alas, were Engineer Laflamme and Captain Caron.

Another accident in the history of North Shore navigation occurred on August 12, 1933. The *North Shore* had to slow down that afternoon because of a thick fog which enveloped the stream. Around 4 p. m. a slight tremor was felt : the boat had run aground on the rocks of the Îlets-à-Caribou. As the Apostolic Delegate, Andrea Cassulo, was aboard, this accident caught some public attention.

A tragic date, also, was October 30, 1934. It became known that a smuggling schooner from Saint-Pierre had run into trouble around Pigou and that the captain had disappeared. The survivors, four men from Saint-Pierre, had walked along the coast and had managed to reach, more dead than alive, the home of Peter Wright, where they received desperately needed help and care in the nick of time. On the same day, the *Saint-Roi-David* was lost with its captain, Albani Brie. It had left Egg Island Sunday, October 28, with Seven Islands as its destination. But the telegraphic transmission was poor, and nothing definite could be learned. On the following day, bags of cabbage addressed to Havre Saint-Pierre were picked up on the shores of Moisie, a barrel of gazoline was found on the beach of Seven Islands, and debris of a grey colour was noticed along different points of the shore. Here was clear evidence of another sea tragedy wherein six lives were involved.

Some time later, in November, an impressive ceremony presided over by Colonel Stanton was held aboard the *North Voyageur* around the place of the casualty. Captain William Tremblay insisted on reciting a prayer for the lost men in the presence of the assembled crew. Then, a wreath of flowers was cast upon the water, a fitting tribute to the brave Captain Brie, who was ever ready to be of service to everyone... These facts serve to point out the difficulties which must be faced by any enterprise of navigation along the North Shore.

After the loss of the *Wolfe*, there began a real crisis in navigation which grew graver during World War I and the ensuing two years. One could only depend on the *Guide*, which was captained by the famous Arctic explorer, Bernier, or the tiny *Labrador*, or the *Savoy* under Captain J.-B. Bélanger. The *Savoy* belonged to Mr. Menier. It was at the service of Anticosti Island and carried passengers and mail for the North Shore. Typical recollections linger in the minds of travellers of that period. Captain Bernier had only eight beds for passengers, and the main dish at meals was usually sausage. This excellent mariner certainly must have known his coast. One day, however, having spread a map on the table of his cabin, he pointed to the exact spot where they actually were and, addressing two missionaries who were following his indications, he said : "To our right is Sainte-Geneviève Island and to our left, a long reef that a good captain must be thoroughly familiar with. We are now between the island and the reef, exactly in the right channel." At that very moment the *Guide* scraped bottom ! "Well, I didn't know about that one !" exclaimed the captain, throwing in a picturesque expression... The old salt was not always easy-going. To a young crew member, whom he saw coming out of the deck washroom one day, he said ; "Well, my boy, is this where you are assigned now ?"

The *Labrador* accommodated a greater number of passengers. It had ten cabins and twenty beds. As they were usually reserved for the ladies, there were often none left for the men. One night, off the coast of Godbout, the sea was very rough, and the *Labrador* was pitching. The men were sitting up in the lounge. As the missionary, who was seated with them, could hardly keep his eyes open, they practically forced him to lie down in the lower berth of a half-open cabin. When he awoke the next morning, he was told that the upper berth was occupied by a venerable lady. This little incident caused much merriment on board.

On the *Savoy* conditions were no better. The vessel very frequently took on more passengers than it could comfortably accommodate, especially at the closing of the lumber camps. Passengers slept in the dining-room, in the corridors, on the benches, and even on the tables. Sometimes, the unwary traveller found himself host to unwelcome parasites, due to this forced promiscuity.

Saddened witnesses of the numerous shipwrecks of the Labrador waters and of a situation as painful to them as to their flock, the Eudist missionaries, through long and persevering efforts, sought ways of relieving it. By incessant negotiations they enlisted the aid of a public man to whom the North Shore owes a great debt of gratitude. Mr. Girard of Chicoutimi, Federal M. P., had visited the region several times ; he understood its needs and responded to all our demands. As a result of his excellent efforts in our behalf, naval lights, buoys, and lighthouses appeared all over the danger zones, and horns blew everywhere during the frequent fogs.

After Mr. Girard, the Honourable Pierre Casgrain hospitably received the same missionaries at his office on Saint-François-Xavier Street in Montreal. The same causes, and others born of changing circumstances, were pleaded in this office. All the problems of the North Shore passed in review. All favourable arguments toward the establishment of a bi-monthly steamer service from Quebec to Blanc-Sablon and of a regular service in winter from La Malbaie to Havre Saint-Pierre were put forward and discussed both in conversation and in writing. Plans were made, also, by the missionaries to obtain smaller vessels that would assume postal service for the smaller localities which were not ports of call of the steamers. Three main sections profited from these negotiations : Rivière-au-Tonnerre – Anticosti Island ; Havre Saint-Pierre – Natashquan ; Natashquan – Blanc-Sablon.

Is there not reason to thank Providence for the circumstances which brought about an interview at Ottawa in 1920 between Sir George Foster, Federal Minister of Commerce, and Desmond Clarke? The Minister asked Mr. Clarke to come to his office and suggested that he organize a maritime company to assume the transportation service of the Gaspé Peninsula and the North Shore. This was a grave question and a project not to be lightly undertaken. Navigation is not easy along the North Shore, as we have already seen. Distances are enormous. Often, the boats must return to Quebec empty. Seeing the hesitation of his interlocutor, the Minister promised the help of his Department and, as the Province of Quebec was directly concerned in such a project, he proposed to enlist the Provincial Government's cooperation, also. He added that he considered this enterprise as indispensable and very advantageous. It was a question of coming to the aid of a nearly isolated population and of keeping up communications with a too little-known region of the Province.

Desmond Clarke is the son of William Clarke. He has three brothers, Frank, Walter, and Wilfrid. All four of them once resided at Clarke City. Frank was manager of the factory; Walter, assistant-manager; Desmond, sales manager; and Wilfrid, head of the Purchasing Department. They did not come easily by these executive positions. People on the North Shore can recall seeing them, while they were still youths, work with other lumbermen, doing their work and living their life, so as to understand them more fully, along the forest limits of Manitou Lake and Manitou River. They know the intense studies and long initiation they underwent in this complicated industry.

To travel from Clarke City to college and back the only means of travel was by boat. The four brothers have, therefore, by their travels and their work, acquired a thorough knowledge of the North Shore and of its needs. Young, full of initiative, desirous of being of some help, they founded the Clarke Steamship Company. Immediately, Desmond sailed to England where he bought two ships; a third one was found in Canada. In a few years, the flag of the new company floated over the waters of the St. Lawrence, and the four white bars on the funnels are a testimony to the continuing excellent service of the four brothers. One can see their vessels along the Gaspé Peninsula, around the Magdalen Islands, Newfoundland, Bermuda, the West Indies, South America, at Georgetown in British

Guiana, in Jamaica, at Havana, and Nassau. Trim-looking vessels, such as the *New Northland* and the *North Star*, bring tourists who are interested in the homecrafts of our rural women and thus carry afar the good reputation of an hospitable, polite, gay population, faithful to its Christian traditions. Thus, the trade of Canada and of the Province of Quebec reaches far, and the riches and beauties of its mighty river become better known and more frequently visited.

Service to the North Shore improved little by little. Winter navigation from La Malbaie to Havre Saint-Pierre was inaugurated and has continued uninterrupted. Finally, the furthermost corner, Blanc-Sablon, was able to communicate with Quebec first by the *La Brador* under Captain Brie, then by the *Sable* under under Captain Antoine Fournier, and the *Gaspesia* under Captain G. Garon. Twice a month, the isolated people of this district now see, with genuine happiness, a boat bring in mail and merchandise.

Is it not interesting today for the section between Baie Comeau and Seven Islands to see trim and seaworthy vessels, gleaming under their white paint, the *Rimouski*, the *Jean-Brillant*, and the *Matane*, cross the river daily and give the illusion of unimpeded commerce between the two shores?

In the *Action Catholique* of August 20, 1946, one can read this excerpt: "In the reconversion of a war corvette the Clarke Steamship Company has found a marvellous solution to weekly service between Montreal and different ports of the North Shore up to Natashquan," six hundred and forty-one miles away.

Politicians, industrialists, business men, clergymen, and other people, who take the beautiful cruise that

Desmond Clarke has made possible, become henceforth more familiar with this region. They are convinced that, now that the North Shore is but a week away from Quebec and Montreal, the Clarke Steamship Company will considerably influence the development of this part of the Province in every respect. Its new vessel, the *North Shore*, can accommodate fifty first class passengers and thirty second class passengers. It displaces 700 tons and sails at fifteen knots an hour. It was blessed at Baie Comeau on August 15, 1946 by His Excellency, Bishop N.-A. Labrie, in the presence of numerous guests and citizens of Baie Comeau. The inauguration of the corvette, *North Shore*, by providing for longer and quicker trips, has indeed added to the ever increasing progress of the North Shore, discreetly, yet perceptibly.

Progress of this sort has resulted in the better welfare of our people. By increasing the number of its vessels, a navigation company creates more jobs for our Canadians. How many French-Canadians have thus had an opportunity to ply their favourite trade, have studied, become mechanics, engineers, etc. Captain Louis Cormier of Havre Saint-Pierre, for instance, his three brothers, and many others picked up their knowledge and skill at this school of practical navigation on the Gulf of St. Lawrence.

The missionaries, the fishermen, and the sick have on several occasions benefited from the progress that has been made. Long cherished projects, supported by the missionaries, have, with the help of the Honourable Mr. Casgrain and of his successor, Mr. Frederick Dorion, been realized. Refrigerated holds have been built in the boats and refrigerated warehouses erected in the fishing centres. The fishermen who do line or net fishing thus receive a higher price for their salmon, halibut, and filet of cod, which can now be sold fresh in Quebec and Montreal.

Understandings were reached between Wilfrid Clarke and the missionaries concerning certain items. Dried caplin, for example, in spite of its highly offensive odour, is transported to Quebec at the very low price of twenty five cents per hundredweight.

Yet, there remain attached to travelling along the Labrador coast many discomforts occasioned by the weather and distance. At any rate, constant efforts are being made to facilitate and encourage travel by the people of the North Shore, especially when most needed. Patients going to the hospital at Havre Saint-Pierre, for instance, travel at half-price. The missionaries travel free. One missionary recalled many trips he had made to Quebec for only two or three dollars, spent mostly in tips to employees, "a sum quite in proportion to my funds," he confided.

One can never forget the fine spirit, friendly atmosphere, and good humour, which have ever been the hallmarks of our boats along the North Shore. All their passengers feel at home. The captains, although subject to sudden changes of mood understandable in men always struggling against the unforseeable difficulties of navigation, against fogs and storms, are beloved by all. Who, on the North Shore, does not recall with particular pleasure meeting Captain Jos. Boucher of the *Labrador*, of the first *North Shore*, and of the *North Star*? Who has not admired the friendliness of Captain Albini Brie of the *Labrador* and of the *North Shore*, or felt the kindness of Captain J. Caron, now aboard the *North Coaster*?

Captain Antoine Fournier, for instance, and his *Sable* were justly popular. Antoine Fournier was a friend whose return everybody greeted with a genuine pleasure, who was always ready to be of service to everyone by accepting errands. When the *Sable* was serving the Lower St. Lawrence region, it was something to see, upon the arrival of the boat in each village, the entire population flock to the wharf and go aboard to find Captain Fournier. Young and old crowded around him to greet and question him, and the good captain smiled, joked, and inquired about their health, their success at fishing, etc.

The Clarke Company has taken the means to favour religious services on board its ships. A little chapel is always ready when there is a priest on board to say Mass, and it is a touching ceremony to see the Holy Sacrifice offered on the majestic river. One could also name a pleiad of young captains and officers of all ranks who maintain, aboard the more and more numerous boats travelling over the waters of the Gulf, this spirit of Christian charity.

The author of these notes discovered by chance at Trinity Bay a document pertaining to navigation and illustrating the devotion which the mariner bears to Saint Anne. It reads as follows :

"We were nine North Shore men aboard the schooner *Trépanier* : Olivier Chouinard and eight companions ; Esdras Langlois, Louis Langlois, Frank Misson, Amable Labrie, Gustave Poulin, Joseph Poulin, Octave Collin, and Pierre Chicoine. During the night of November 9, 1906, a very violent storm suddenly arose so that in a few minutes we were unable to direct the boat, and it ran aground at Pointe-Paradis, west of the Manicouagan River. By morning, the schooner was tilting dangerously, and it was impossible to think of using the lifeboat in this boiling sea. Our situation soon became desperate. Captain Trépanier, who was a profoundly Christian man, drew a little statue of Saint Anne from his pocket and, with the help of a companion, fastened it to the fore-shroud. Then, we all knelt down and implored Saint Anne to help us and to preserve our lives for the sake of our wives and children. We promised to have many High Masses sung in her honour. After this, we arose and set to work trying to straighten the vessel. We succeeded, and the schooner was carried out to sea by the waves. Still, the waves were getting continually bigger, the wind became icy, and the seas seemed ready to swallow our little vessel at every moment. We had a cargo of many bales of hay. By nightfall we felt there was little hope left. After having commended our souls to God, we turned to the statue, which darkness prevented us from seeing, and kept repeating the prayer : 'Good Saint Anne, have pity on us and our families.' Around midnight, the wind dropped, and the sea became very nearly calm. With what joy and relief we thanked the good Saint for her manifest protection. At the break of day, a steady, westerly breeze pushed us along towards the harbour of Pentecost, where we dropped anchor less than 24 hours later."

Needless to say, the sailors expressed their heartfelt gratitude to Saint Anne, in the little chapel erected on the rock at Pentecost, for having saved their lives, whereas so many other mariners lost theirs in that fearful storm of the night of November 9, 1906.

CHAPTER TWELVE

PROGRESS

III

Health. — Dispensaries. — Saint Jean Eudes Hospital.

WHEN the pioneers settled on the sites which they had chosen along the North Shore, they little worried about their health. All they relied on were the home-brewed remedies prepared by the women over the kitchen stove with the pure water of the spring and the medicinal herbs which grew in the forest. They called on Divine Providence, for the most part, to take care of them. Yet, as the communities became more populous, epidemics spread throughout the settlements, and even the most conservative realized that something had to be done.

As for the missionaries, the most expert writer could hardly describe adequately the physical and especially moral sufferings which they had to undergo. Two dates remain horribly vivid in their memory : 1904, the year of diphtheria, and 1918, the year of Spanish influenza. In the November, 1904 issue of the *Écho du Labrador* is the following announcement in an article entitled : "Hours of anguish," — "One of our missions has been visited by an epidemic of croup."

At the first call, the missionary set forth to visit the stricken families. The season was far advanced, snow covered the ground, ice was beginning to form on the rivers and had already formed along the shores, thus making it difficult to travel in a frail canoe. One had to be extremely careful. The shining surface of the thin ice sometimes hid abysmal depths beneath. To make matters worse, chunks of ice were strewn on the beach by the tides and made walking particularly difficult. But of what consequence were these inconveniences compared with the sadness which inundated the soul of the missionary when, after 20 miles of travel, he reached the village only to find that the sickness had spread to all the houses?

He entered the first dwelling along the way. Both father and mother stood there with tears streaming from their eyes. His arrival cheered them up somewhat, and they asked him to do something to save their little child, begging him on their knees to deliver the child from this sickness which was already choking him. Yet what could the missionary do? He was powerless before this relentless disease, the gravity of which he was so well aware. Only a doctor could help, but the nearest one was sixty miles away. Such moments of anguish cannot be forgotten and incidents like these recurred both night and day for three weeks!

And yet, they are still not to be compared with the sufferings brought about by the Spanish influenza of 1918. This new malady appeared suddenly at one house. It was a strange disease which struck without warning! It spread like wildfire, striking one or more victims in every home. Every one was exposed to it, both young and old, and it took on sundry aspects with different persons. For some, the symptoms of diphtheria were evident, for others, those of typhoid fever, pleurisy, or meningitis.

Only a few days after its first appearance, it reached the main localities and invaded the majority of the homes. Every day, the mortal remains of some villager were carried to the church and laid to rest in the cemetery. A pall of gloom settled over this part of the country. Information about the deaths that had occurred was exchanged almost in whispers. The bells even stopped tolling so as not to aggravate the general grief.

Fortunately, great charity was exercised throughout the stricken areas. Those who had not become a prey to the sickness devoted their time to helping sick relatives and friends. But, as time passed by, even they became fewer and fewer until it was sometimes difficult to find someone to cook meals, administer medicine, lay out the deceased, and accompany them to the cemetery.

The missionary then had to give of himself unreservedly, both in time and energy, and attempted, though limited in means, to allay the sufferings of his parishioners. He distributed small doses of quinine and gave whatever advice seemed appropriate. Alone, without a doctor to come to the aid of a population of eight to twelve hundred people scattered along a stretch of more than forty miles, he was continually on the road. He ran from one house to another, soothing, confessing the sick, distributing the Holy Viaticum, and performing the last rites.

One of them wrote after the nightmare was over : "I have had to travel alone at night through the forest, three times, over a distance of ten miles, with only a miserable lantern to light my way and big boots on my feet because of all the water along the way. When one motor boat brought me back from a village to the west, another was waiting to take me to a locality to the east. In spite of this, in one mission twenty miles away from my rectory, where it was impossible for me to arrive on time because of bad weather and the deadly rapidity of the disease, nine parishioners died without receiving the Last Sacraments. Thank God, I was able to reach the other thirty on time."

Father Le Strat, pastor of Havre Saint-Pierre, recalls here some incidents of which he was a witness during this fatal year of 1918.

"One fall evening, I was returning from Magpie where influenza was as virulent as at my resident mission of Rivière-Saint-Jean. The work of the mission, the visits to the many stricken parishioners, the burial services, and the long trip had just about exhausted me. I felt the need to take some food and rest awhile. At the entrance to the village, however, somebody stopped me with the information that a young man had died two days before. His mother was alone, ill with the same disease, and nobody had come to lay out her beloved departed one ! On the morrow, corruption would certainly have appeared. Heeding the call of charity, I immediately turned my steps towards the stricken home. I succeeded in persuading a local man to accompany me, assuring him that I would do most of the work and that he would not be in any danger of contracting the disease. The neighbours had prepared a casket but had not dared enter the house. We went in and laid the casket inside near the door. A heartrending scene met our gaze. The bereaved mother had collapsed on a chair, weeping over the death of her son and over her own powerlessness. I spoke a few words of sympathy and tried to comfort her as best I could. At the far end of the only room in the house, on a miserable bed, lay her son in the position in which death had left him. I recited a short prayer by the body, then wrapped him up in a shroud and, this time with the help of my companion, I carried him to the casket, which we nailed down before the unfortunate mother, who, in spite of her grief, found enough faith to say : 'Thank you, Father. It is hard, but it is the will of God.' Our task was done, as we had rendered the last earthly service possible to a deceased Christian."

The 1918 epidemic of influenza on the North Shore reminds me of a similar epidemic, notable in the annals of the city of Caen in Normandy. Saint John Eudes devoted himself to its victims even to the point of sleeping for several years in a cask kept purposely for him in a meadow, so that he would be more at liberty to give of himself and his time unstintingly to the help of the stricken people of the city. Nothing, likewise, prevented the followers of Saint John Eudes, during the North Shore epidemic of 1918, from doing what was humanly possible to succour their unfortunate parishioners.

For all the villages strewn along the one hundred and fifty miles of coastline where this epidemic struck its lethal blows, there were only two doctors, one at Havre Saint-Pierre and the other at Clarke City, two important localities which already kept them quite occupied. Only rarely were they seen in the other communities because of the distances to be covered, the expenses which such travel entailed, and the habits contracted by the mere force of circumstances.

At Natashquan, for example, the doctor of Havre Saint-Pierre was called only for the gravest illness and solely by those capable of paying the expenses of the trip. He was once called to attend a patient who would most assuredly have died without a surgical operation. The patient regained his health but found himself a considerably poorer man.

It is painful to be called upon to attend a sick person when a doctor would be needed, but it is even more painful to realize one's absolute incompetence in most cases. In all the missions, the Sisters, who were, from 1903 to 1917, our devoted collaborators, rendered remarkable services to the sick, and it was with much regret indeed that the population saw them leave.

At Natashquan we had a little pharmacy. We communicated then with Doctor Joseph Schmit, who who was considered an excellent physician at Anticosti, where he was retained by the millionaire, Henri Menier. In 1908 this good friend had bought us precision scales in Paris for light medicines. We also had a good medical book to which we often referred.

Finally, for more than thirty years, letters addressed to the Reverend Mother Superior of the Sisters of the Hôtel-Dieu of Quebec City were often mailed from some Labradorian rectory. These letters all had about the same contents : they spoke of medicines then in fashion, of sterile gauze bandages, of antypirine pills, quinine, cascara, creosote, and iodine. They thanked the Sisters for the excellent medicine received. One of them expressed anxiety, as the fearsome tuberculosis seemed to be spreading among our population. Four young people had left us around then, seemingly struck

Fr. JOSEPH LEGRESLEY WITH GROUP AT CAMP OF OUTARDES

FATHER TORTELIER

FATHER LEJOLLEC

FATHER BRÉZEL

TRAGIC
DEATHS

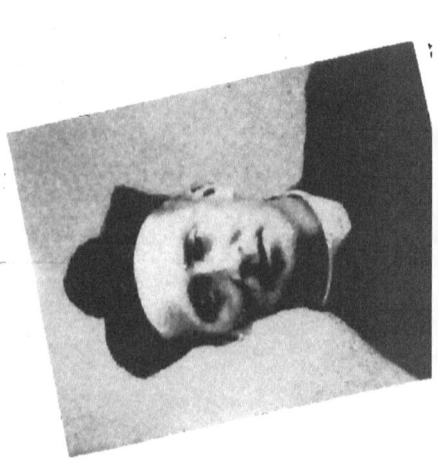

by this disease... Changes in the weather were so sudden and dangerous there !

Around 1925 we came up against a sickness that had been heretofore unknown or nearly so on the North Shore. In April of that year a talented young man had been sent to study in Quebec. The missionary was hoping that he would become a schoolmaster for his boys' evening school. He fell sick, however, and the doctor diagnosed his ailment as chronic appendicitis. He was advised that, if he took proper care of himself, he could wait until spring to be operated on, but Horatio Duguay died after Christmas.

This was an object lesson that demanded decision. At all costs a way had to be found to send to the nearest hospital (in our case the Hôtel-Dieu in Quebec City) all persons found suffering from this disease. Many were the patients who took the long, costly journey to this house of charity.

A letter written at the time alludes to the charitable demands that had to be addressed to this hospital : "Here comes the protégé of the Hôtel-Dieu, humbly, with yet another request. The young girl who brings this letter is suffering from the common ailment, chronic appendicitis. I have sent her, fully confident that you will receive her. Her father has been wholly unsuccessful with his fishing because of the porpoises. I shall help her a bit myself... Your kindness will probably do the rest." The Sisters of the Hôtel-Dieu have been very kind to the population of the North Shore. Indeed, there was a time when the word "porpoise" was associated with all new arrivals from a certain Labradorian region. "Another porpoise has come in," they would say.

Thus, the missionaries did all in their power to relieve physical suffering on the North Shore. Nearly all concerned themselves with medicine, giving advice and recommending known remedies. Many became experts at tooth extraction. Father Louis-Philippe Gagné recalls that, in one single evening, one hundred and eight canines, molars, and incisors were uprooted by his forceps. He was then making the rounds of his missions and had stopped at the village of Romaine. In many cases all they could do for their patients was to pray for them. Frequently have they come out of the sick room worried, perplexed, not knowing what to do or say. How often could not the words which a poet wrote about the priest have been applied to them:

"Mes larmes tomberont du cœur avec les vôtres,
Je n'en ai pas pour moi, mais j'en ai pour les autres." [1]

All these facts demonstrate the ardour and the perseverance shown by the missionaries towards improving this miserable situation. I began my activity in this matter in 1912 and never let up thereafter. Our first aim was to obtain doctors for the most important localities. Doctors! that is all we could think of! At first I knocked at the wrong door. I wrote to Ottawa, to our Federal M. P., Mr. Girard, whom I knew very well.

Mr. Girard was one of my most important correspondents, and he always answered me very faithfully. He had obtained a new wharf and other improvements in our behalf. I thought he could help us in other fields

---

[1] "My heart's tears will mingle with yours,
None have I for myself but only for others."

as well. He did not refer me, moreover, to anyone else. I described our situation in the most doleful manner and compared it with that of the population of the eastern part of our region, which was farther away from cities than we were yet getting a better medical service. The Protestant enterprise, the "Deep Sea Mission" directed by the famous philanthropist, Grenfell, had, in fact, built a hospital at Harrington, from which a doctor now and then set forth and visited points between Natashquan and Blanc-Sablon. Yet, our more populated villages to the west were entirely without medical service. Good arguments, indeed, but to no effect : medical assistance was not a service of the Federal Government. It was only later that I learned whom I should contact.

The terrible memories of the epidemic of influenza spurred me on to greater efforts. Having become, as a jesting colleague ironically called me, Engineer of Bridges and Highways for my mission district, I was in constant communication with the Honourable J.-E. Perreault, who was Minister of Colonization at the time. I wrote to him by every mail ; he never let a letter of mine go unanswered. Every time I went to Quebec City and met him at his office, I would tell him about certain humorous incidents of the district, but we also discussed very serious subjects. One day, I told him about the great desire which had obsessed me for a long time, that of obtaining some kind of medical service for the district most forsaken in this matter, namely, the area between Seven Islands and Natashquan. "This is a matter for the Director of Public Health," he answered me. "Why don't you contact Doctor A. Lessard ? He is kind and humane. I am sure he will do something about your distressing situation." The Minister was kind enough to lead me through the labyrinth of corridors in the Parliament Building to the office of the Director. He happened to be absent. "Take a chair, Father," said the Minister, "Doctor Lessard should be along presently." How long did I wait? I could not remember, for the Doctor, who was then a perfect stranger to me, had to wake up the intruder to get acquainted with him... I had fallen asleep.

I regret not being able to remember the exact date of my first meeting with this man, who subsequently became one of the greatest benefactors of the North Shore. It must have been around 1922.

From this day on I kept up a constant exchange of friendly letters with Doctor Lessard, discussing our hopes, plans, projects, and their fulfilment. I explained our painful situation and insisted that the presence of a doctor was a necessity in all the main localities and that a hospital should be built for this forgotten part of the country. Of course, the much too limited resources at hand had not permitted us to promote this enterprise, but the point was to see whether it should not be undertaken by the Department of Public Health. Doctor Lessard always took careful note of my letters and patiently listened to me in his office when I presented myself there twice that year, but he was fearful of too high expenses and, like all Quebec people of that period, had only a vague knowledge of the North Shore. Finally, in the fall of 1923, some action was taken.

An elderly American lady, Doctor R. Emerson, was residing in the little village of Moisie, where she found only a limited practice. This woman physician had been, prior to her arrival at Moisie, in the employ of the Protestant organization of welfare, the "Deep Sea Mission" in the easterly village of Harrington. She was competent and offered to come to Rivière-au-Tonnerre. Doctor Lessard, accordingly, sent her to us. This original and eccentric woman died, however, the following year in the house which served her as dwelling and consultation room. This was a great blow for the missionary, and another period of vexations known only to God and himself began.

However, the idea of retaining the services of a graduate nurse had taken hold on my mind. I was then on a holiday in France and wrote to Doctor Lessard about this project. The answer shone like a guiding star : "Your idea of acquiring nurses to relieve the distress of the sick in your district seems to me good and practical."

About the same time, moreover, another event eliminated the hope of ever getting resident doctors for the region east of Seven Islands. After being sent by Doctor Lessard to investigate the situation on the premises, young Doctor Savoie, freshly graduated from Laval University, met me upon my return from France. "Well, Doctor," I said, "what do you think of the North Shore? Are you taking the boat with me tomorrow? You are young, with a long future before you..." "I would go with you for a year, Father," he answered, "provided I was paid $360 a month." This was far too much at that time.

From then on, the word "doctor" was to be forgotten and not mentioned any more, but where were we to find nurses courageous enough to come to this unknown

North Shore? By a strange coincidence I received a very well-written letter in 1925 which greatly impressed me. A young girl by the name of Eveline Bignell stated therein that she was ready to do some social service on the North Shore and to devote herself body and soul to the task. Social service? A most obscure term for me at the time.

Bishop Leventoux was then in Quebec City. I requested Miss Bignell to contact him at the Saint-Cœur-de-Marie rectory. At the same time I inquired of His Excellency whether her request should be taken into consideration. He replied that this person appeared to be sincerely desirous of doing some good and would be happy to find a position which would permit her to support her aged parents. I then wrote to Miss Bignell that, in these isolated missions, we were in desperate need of a competent nurse, expert in obstetrics and able to treat ordinary illnesses. "I see no obstacle there," immediately answered this forerunner of the *Équipières Sociales*. "I am ready to study and shall quickly acquire the necessary experience." Doctor Lessard, upon being apprised of this generous offer, accepted it, and she set to work under Doctors Samson, Laliberté, and Philippe Hamel. All three had nothing but praise for the talent and remarkable aptitudes of their pupil.

Miss Bignell arrived in our village on August 26, 1926. A spacious house, but, alas, unfinished and little fitted for the use for which it was destined, was rented and furnished for our nurse and her parents.

This first dispensary set up in the Province soon became a source of considerable expense. The bills which passed through the office of the Director of

Public Health began to worry him. Finally, he decided to come and appraise the situation himself. This news made us leap with joy. He was accompanied by a friend, Mr. Oscar Morin, Deputy Minister of Municipal Affairs, whose help we had already requested for the possible erection of new municipalities in our district. Was it not time to give more importance, from the civil point of view, to our humble hamlets?

We received the two gentlemen with all possible deference. On Sunday, at the sermon, I greeted them and thanked Divine Providence for having sent them to realize, *de visu*, the extent of our distress. During this little talk I could not restrain the tears that came to my eyes and later excused my emotion as due to the already advanced age of the orator. But the painful memories, which were recalled at that moment, caused the emotion to well up from the depths of my soul. It did not leave our two visitors indifferent, nor their wives and several parishioners, whose eyes also became moist.

A great step was taken. On the first fine day, I accompanied my distinguished guests to the residence of my neighbours to the east, Father Le Strat, at Rivière-Saint-Jean. This colleague, who was mischievous and has remained so, had discreetly informed his parishioners of the expected visit. Very nearly all were sick on this occasion and came, one after the other, until a very late hour, to consult the Director of Public Health. "Ye Gods!" exclaimed the Doctor when finally the last patient went out of the door, "how I pity you having to live among such unfortunate people!"

On the following day we proceeded towards Havre Saint-Pierre. Doctor Lessard examined patients and questioned many of the inhabitants.

After the Sunday High Mass he spoke to the parishioners. All were there, in great anticipation. "I have come among you," he said, "to study the situation here from the point of view of hygiene and public health. It is really deplorable. I realize that all that your missionaries have told us is very true. In the presence of my friends who have accompanied me, I promise that a hospital will be built in your locality." A hospital at Havre Saint-Pierre was the main thing our district needed. All there was left to do was to see to it that the authorities would fulfill their solemn promise.

The dispensaries, meanwhile, gave us a few worries. The nurse at Rivière-au-Tonnerre had brought her father and mother to live with her. She also hired an assistant, Miss Antonia Roy, a chance acquaintance whom she had met at the Hospital of the Child Jesus in Quebec. Then she took advantage of Doctor Lessard's kindly disposition to extend and equip her modest establishment with unflagging zeal. Rivière-Saint-Jean, Natashquan, Aguanish, Baie Johan-Beetz, and other posts complained, and rightly so, that they needed a dispensary just as much as Rivière-au-Tonnerre. They had become envious of our good fortune. We therefore had to keep up the struggle.

I shall never forget the hard days which Doctor Lessard made me spend in the old city of Champlain. It must have been during the summer of 1927. A trip to Quebec was decided upon and, of course, an interview with our good friend. Father Le Strat, a recognized builder in our district, had entrusted some precious papers to my care : a plan for the new dispensary to be built at Rivière-Saint-Jean and a complete list of materials required. Doctor Lessard was then busy with a patient at the Hôtel-Dieu. "We are getting more and more involved, Father," he said to me. "Before going any further, I demand that you have a talk with the Honourable Prime Minister. That is indispensable."

I had to wait three days for the privilege of this interview. The Prime Minister, on this occasion, seemed cold and reserved. He received me in his office, had me sit down before his desk, and listened. I described our situation and explained that, considering how things were up our way, it was absolutely necessary that a hospital be built at Havre Saint-Pierre. Furthermore, dispensaries, under the direction of competent nurses should be organized in the more populated localities. The nurse could receive and treat patients and would, when necessary, attend them in their homes.

I was well acquainted with the situation, having considered it under all its aspects for so long. Thus, for a quarter of an hour, I was able to give the Prime Minister what I hoped was a complete exposé of the reasons in favour of this project. "How much would these dispensaries cost?" the Honourable A. Taschereau finally inquired. "Between five and six thousand dollars, Sir," I replied. "Very well. With that amount you should have a decent house." The Prime Minister then arose, shook my hands, and added : "We cannot abandon the inhabitants of the North Shore, Father, and we shall give them definite aid."

I wondered just what he meant by these words. If they were enigmatic to me, they produced an excellent effect on Doctor Lessard, to whom I reported them faithfully. In fact, he authorized me to purchase the wood necessary for the construction, a furnace for the basement, a cooking stove, a bath, pipes, and all other supplies listed by Father Le Strat. Then, he made an appointment with me for the following day, when he gave me a cheque to the amount of four thousand two hundred dollars.

Two months after this decisive interview, the missions of Father Le Strat with their one hundred and fifty families had their dispensary. This proved to be a great boon. Nurse Pelletier, one of the first nurses, is still vividly remembered. Doctor Lessard used to say of her that she was a first-rate nurse whose work he greatly appreciated.

A year later, Natashquan had its dispensary, also. Miss Éveline Bignell, who later on went to Moisie, organized that of Aguanish, moreover, and continued to do her "social service" in a dispensary of Lake Saint Jean in spite of her frail health.

The Canadian nurse is seen everywhere now. One meets her even in the smallest and most out-of-the-way settlements of Provincial colonization.

Built in the centre of the village, if most convenient, or else alone on a hill, if more accessible there to all, her little house appears trim and attractive. Everyone is welcome, rich or poor. At the entrance is the waiting room ; then a neat, little kitchen, a concrete basement, and a bathroom. It is cozy, this model house, clean and well-kept. It must be remembered that "our nurse", as her many friends call her, spends most of her life in this home built for her. She bakes her own pies and makes her own soup when her mother or maid is away. She is often busy with some sewing or embroidery for the church or the poor, resting, in between consultations, by doing some other work. There is no room for boredom in the life of a district nurse. Active and self-sacrificing, she answers all calls, gets into any conveyance ready to carry her to all corners of her territory, whether it be barges, sleighs, dog-sleds, trucks, automobiles, etc. Every day, and often at night, she must go out. She presides at all births, attends the wounded, and extracts teeth. She often gives real medical consultations, prescribes diets, and stresses preventive medicine. Fortunate, indeed, are the sick who can be attended by this heroic woman. She sees to one's hospitalization, when necessary, and prepares him for whatever sacraments required by his state.

Here, then, we have a problem which had previously been a source of great distress and anxiety and to which the most workable solution has been brought for the North Shore and its poor and isolated communities.

Indeed, criticisms have been made and even protests raised since then against this system. Once, having entered a bookstore in Quebec City, I heard a man violently condemning the dispensaries of the North Shore in these words : "They have been put under nurses who are paid high salaries, remunerative enough even for young doctors starting out, etc . . ." Surprised, I deemed it necessary to intrude into the conversation and affirm myself partly responsible for the development of this system. It was easy to prove that, because of the circumstances and the nature of the region, it had been impossible to do otherwise or to find a better solution.

As Doctor Lessard had promised, the Saint John Eudes hospital was built at Havre Saint-Pierre in 1927. Unfortunately, Doctor Lessard had been too timid, too conservative, too afraid of getting involved in tall expenses. It was not a twenty-five bed hospital which was needed, but one at least five times larger.

During the summer of 1940, however, the North Shore was honoured with the visit of the Honourable Mr. Godbout. He was accompanied by several of his Ministers and by Desmond and Wilfrid Clarke. There was some question then of enlarging the first hospital. "No," said the Honourable Mr. Godbout, "times have changed. One does not built in such a paltry way nowadays. We shall give you a modern hospital." Subsequent to this praiseworthy resolution, His Excellency Bishop Labrie, the Honourable Edgar Rochette, and later Dr. Arthur Leclerc worked in collaboration with the Sisters of Charity to endow the North Shore with a first class hospital at Havre Saint-Pierre.

A letter written from that hospital in 1935 by a missionary points out the merits of this establishment, so long awaited : "I have been at the Saint John Eudes Hospital for a month now, receiving my little quota of sufferings that God sometimes sends to His friends. As a consequence of a neglected head cold and trips taken through neighbouring missions, I now see myself a prey to acute running otitis, something new to me. I consulted the big medical dictionary, but where would I find the medicine recommended in this learned book? I therefore telegraphed Bishop Leventoux who, in turn, got in contact with Doctor E.-E. Binet. This good doctor decided to visit me. Think of it ! Sixty miles of sea in a fisherman's barge and seven hours of land travel. The following day, Sunday, the doctor returned, bringing his patient with him. Another crossing ... Ten hours on the sea, ten hours of rest for me in the only cabin on board, warmed by a little sheet-iron stove in the corner, a precious comfort to a feverish man.

"All this to tell you that now we are not reduced to the forlornness of times gone by. Without the help of Doctor Binet, so conscientious and so courageous, without the good care of the Sisters of Charity, what would have become of me? A double running otitis followed by an œdema, stubborn enough to resist a fortnight of ice applications and poultices, isn't that enough to make me thank God that I could become a patient at the Saint John Eudes Hospital where I have received excellent care from the doctor, the Sisters, and the nurses?" How many people could not today unite their voices to that of the missionary in similar heartfelt thanksgiving?

The Saint John Eudes Hospital, to which patients come from sometimes more than three hundred miles east or west, is the fine culminating point of the magnificent deeds of Doctor Lessard in behalf of the North Shore. This good doctor, one day, nearly paid dearly his devotion to the Labradorian population. He had stopped one night at Mingan, a village with an excellent seaport. He was on his way back from Havre Saint-Pierre with the hospital contractor, Léo Ratté, and wanted to reach my rectory of Rivière-au-Tonnerre that very night. Neither he nor his companion was fully aware of the dangers of the sea. There was a very strong, westerly wind. As I had been informed of this departure by telegram, I could not shake off a sense of impending doom. I recited my rosary and kept praying for the travellers. It was then about five in the afternoon. At seven o'clock I received another telegram from Doctor Lessard, which read: "Shipwrecked. Will stay overnight at Long Point and proceed tomorrow." They had been imprudent enough to forget the heavy seas between Perroquet Island and the village of Long Point. A huge wave crashing on them had, in fact, made an opening in the frail hull of their boat. Fortunately, Eugene Francis, an experienced sailor, was on board. This brave man kept his wits about him and took immediate command of the situation. He stopped the motor, vigorously raised the foresail, and ordered the others to steer the boat towards shore through the foaming waves. He then seized a pail and bailed out the water, that dropped into the hold, as fast as he could. A quarter of an hour later, the barge ran aground on the beach, three miles from Long Point. By some stroke of fortune it had slid in between two sand bars on which it could easily have been smashed. The following day, a calm sea permitted me to get aboard a small craft and start off to meet our distinguished visitors. I sighted them about half way. Doctor Lessard was standing in a frail Labradorian skiff, pale, still shaken by the emotions of the preceding day. "Father Garnier ! Thank God you have come !" he exclaimed. "I feel better already !" " That is why I came, Doctor," I told him.

A letter written by Doctor Lessard on January 16, 1949 would make an excellent conclusion to this chapter, as it sheds a wonderful light on all that has been recalled in it. "Your letter," he wrote, "has pleased me greatly. It has brought back a host of memories that the passage of time blurs somewhat but can never destroy altogether. I thank you for the good wishes you have expressed for myself and my family and beg you to receive ours in return. May the year 1939 prove a happy one and bring you more satisfaction than those which have preceded it. You are still living in your little North Shore hamlet, I see, amidst rocks, moss, and sand in the summer, confined by storms and cold weather during the winter and ever contemplating the depths of human misery. What merit is yours!

"I often think upon our relations of past years and of the good which we tried to accomplish together.

"How often, every year, did you not write to me to appeal to the generosity of our government. My first movement was always one of denial, and I would say to myself : 'If I listened to Father Garnier, everything would go to the people of the North Shore !' Then I would think better of it, read your letter over, picture the utter penury of those poor people, and finally, I would end up by granting what you had requested. I sincerely believe that we have accomplished some good in your district.

"Sometimes, I close my eyes and conjure up your barren country, Rivière-Saint-Jean, Havre Saint-Pierre, the Mingan Islands, and that Perroquet Island where I nearly perished on August 12, 1930. Such a throng of memories ! And your warm and cordial welcome !

"I was very ill last summer. For two months I was hospitalized at the Hôtel-Dieu in Montréal, where I underwent a serious surgical operation. I had, as you can well believe, committed myself entirely to the will of God. I only ask that I gain some small part in the merits of the missionaries, as I did my small share, when I could, in bringing them help and assistance.

"In closing, I sincerely hope that you will be able, before long, to enjoy a well-earned rest in your beautiful country of France, particularly in your own Brittany. You know, I have always loved France. It is the country which, in spite of its errors, still brings the greatest consolations to the Vicar of Christ."

God must have well rewarded this charitable man, this true and sincere friend. When two men regularly exchange letters for a just cause, for the purpose of helping their fellow-men, there soon grows between them a strong attachment that nothing can break, a friendship as solid as that resulting from daily contacts. This admirable final letter of Doctor Lessard, which so fittingly concludes this chapter on health, is a striking example of what a genuine friendship can accomplish with the help of God for the welfare of some unfortunate brethren.

HAVRE SAINT-PIERRE ... CHURCH, CONVENT AND HOSPITAL

THE « NORTH SHORE », 1947

CHAPTER THIRTEEN

PROGRESS

IV

Colonization. — Pointe-aux-Outardes. — Ragueneau. Taillardat. — Sainte-Thérèse-de-Colombier.

NEVER had anybody thought of agricultural colonisation east of the Saguenay. For three centuries after the first European establishments, this endless rocky coast remained the exclusive domain of trappers and fishermen. Under the French régime, the *seigneurs* and the holders of concessions set up trading posts for the commerce of furs with the Montagnais Indians and built fishing establishments, fish being then particularly abundant in these cold waters. Towards the end of the nineteenth century, a few timid forestry ventures were born and died without great success. This part of the country seemed to be irrevocably condemned to remain a wilderness and would have brought smiles at any suggestion of growing wheat and oats.

Nevertheless, the few Europeans who settled there for the purpose of hunting and fishing succeeded in harvesting delicious vegetables, and small cultivated meadows advantageously supplemented, for the feeding of the cows and few horses, the wild hay and peas gathered along the beaches. This region of austere aspect was not, therefore, entirely devoid of agricultural qualities.

Moreover, a few families from the South Shore or from Charlevoix remarked the particularly rich soil of the Manicouagan Peninsula, and they accordingly began farming at Pointe-aux-Outardes. The first ones were the two Ross brothers from Métis, of Scottish origin, and Alexandre Tremblay from Charlevoix. Their descendants still constitute the greater part of the population of Pointe-aux-Outardes. Édouard and Théophile Jean and their brothers-in-law, Jimmy Boulay and Louis Tremblay, settled north of the Outardes River. If these last named managed to acquire moderate means by selling the products of their little farms to the Montagnais, if those of Pointe-aux-Outardes cleared off a small portion of their large and beautiful farms, these agricultural ventures remained so modest as to be hardly worth mentioning. Farming was perhaps carried on in such villages as Mille-Vaches, Escoumains, and Bergeronnes on a grander scale, but the fact remains that the population of this part of the North Shore was, first and foremost, a population of trappers and woodsmen and will long keep its woodsman mentality, just as the eastern part will remain a country of fishermen.

The foundation of the first agricultural community worthy of the name goes back to 1886. Not far from Tadoussac, hidden by the mountains of the Saguenay, it nestles in the hollow of a splendid valley. The navigator who sails up the river would never surmise that, behind these frowning ramparts, grain fields undulate in the breeze, or that fine sleek herds provide one hundred thousand pounds of butter every year to the Co-operative Dairy of Sacré-Cœur. Today, it is perhaps the most prosperous parish of the new diocese of the Gulf of St. Lawrence, because it rests on the incomparable security that only the soil can give. I do not at this moment possess the details necessary to constitute its history, but it would be the subject of an interesting local monograph. Furthermore, it has been my intention, in the writing of this book, to limit myself to the boundaries of the former apostolic vicariate.

It was not until 1921 that another apparently serious attempt was made in agriculture, this time on the shores of the Outardes River. The little Rosiers River to the west and the falls to the east formed the natural boundaries of a tract of good clay. The results obtained on the small farms of the families already established there augured well. Scarred by the valleys of two small rivers, this district of Ragueneau was, on the whole, reasonably level. It seemed easy to clear. The fifty families that settled there came mainly from Saint-Paul-du-Nord. Two or three of them built themselves houses as soon as they arrived, but the others contented themselves with log cabins on the banks of the river for a long time.

One would like to attest to the farming qualities of these families as well as to their edifying faith, but evidence is ever present to tell the passerby that these first settlers were not true pioneer farmers. If exception is made for a few small areas reasonably well cultivated, all that is left of the green forest are half-burnt stumps, slowly decaying in tangled brush. A church and a few houses along the road point to a certain prosperity, but the absence of barns and herds proves that it is not the prosperity of the soil. Colonized by lumbermen, Ragueneau still has a woodsman's mentality. One cannot improvise oneself into a colonizer or farmer.

The fault does not lie entirely with this improvised colonizer, if the results have not fulfilled the hopes set upon him. To colonize, plans, programs, and means are needed. The education of the colonizer, in particular, should be carried on simultaneously with an efficacious control of his activities. None of this was done, and so one cannot lay all the blame on the colonizer for his lack of success. Nature offered him the elements of success : a fertile soil, a favourable climate due to southern exposure, and a forest which provided means of subsistence for the first years. But this same nature also placed obstacles on the road to progress, obstacles which the colonizer was unable to overcome by himself.

Let the reader picture some fifty families settled on the shores of the river, which was their only means of communication. At low tide it was possible to walk on its beach, provided one was willing to smear one self with clay up to the ankles, even up to the knees. They did not all possess boats and usually the current, wind, and waves made sailing dangerous in the miserable canoes at their disposition. There were no overland roads. Each settler was separated from his neighbour by a forest so deeply rooted in damp soil that it was practically impossible even to make paths. Winter smoothed the way to easier neighbourly communications by covering the river with a thick coating of ice, but fall and spring brought added dangers, and many were the teams that suddenly plunged into the icy water.

Little encouragement came to stimulate the settler to clear more land, except an occasional insufficient bounty. His only means of subsistence was the sale of pulpwood and logs to the Tremblay and Martel sawmill, set up a year or two after the opening of the area. The price of wood at that time was very low.

On the whole, if the men, trained to the hard work of the lumbermen, could get used to this precarious existence, nothing came to brighten the days of the women in their miserable dwellings, and they needed a superhuman courage to live around Ragueneau.

There were very few or no schools for the children and, moreover, whoever substituted as a teacher had to give lessons in wretched quarters. The privation of religious assistance, however, was the hardest of all things for these poor people, who had been accustomed to parochial life and whose spirit of faith and confidence in the priest were so great as to border upon superstition. Contrary to other groups of settlers, they had left without bringing any priest with them. They depended on the Oblate Fathers, who were already very busy with the Montagnais and ministered to the 70 mile stretch between the Portneuf River and Baie Comeau. They could stay only a very short time, therefore, in each of the ten localities for which they were responsible. Moreover, there was no chapel in Ragueneau, and the priest practically had to go from door to door, so as to group five or six families together in one house and there exercise his ministry. Even though these humble ceremonies may have lacked solemnity, they created between the priest and the settlers a bond of friendship which still lasts and memories which are recalled with emotion.

It is no wonder that, under these conditions, colonization was not very successful and that, even today, if one excepts a few families that have become well-to-do through their own initiative and ingenuity, the first settlers have remained poor and discouraged.

In August, 1929, Father La Brie was sent to Pointe-aux-Outardes by Bishop Leventoux. Conditions had improved by then, for his territory was limited to the Manicouagan Peninsula and Ragueneau, but his arrival was the starting-point of another adventure. The Father, unfamiliar with the problems of colonization, spent the first year studying them as best he could. He presumed he had found a solution by encouraging new settlers to move in to form two complete parishes, one at Pointe-aux-Outardes, the other at Ragueneau. The plan was to start with the first locality. A few good farms were left on the peninsula, and well-chosen families would be established there. A grant would permit them to build suitable dwellings at the very outset. Roads would be made before the arrival of the new settlers. Schools, situated at reasonable distances, would be requested. Then, when this district was under way, the second and third concessions of Ragueneau would be progressively opened by the same method, which seemed prudent and practical. During the summer of 1930 the Father, accompanied by the agent of colonization, Mr. Télesphore Marin, called upon Mr. Edgar Rochette, the area's Provincial Member of the Legislative Assembly, to explain the project. Mr. Rochette, who was ever eager to contribute to the progress of his country, was very encouraging and pledged his wholehearted support.

The travellers returned home happy and confidently awaited the results of Mr. Rochette's negotiations. Unfortunately, Mr. Rochette had circumspectly talked it over with the missionary-colonizer of the country, who took it upon himself to get things humming. In September, Father La Brie had hardly left for his annual retreat when he received the following telegram from Mr. Marin : "Return immediately, the settlers are coming." In fact, the Father found eighty-six settlers stranded on the shores of Pointe-aux-Outardes the very next day. Others were to follow. One can easily imagine the confusion that arose as a result. "Choose yourselves some lots," was the only instruction given them. Who had given this order? What was to be done with all these people? Caught wholly unprepared by this untoward turn of events, all they could do was to watch while all these people feverishly overran the peninsula and the first and second concessions of Ragueneau. It was a real invasion. The residents, not wishing to be outdone or to leave to the strangers some lots which they had coveted, joined the *mêlée*. There was nothing to check this big push. Before the end of the month the population had increased by more than a hundred families.

This period of enthusiasm soon gave way to one of grievances. The pastor and the agent did not know where to turn. They had to be everywhere at once, work incessantly to fill out the necessary papers, find, at all costs, some temporary shelter, visit the sick and arbitrate in quarrels between neighbours, so that the nights and days did not suffice any more. It was already late in September. How were all these people to be housed before winter?

Fortunately, the Ministry of Colonization, whose intentions and plans had been exceeded, proved forgiving and generous in the circumstances. The missionary-colonizer, who was always suspected as being responsible for this disservice, put forward his best efforts and influence to set things aright. They were permitted to buy lumber, windows, glass, and nails. Everyone set to work, and when the first snowfall came, everyone had a roof over his head. The more skillful and energetic ones even succeeded in building very convenient and spacious homes. Two schooners, loaded with horses and cattle bought in Charlevoix, were sent by the Ministry of Colonization. Although not of the best breeds, they proved very useful after they had been distributed as equitably as possible, even considering the disputes that occurred on their account.

As can easily be surmised, the choice of the new arrivals had been too hasty to have been a completely happy one. Many families had to return to their former villages in the spring. This new experiment turned out to be little more profitable than in 1922. Still, at the present moment, a few colonizers of Baie Saint-Ludger, of the concession of Pointe-aux-Outardes, and of the double concession of Ragueneau can show with a certain pride reasonably well cultivated farms. All the cares which this project had demanded were not entirely wasted.

A curtain cannot be drawn over this episode without recalling the disaster which devasted the double concessions of Ragueneau during the summer which followed hard on its opening. A forest fire, fanned by a high wind, swept over the whole length of the settlement in one day. One can imagine the anguish of the missionary, unable to cross the river because of the gale, forced to be nothing more than a helpless witness of the destruction of an enterprise he had built with sweat and worry, and dreading the fate of families caught in that inferno of smoke and flame. In fact, a few families, determined to defend their property, refused to abandon their homes and belongings. By what courage or miracle did they succeed? It defies explanation, but the fact remains that these families saved everything, whereas the eleven families who fled saw all their possessions go up in smoke.

Later, in 1944, a still more devastating fire consumed twenty-six houses of the district. In both cases, however, a truly Christian charity helped the victims to get started anew.

Father La Brie remained only two years at Pointe-aux-Outardes. His first contact with colonization had not been entirely successful. He was succeeded by Father Ludger Lebel, who also remained only two years with the colonizers, but he left there, as everywhere he went, a memory of limitless devotion and great kindness.

The task of definitely organizing Ragueneau was the work of Father Taillardat, a Frenchman from the province of Auvergne. Ragueneau had grown much more rapidly than Pointe-aux-Outardes, and with the national highway now cutting through it, an even more rapid development could be hoped for. Consequently, Bishop Leventoux requested Father Taillardat to reside at Ragueneau rather than at Pointe-aux-Outardes, where Father Sirois was to come later, succeeded in turn by Father Joseph Le Gresley.

Father Taillardat possessed all the energy and determination of his native province and, moreover, practical knowledge of agriculture and gardening. In 1938 he became missionary-colonizer, which post added to his prestige and heightened the efficacy of his work. He applied himself to the task and soon, a church, rectory, parish hall, and barn arose on the hill above the highway. Simultaneously, the stumps disappeared from the church land and gave way to a beautiful grain field, a waving meadow of hay, and the best vegetables of the region. As missionary-colonizer, he kept in check those who would have taken advantage of his flock and worked incessantly to find the best markets for their wood and other products. He secured the services of agricultural experts, helped in the foundation of a parochial bank and a consumers' cooperative, and had many good schools built.

With such a model and under the influence of such tireless and energetic activity, one could have hoped that the colonizers would have followed his example like a well-disciplined group. It was only a small number that did so. Even today, the pastor cannot say that results come up to his expectations or are equal to his devotion to the cause. Yet, one must not give up hope. The good earth is there. It has been watered by sweat accompanied by fervent prayer. The day will come when the golden grain will whisper its autumn song all along this beautiful river.

After His Excellency Bishop Leventoux had retired, he enjoyed coming every summer for a rest at Father Taillardat's settlement. From the balcony of the rectory, where the good old man liked to sit in the sun, he could contemplate the wide estuary of the river, Pointe-aux-Outardes, and the whole of the coast of Betsiamits where the graceful belfry towers over the white sands. Before this matchless panorama he, also, must have invoked the blessing of ripe wheat and abundant milk for this land. May it please Heaven that his prayers be heard and that the good pastor, in his old age, may view from this same balcony the realization of his dreams.

The settlement of a few colonizers has been tried at Pentecost and in the localities of Arnaud and Letellier around Seven Islands Bay, but in spite of the zeal of Fathers Regneault, Robitaille, and Doucet, this enterprise was never seriously looked upon by the Government and continues to struggle in mediocrity. We have not made a thorough study of these places and so we cannot say that they are wholly unsuitable for colonization. A little more encouragement and enthusiasm might produce results. The future may be revealing. Nevertheless, it is a matter for rejoicing to see that a few families have been able to make a living and, although not wealthy, are free and not dependent on a foreign company for all their needs. If each worker received his parcel of land coupled with the essential liberties of commerce and industries, of schools and associations, instead of selling to foreigners more land than is needed for their industrial establishments and constituting so many closed towns, there would be no need for a struggle to regain these rights. Our population would be better aware of its duties, of the possibilities of individual or collective enterprise, and it would feel a greater pride in its ancestry and in its human, civil, and Christian dignity. To be sure, everything would not be perfect (many things, and rightly so, have been a reproach to the colonizers) but experience has demonstrated that a society composed of proprietors soon builds sounder and more wholesome foundations morally, socially, and economically. On the North Shore as well as anywhere else, so long as the worker will not be permitted to own house and land near his work and enjoy all the freedoms championed by a Christian society, there will exist only an amorphous population of automatons.

Another attempt at colonization, this time organized in a more rational manner, was made in 1936. In the month of July, a group of settlers coming, for the most part, from the agricultural community of Sacré-Cœur, disembarked at Anse-Noir, near the Colombier River. This little river flows leisurely in the heart of a wide valley. The rich soil and luxuriant forest made it an ideal site for a new community. The colonizers settled there according to a methodical plan and immediately set to work.

Upon the recommendation of Mr. Arthur Leclerc, who represented Charlevoix and Saguenay, this colony was inaugurated under the auspices of the excellent Minister, Mr. Henry Auger. Those who have known him are well acquainted with the heartfelt solicitude with which this good Minister accomplished his task, but we are tempted to believe that, of all the districts colonized, Colombier was his child of predilection. He always spoke of it with a hint of emotion in his voice. During the summer of 1938 he even visited it, an honour which will long remain in the memories of the settlers. He liked to tell the following anecdote about Colombier : "For a whole year we had timber ready to help the settlers get started. This wood was piled at a cross-road, far from all habitations, and without a watchman. The settlers went back and forth continually before this pile of wood, yet, at the end of the year, not even one plank was missing. In certain other colonies there would have been nothing left." This fact, a source of edification for the Honourable Mr. Auger, is sufficient proof of the moral character of these good people. As early as September 1938, both the Minister and Mr. Leclerc insistently asked Bishop Labrie to appoint a resident pastor at Colombier.

This appointment had, in fact, already been decided. Bishop J.-M. Leventoux had suggested to his successor that he send Father A. Gallant. Father Gallant was ready to leave. Due to his talent as organizer and to a generous contribution from the Government, a modest but very suitable church was built in 1939 beside a little rectory. An attractive parish hall soon followed. Now, from the top of the hill overlooking all the concessions, the Little Flower, the patron saint of the parish, gazes on a scene that changes with the seasons, now upon growing piles of wood, now upon the plough opening furrows in the fertile land. With the good saint's blessing and the yearly retreat of the forest, new fields of fine grain and succulent vegetables appear. Agricultural success has already repaid in part these energetic efforts. The day is not far off when the happy pastor will have before his eyes, in this rich valley, only golden meadows and white farm buildings amid clumps of green trees.

All is not idyllic, though, in the foundation of a new parish. "I can recall," says Bishop Labrie "having found Father Gallant, one evening in 1944, when a forest fire was raging, blackened with smoke, eyes bloodshot, and dripping with perspiration. When he saw me, he could not speak for the sobs constricting his throat. He found some solace and encouragement in the unexpected visit of his bishop. My travelling companion and I led him to his bed and promised him to keep watch ourselves over the harassed parish."

For a week, and with all his flock, he had been fighting against the fire. Everyone felt exhausted, and great damage had been inflicted, but only one house had burnt. Now, alone in the calm night to keep watch over this misery, we let our minds wander, "How great are these humble folk !" we told ourselves. "By dint of sweat, hard work, and struggles against the elements, they are accomplishing a heroic task. The wealthy can spend millions to wrest raw materials from the earth, but they can never be builders of a country like these people, who give their lives in order to take possession of the soil and protect its God-given fertility, either by preserving the forests or replacing it with fertile fields. How great are the priests who, to anchor faith in the heart of the settlers, faith without which their courage would falter, willingly share their toil and miseries. Our Catholic Canada has been built of just such heroism." On this night, the fire was a terrible reproduction of this struggle. In the calm of the night, the thousands of long and brilliant flames which, every now and then, in a sudden wakening, drew dismal groans from the tortured firs, foretold that, on the morrow, the community would awake to take up the battle anew and finally triumph. "At midnight, large raindrops spattered the window. An hour later, a torrential rain doused the fire. Darkness settled everywhere. We too, were now able to sleep."

On the following day, when we took our leave, the scorched faces of the settlers radiated hope and optimism. The fruitful labor was picked up and carried on as before.

While Colombier was growing, other colonizers established themselves on both sides of the national highway at Latour and opened a series of new farms, while a third group settled the district of Laval. This group left Colombier in order to join the new industrial community of Forestville, where Father Luc Sirois is still its first pastor.

Because of the good road built and annually improved by the Provincial Government, because, also, of the proximity of industrial centres offering good markets, these settlements can hope for a rapid development. If these new farmers will only realize the opportunities which thus present themselves and accordingly intensify their efforts, they will find a comfortable living on their productive land.

Can we hope for many other communities similar to these? Although the problem has not been fully studied yet, the general topography of the region does not give much hope. There still are a few districts where it will be possible to group a few hundred families, but, on the whole, Saguenay County will never be an agricultural region.

Another form of colonization remains possible, however, one which would allow of a population five times as large as the present one, which would assure industry more stable, more experienced, and more specialized labourers and happily provide for the agricultural population of the Province a natural market for its products. The North Shore possesses, at the present time, one of the greatest and best preserved forests of the Province. If improvident industry lays waste this vast domain, what will be left, since, unlike other regions, not even soil will remain? As it is impossible to grow grain upon this land, why not help it grow, better and faster, the firs which form its wealth? This is far from being an impossible dream! It has been accomplished elsewhere. A forest-minded population, finding its subsistence in the products and by-products of wood and helped by conscientious technicians, could as well live here in happiness and financial security, developing industry, accelerating reforestation by a thirty-year plan, and saving beautiful trees from murderous forest fires. This is no time for utopian theories. Let us hope that one day someone will demonstrate the practicality of this one and that a wise government, assisted by social-minded industrialists, will put it into practice. It is a question of stability for a rich national industry, of dignity for a whole class of labourers, who should not be nomads seeking seasonal employment from camp to camp, but proud men carrying on our traditional Christian civilization with all the robust energy and freedom of builders of countries.

SAINTE-THÉRÈSE DU COLOMBIER ... COLONIZATION IN PROGRESS

VILLA MENIER ... ANTICOSTI ISLAND

CHAPTER FOURTEEN

ANTICOSTI

Physical aspect. — A little history.
From Louis Jolliet to Henri Menier. — Recollections.

THIS record of the North Shore would not be complete without some mention of its great neighbour — Anticosti Island.

The island of Anticosti is a lengthy strip of land, its length approximating to the ebb and flow of the tides, situated in the centre of the Gulf of St. Lawrence. The island divides the gulf into two large and unequal bodies of water. The northern channel, at its narrowest point, between Pointe-du-Nord and the southern tip of Mingan Island, is 22 miles wide. The width of the southern channel is 55 miles. Remarkably regular in outline, it closely resembles the shape of a fish. Picture this fish lying on its side, the head to the east and tail to the west, the back would represent the northern side of the island and the stomach the southern side. Anticosti is 130 miles long and 32 miles wide at its greatest width. Along the north, a series of sharp cliffs rise to a height of 300 feet, with only four coves in which vessels may safely anchor. Five rivers and the odd creek alone break the rugged monotony of this shore-line which at first sight appalls one. Whereas, along the south, the shore is low-lying, sloping gradually to the sea where, at low tide, the beach stretches out for as far as a mile and even two miles. Here are to be found the dangerous Anticosti reefs, witness to many a tragic shipwreck and in winter covered in a great white mantle of snow. This shore can be very attractive and, in summer, offers great variety of scenery because of the many rivers which fall into bays and scatter their waters among the low-lying rocks, or drop in cascades to the shore.

Who first inhabited Anticosti Island? It is thought unlikely that the Indians stayed there for any length of time. The northern mainland would suffice for them. Louis Jolliet, who died about 1700, was the *seigneur* and, according to a certain geographical map of the time, busied himself with fisheries at Baie-Sainte-Claire and Rivière-à-l'Huile, points well chosen for the abundance of fish. A hundred years later, the legendary Louis-Olivier Gamache settled down to live the undisturbed life of a hermit in the depths of the woods around Baie-Ellis, by cunning stratagems driving unwelcome visitors from his domain. In 1870 there appears a record of two families, Béliveau and Wright, at English Bay, now Baie-Sainte-Claire. Others, the families Doucet, Frank Bezeau, Pierre Poulin, and Anthyme Noël are recorded at Anse-aux-Fraises (Strawberry Cove).

About this time the Foresyth Company made a fantastic claim to rights over the whole island and deluded a group of unfortunate Newfoundlers who, to save them from starvation, the government had to repatriate. On the bankruptcy of the Foresyths, the creditors became owners of the island and, in an attempt to recoup their losses, sold it to the Stockwel family of England.

Under the reign of the Stockwels, which lasted twenty years, the pretty little village of English Bay attained a certain amount of fame. The census for 1891 shows a total of 676 inhabitants dwelling on the island — 374 French, 264 English 69 Irish, and 31 Scottish. Many of these people refused to relinquish the rights to their property, even to Henri Menier, when he came at a later date. Henri Menier desired tenants only and the census of his time gives the figure of 50 inhabitants to which, due to Mr. Menier's many enterprises, must be added a floating population of 200 to 300 workers from France, Québec, and the islands of Saint-Pierre and Miquelon.

This was the "Golden Age" of Anticosti Island. Henri Menier spent freely to make of his kingdom a "Corner of France". Three farms were located respectively at Baie Sainte-Claire, Rentilly, and Ellis Bay ; a chateau was built at the extremity of this latter bay which became known as Port-Menier. Today, visitors to the island may admire the artistry with which this palace was built and the richness of the many tapestries and furnishings.

However, these attempts at large-scale farming could not endure. As forest covers three quarters of the islands, fir, spruce, and birch intermingling profusely, and the remaining quarter is covered in savanna and lakes, but few places remain in which the soil is sufficiently deep for intensive cultivation. Any attempt at plowing turns up quantities of the limestone which is to be found throughout the island. The inhabitants must, therefore, be content with their small bit of garden. The sea-weed, which stormy waves drive up on the shore, may be used as fertilizer for all those vegetables which require no more than three and a half months growing period. According to local gardeners, growth is very rapid from the end of May into June, but comes to an end by the tenth of September.

The enterprises launched by Mr. Menier : cultivation of the soil and roads linking the farms, gave a distinctive character to Ellis Bay and the surrounding country. ... Here, the nocturnal howling of dogs is not heard, and the dog-sled remains unknown. In contrast, the most interesting of our wilderness animals were imported for the pleasure of the Anticostians and visitors ; this was certainly a happy thought on the part of the promoters. Four species are mentioned prior to 1903 : bear, fox, otter, and marten. With the coming of deer and the opportunity of securing venison, the marten disappeared as this meat is deadly to the young marten.

How came these animals to establish themselves on the island ? Were they brought by man, by Louis Jolliet, or by Olivier Gamache, or were they trapped on ice floes from the North mainland and eventually carried by wind and current to the island ? In his time Henri Menier also felt the desire to increase the quantity and species of wildlife on the island. Two pair of imported mink were caught in traps meant for beaver. Opossum suffered a similar fate. Pheasants, released in the forest on two separate occasions, were devoured by birds of prey. Of three wapiti, one male and two female, one injured a leg and the other two disappeared, without doubt falling victims to the poachers' rifles. As for the moose, these quickly increased from three to six and more, and it was found necessary to kill them off, as the inhabitants of the island went in fear of these animals.

In 1932 the Consolidated Paper Company let loose 300 pair of muskrat on the island. These unfortunate little animals had great difficulty in escaping their cruel enemy, the fox. As for these latter sly old blades, they maintained themselves on the island in great numbers, feeding on venison and the tender flesh of rabbits and partridge.

It is quite probable that the entire population assembled on the wharf at Ellis Bay to greet the first elk, a mother and its young in 1901 ; a male in 1912 ; and another female in 1919. Undoubtedly, these choice specimens became a great temptation to poachers... today, some fifty or possibly a few more now rove the island.

The beaver soon learnt to protect themselves against the possibility of falling into an Indian's trap or the many wiles of their enemies of the North. In this island they settled where they wished ; even alongside the roads, proudly displaying their building skill before mankind.

From the very first the deer made Anticosti their home. Twenty couples were let loose in the woods in 1896, forty in 1897, and another twenty in 1900. Today they number in the thousands. The tender herbage over the old farm sites, along the shores of lakes and streams, attract these gentle creatures who, at the slightest sign of danger, are so swift in leaping over the plains or through the woods. It would be a sad event, nay a calamity, should these creatures disappear from the haunts in which they so gaily disport themselves. The story is told that on a certain evening three jolly companions set out by carriage from West Point to Ellis Bay, a distance of some twelve miles.

On a route so flanked by firs this might be expected to be a monotonous trip. But, not at all ! The trio decided to count aloud all the deer seen 'en route'. One, two, three, four, ... twenty four ! ! ... eighty ! ! ! Eighty was the final number counted on this trip.

Another attraction of the island is its fifty rivers and numerous brooks in which the sportsman may tempt an excellent trout, with no fear of the mosquitoes which abound on the Labrador coast. And, finally, there are the twenty salmon streams on which can be practiced that pleasant pastime of catching the king of fish on a rod and line with fly. Some prefer the foot of a rapid ; others, the juncture of two streams ; still others, the many pools high up the streams — even as far upstream as five, six, or ten miles. The river Jupiter, as an instance, offers the sportsman many fishing pools, the farthest upstream being no less than thirty-six miles from the sea. No man fishing here need worry about reaching these places, for the flat boats such as in use here may be used as a conveyance, or he may easily ride horseback to his chosen pool. Each year this island attracts fishermen in sufficient numbers to fill all the camps placed at their disposal by the owning-company. This sport of salmon fishing, inaugurated by Henri Menier, will continue to be enjoyed on Anticosti Island by the faithful followers of the sport and all the more so in that there now exists a local salmon protection law limiting each man's catch to five fish per pool.

The population of Anticosti Island has never reached the numbers that this large territory, with its many possibilities, would seem to demand. For a long time the few Catholics on the island were visited but once a year by a missionary from either the North Shore or from Quebec City. Bishop Guay lived on the island for a short time and Bishop Labrecque made a confirmation tour which almost cost him his life. Tired of awaiting the end of a forced stay at a small cove some thirty miles from English Bay, he set out to cover this distance on foot. He did not reach the village until the following day, more dead then alive and resolved never again to risk such a march over the rocky shores of Anticosti.

In 1895 Henri Menier purchased the entire island. From that time on, one word, and that one word only, was in particularly constant usage : "administration". The "governor" was the head of this powerful organization, and numerous were the subordinates — directors, assistant-directors, accountants, and assistant-accountants of the various branches and departments of the administration.

As regards the Church, the administration undertook the upkeep of the church, rectory, and schools and assured a suitable monthly salary to the officiating missionary. Although in many respects very helpful, such as in relieving the priest of material worries, nevertheless, this system was responsible for the fact that no church was built at either Baie-Sainte-Claire or Ellis Bay.

The holding of regular services in the principal church and at the convent, visiting the schools and neighbouring missions, either by automobile or on horseback, touring the island at least once a summer, and missions to the logging camps in the winter, of such was comprised the work of Fathers Travert, Robin, L. Garnier, J.-M. Leventoux, J. Le Strat, Ls-Ph. Gagné, A. Brault, F. Hesry, J. Huland, and L. Roy, who succeeded each other over a period of forty-five years. The

Fathers were all delighted with Anticosti Island. They had real cause for satisfaction in the friendly relations maintained with the administration and took delight in fulfilling their ministry amongst their well-disposed and respectful parishioners, whose children were well trained first by the teacher, Mr. Y. Lerouzès (who has since become a school-inspector in Montreal) then by the admirable Sisters of Charity.

Undoubtedly, until the advent of aviation, they must all have suffered greatly from isolation, much more so than their confrères on the North Shore. When, in the springtime, the newspapers arrived in large quantities, the more eccentric characters would solace themselves in an original manner : the papers would be sorted in order of date and read one per day, thus creating the illusion of being regularly received. Several of the Fathers gave lessons in Latin to students at the rectory ; and, during his sojourn on the island, Father Travert was musical director of a celebrated instrumental group of that period.

The Rev. Father J.-M. Leventoux, future Apostolic-Vicar of the Gulf of St. Lawrence, was missionary on Anticosti from 1912 to 1922 ; eight of these years he worked alone, while for the remaining two years he had the assistance of a curate. Sister Saint Jean of The Trinity, whose first steps on the path toward the cloister he directed, has provided us with many precious memories of this missionary's sojourn on Anticosti. Unhappily, it is not possible, in the limited space available, to reproduce all of these. Noteworthy among these recollections is the eagerness shown by Father Leventoux in visiting the sick, receiving visitors, and in using the colloquialisms in common usage among the members of his flock, thereby creating a closer understanding with them. Father Leventoux made it a habit never to mount the pulpit without first fully preparing his explanation of the Gospel for the particular Sunday ; similar preparation he also made for all his sermons, which were particularly appreciated and admired. Today, mention his name to any old Anticostian, and you will be told : "Monseigneur Leventoux ! We loved him greatly . . . he was so good a man ! . . . and he preached so well !" All these qualities were grounded on a base of sincere godliness. It was the Father's habit to rise at 5.30 in the morning, pass a half-hour in prayer and meditation before the altar of the Virgin Mary ; thence to the confessional where he was at the disposal of all until the hour for Mass. In the afternoon, from four to six o'clock, he was very often again seen in the church. Here, to Anticosti Island, the Sovereign Pontiff sent in search of this humble missionary to raise him, in spite of himself, to the episcopacy. One old islander, proud of this recognition of the Father's worth, but much grieved over his departure, remarked : "He was so good, so fine a man, our Father — I knew well that some such thing as this would happen to him."

Special mention should be made of Father A. Brault's stay at Ellis Bay, to which missionary post he was appointed on two separate occasions. Here he founded the convent of the Sisters of Charity who have rendered so great service to the families of this locality. To him also goes credit for the succession of buildings serving as rectory, sacristy, and church.

As we saw happening on the North Shore, so here on the Island the missionaries visited the logging camps.

Fathers J.-M. Leventoux, J. Le Strat, Ls-Ph. Gagné, A. Galland, Bréard, and A. Brault encouraged and strengthened the lumberjacks. These Fathers, each in turn, made the circuit of the island. This was a long and hazardous trip, especially when the only method of travelling was by aid of sail or oar.

Nowadays, every fifteen days the twenty game-wardens and six light-house keepers eagerly watch from the threshold of their homes for the arrival of the mail boat. These lighthouse keepers and game-wardens, the first inhabitants working to overcome the island's early bad reputation of "the sailors' graveyard", and the second to preserve the fauna of the island from the depredations of the hardy poachers from the North Shore, are now no longer as isolated as were their predecessors. Today they may communicate with one another by telephone, as well as with the priest, the doctor, and even their children in the convent. Replenishing of supplies is assured during the summer of each year. It is therefore a pleasure for the present-day missionary to make his circuit of the island and visit his parishoners.

Developments in communication, especially aviation, have greatly decreased those accidents and misadventures usual in the six months of winter's snow and ice. As instances of such hardship, three episodes are here set down.

One beautiful summer's day in 1919 two men, Georges Fafard and Antoine Chiasson, who lived at Point North lighthouse, decided to go codfishing along the shore. Finding a large box, approximately eight feet by six feet, which had been used for the mixing of cement during construction of the lighthouse, they set out with the aid of home made oars and cast their lines into the water. Whilst they discussed the weather and the chances for a good catch, a light breeze sprang up from the south and rapidly grew in strength. They then attempted to regain the shore but all their efforts were in vain. Their flat-nosed little craft was unable to breast the waves and made no headway ... they could but drift at the will of wind and wave. It therefore happened that on the morrow Hector Vigneault and Richard Collin, guardians of *Le Perroquet* lighthouse near the North Shore, while scanning the horizon for any chance piece of driftwood which might come in handy for use in their stove, perceived afar off a large dark object. "A real prize" cried Vigneault. "Better still" replied Collin, "there are even wild fowl flying over it ! Get your gun quickly, and we'll be after them in the canoe". ... The two castaways had found the night long and trying while they attempted with their makeshift oars to keep the box from capsizing and, with their hats, baled out the water which surged in with every high wave. This well-nigh miraculous crossing of these two men from Anticosti's North Point was for long after the main topic of conversation ; a good seventeen miles on the stormy open sea in this new mode of boat travel.

1927. Wilfrid Therriault and Béloni Vigneault, nicknamed "Maitt John", were working on Rivière-au-Saumon (Salmon River). Finding the long winter wearisome they decided, at Christmas, to visit the Perrey family at "Table Head". They set out by canoe but found their route blocked with drift ice. A leak appeared in the hull of their frail craft, and it was only with great difficulty that they eventually reached the shore, their clothes dripping wet. They had then to scale the cliffs in order to effect the portage. When Therriault and Vigneault were found missing from Salmon River, a search was started. It is said that Nazaire Cormier was the first to find his friend, "Maitt John", and that he was so overcome he imagined he saw a ghost. "I saw him" he cried to his companion. "Yes, of course," replied the latter, who was more aware of reality, "it is in fact Maitt John. Look, it is really he, crouched in a cranny of the rock, his head resting on his hand." The unfortunate Béloni Vigneault (Maitt John) was unable to reach the summit of the cliff and died in the attempt. As for the body of Wilfrid Therriault, it was found lying face downward some distance further along the portage. Alongside the body were a few twigs and a box of damp matches, showing that the poor chap had put forth his last strength in an effort to light a fire by which to dry his clothes and warm his frozen limbs.

Four years later, in 1931, Armand and Patrick Bourque, game-wardens on the same river, felt a similar desire to visit their fellow-men and enjoy companionship for Christmas. The bay appeared to be covered in solid ice. The brothers set out over this, but it gave way under them, adding two more drownings to the waters of the St. Lawrence. Search for the bodies was for a long time unsuccessful, until a passing forestry engineer observed a mitten on the ice. A hole was made at this spot, and the bodies of Armand and Patrick were found together in ten feet of water.

The pages of this chapter will give the reader a general idea of this famous island, the remoteness of which, with the tales recounted by mariners and travellers, has fired the imagination of many writers and story-tellers.

For ten years woods operations were carried on by the Consolidated Paper Company. But the loading of wood in open water and its transportation to Ellis Bay proved so expensive that this enterprise had to be abandoned.

In 1947 the Company decided on another plan. It is now hoped to build a road from Ellis Bay to Potato River. With good harbours at each of these points and a main road with many side-roads, the cutting and transportation of wood should be greatly facilitated. If this new plan proves the success it is hoped to be, and for the good of the population and woodsmen who here earn their living this success is much to be desired, then Anticosti will continue to be the meeting-place of sportsmen and tourists.

With such a roadway the fishing industry should also develop. One missionary from the North Shore, after much intercommunication with Quebec, Ottawa, and the directors of the Consolidated Paper Company, has succeeded in organizing a fishing industry at Baie Sainte-Claire. With the appearance of refrigerated warehouses and fishermen's co-operatives, this industry is making interesting progress. One of the managers of the island, Mr. H. Graham, as well as Mr. Faure, president of the Consolidated Paper Company, has supported the Baie Sainte-Claire fishermen by giving them complete freedom from restrictions in the exercise of their hard calling.

All this would seem to offer encouraging prospects for the Company and the fishing industry on Anticosti Island. Around Baie-du-Renard, for instance, fish are even more abundant than at Baie Sainte-Claire. Herring, mackerel, salmon, halibut, lobster, and especially cod take turns at visiting its haunts in spring and summer.

CHAPTER FIFTEEN

RELIGIOUS AND MORAL LIFE ON THE NORTH SHORE

First episcopal visit of Bishop Blanche.
Religious feasts. — Churches. — Schools.
A Normal School at Havre Saint-Pierre.
An example of Christian Life and Catholic Action at Franquelin.

REVEREND Father Gustave Blanche was appointed Apostolic Prefect of the Gulf of St. Lawrence on July 18, 1903. Although he had to spend the winter at Chicoutimi in the interests of the Eudist Congregation of which he was Provincial, he decided to visit his new apostolic domain in the fall of the same year.

The inhabitants fully understood the great privilege granted them by the Church ; they prepared to welcome their spiritual leader with honour and celebration. Their happiness was complete when they learned that he would be accompanied by teaching Sisters, the Daughters of Jesus from Kermaria in Brittany, for all the important villages. This was a great step towards the development of education on the North Shore.

The impression which the Monsignor took away from this first visit was somewhat touched with sadness. He sollicited help for his missions, which he found destitute of worldly goods. In order to interest generous souls in his missions he wrote : "The Prefecture of the Gulf of St. Lawrence, which the Holy See has entrusted to our care, comprises a far vaster territory than that of the whole of France. About seven thousand fishermen live there in small scattered groups all along the Gulf. In the interior two thousand natives live by hunting. These Indians, given the name of "Montagnais" because of the mountainous and rolling country over which they roam, come down to the sea in the summer to sell their furs and perform their religious duties. All these people are good, honest, and profoundly atached to the Catholic faith. But the poverty of so many among them makes their situation dificult from the spiritual point of view. Each hamlet cannot have a resident priest ; many are thus neglected. The districts dependent on two missionaries often extend over areas thirty to a hundred miles long. The most extensive, which at first was given to a single priest, is more than three hundred miles in length. The visits of the pastor to his flock cannot, therefore, be very frequent. This religious population shows great zeal for the building and decoration of churches. But what churches ! Mere chapels, very small and very poor. Some do not even offer shelter against the elements, while some rectories are uninhabitable. A great opportunity is thus offered to the generosity of Christian hearts."

Bishop Blanche was an impulsive man, always ready for action. His young priests like to recall one of his militant phrases. As they had never travelled out of France, they dreaded the long voyage ahead of them : the English Channel, England, the ocean, Canada, the unknown ! Father Blanche curtly solved the difficul-

FORMER EPISCOPAL PALACE AND PRESENT RECTORY OF HAVRE SAINT-PIERRE

ty : "My good friends, you simply leave... then you will arrive !"

His Excellency Bishop Labrie vividly remembers the following amusing incident. One of his colleagues and he had brought Bishop Blanche to Egg Island. The following day, after the mission was over, the Apostolic Prefect wished to leave the island.

"But, your Excellency, the sea is too rough !"

"No, my friends. The weather is beautiful, there are only a few insignificant waves. We'll just have to row a little harder, that's all !"

"Your Excellency, just look ! The waves are getting higher and higher."

"Now! don't get frightened at nothing. Let us go."

The young men, respectful of their chief's authority and decision, pushed the rowboat in the water, but their secret desire was realized with the first strokes of the oars. Waves crashed into the boat, drenching them and tossing the small craft about like a shell.

"Let's return quickly, my friends," demanded the prelate, "we'll leave later." His Excellency had been seized with a salutary and very opportune fear.

His first visit on the North Shore was without incident. It lasted only from October 2 to November 16, and all the posts were visited up to Natashquan. His ardent nature was put to a hard test when he was forced to wait three weeks for the boat at Rivière-au-Tonnerre. The Fathers, already accustomed to the exigencies of circumstances on the North Shore, took an innocent pleasure at hearing the loud and oft-repeated complaints of their chief : "This strange country where man can move neither by land nor by sea !"

Mgr Blanche was a former soldier. He was brave, courageous, a man of duty ; nothing could stop him. The following spring, the little paper, *Écho du Labrador*, announced some important news : "The Very Reverend Father Blanche has left Quebec for the North Shore." He wanted to visit his flocks again and administer the Sacrament of Confirmation. Without flinching before the distance to be covered and the setbacks he was likely to encounter, he wrote : "I shall go first to Esquimaux Point, then to Natashquan. I shall cross to Anticosti Island after and sail up the river with stops at Seven Islands, Pentecost, and Manicouagan." Excellent news, indeed.

Mgr Blanche succeeded in bringing with him a famous preacher, Father Collin, whose powerful voice and solid doctrine had produced happy results with numerous audiences in Brittany. The new Apostolic Prefect was first and foremost a priest and an apostle devoted to the welfare of souls. He desired to inaugurate his ministry on the North Shore, to which he was henceforth to dedicate all his energies, by giving all the faithful the opportunity of following a good retreat. Many had never experienced such a spiritual boon and looked forward to it all the more eagerly.

Everywhere, both at his arrival and departure, the whole population assembled to greet the pastor and receive his blessing. The roads were lined with fir trees, and the prelate thus made his entrance into each village between two hedges of greenery. Flags waved from every house. Guns were requisitioned by the young men. Often, a much bedecked barge bearing a dozen of them left the harbour to meet the Bishop, welcomed him with volleys, and accompanied him to the landing-place. "Before the rectory," reads a chronicle of the time, "a choir of young girls, accompanied by a harmonium, hailed Mgr Blanche as the envoy of God, while the bell rang merrily in the zinc belfry." The churches dispayed their brightest decorations, sheaves of flags were disposed on the walls, and garlands of fir boughs, laced with variegated flowers, made an artistic pattern. The day following his arrival everybody set to work. Father Hesry at Moisie and Seven Islands, Father Conan at Pentecost, and other Fathers elsewhere prepared the children for First Communion and Confirmation. In every mission, for three days, according to the itinerary decided upon in Quebec, the faithful assembled in church to hear the apostolic words of Father Collin.

Everywhere, for once, one could have thought himself present at an elaborate cathedral ceremony. At Rivière-Saint-Jean, the third day marked the blessing of a cross erected at the entrance of the river, on a high promontary. This gleaming white cross, which can be seen far out at sea, protects the harbour and guides the fishermen, who never fail to salute it upon entering or leaving the harbour.

The Indians were not neglected, either. Mgr Blanche took as great an interest in their souls as in those of the white men. They amazed him, moreover, with the way they greeted him, all by themselves, notwithstanding the absence of their missionaries. They stood in a long line on either side of the road and, after kneeling for his blessing, arose and fired a loud salvo. Then, in their chapel, transformed by rugs and garlands, they intoned the *Magnificat*. The men on one side, the women on the other alternated the verses in the Montagnais tongue. These bronzed and impassive faces, these strange yet elegant vestments presented an amazing and ravishing sight. Mgr Blanche wished to address them. As for diplomatic relations in far-off countries, he made use of an interpreter. He expressed the interest he had in them, his wish for a successful hunt, and his hope of confirming them in their own chapel later. One would think for a moment that the interpreter was cheating, that he did not translate everything, but Father Sirois can assure us that Montagnais is a very synthetic tongue : many things can be expressed in very few words.

When weather and sea permitted, a little fishing barge took the party to another mission immediately after the conclusion of the retreat. Once again, the inhabitants gathered at the harbour, this time for a grateful leave-taking. For a long time they watched the boat recede over the water, filled with happiness over this visit, yet experiencing the sadness of parting from persons who have done good to their souls and who are well loved.

This rejoicing of a Christian population at the visit of their spiritual chief repeated itself at every subsequent episcopal tour. Their Excellencies, Bishops P. Chiasson, J.-M. Leventoux, and N.-A. Labrie have everywhere met the same spontaneous, warm, and even noisy welcome.

As for retreats such as were so successfully conducted by Father Collin in 1904, the North Shore was thereafter deprived of them for a long time. Eloquent voices of celebrated preachers such as Fathers Travert and Blondel profoundly moved listeners during their sojourn on the North Shore, at Anticosti, Natashquan, and Havre Saint-Pierre. From time to time, whenever possible, a retreat was organized in the principal missions. But the difficulties and uncertainties of travel, the great loss of time, in particular, prevented regular retreats, with all the spiritual graces which a time of reflexion and prayer bring to a parish, for many years.

Modern aviation proved a great boon. For a few years now, it has been repeating its feats on the North Shore, a region most suitable to its future expansion in Canada, transporting missionaries, industrialists, and workers of the first and eleventh hour. Thanks to this mode of travel, nearly the whole of the North Shore has profited by the fruitful retreats given in 1946 by the Redemptorist fathers of Saint-Anne-de-Beaupré.

In 1903, the Apostolic Prefect opened a dozen new missions on the North Shore. The apprenticeship of a new life began : a nearly parochial ministry at the village of residence, trips left and right, according to needs and calls received, in small rowboats, with frequent long waits in the fog at sea or in some shelter while storms raged on, and trips by *kometik* over the snow, with forced stops in hunters' camps built at intervals along the trails to shelter travellers in distress or tired of snowshoeing.

On September 12, 1905 the prefecture became an apostolic vicariate. Bishop Blanche then decided to establish his see at Seven Islands. He had the chapel of the village repaired and enlarged and made it his cathedral. Soon the episcopal palace arose, facing the immense bay, ready to accommodate the Fathers of the vicariate whenever they met for the annual retreat. Bishop Blanche dreamed of opening a secondary school, a juniorate or small classical college, for boys in this village. He also thought of a convent for girls.

It is regrettable that, suffering from heart disease, too old to undertake important enterprises, and lacking sufficient funds, he was unable to realize for the North Shore the great educational achievements which he had accomplished in his youth in France and in Acadia.

The Honourable Alexandre Taschereau used to come quite often to Moisie at that time to try his luck at salmon fishing. He later wrote to a friend on the North Shore : "I have kept an excellent memory of Bishop Blanche who, one day, as Sir Lomer Gouin and I were caught by a storm, most cordially received us and extended such hospitality as we shall not soon forget."

We owe to the pen of the famous Prime Minister an amusing anecdote, which was often repeated at the time. Bishop Blanche was having some construction done under the direction of a Quebec architect. One day, he sent his architect the following telegram : "I am very eager to see you. Signed : Blanche." When the message was delivered at the architect's home, he happened to be absent. His wife, believing the matter urgent, opened it, and read it with boundless indignation. Soon after, her husband appeared. He read the telegram and promptly told his wife that he had to leave without delay. The following conversation then ensued :

— "I must leave immediately on urgent business."
— "You will not leave, no, no, and no !"
— "Why not, my dear ?"
— "I am telling you that you will not leave !"
— "Will you tell me what this is all about ?"

— "I have more than enough of your Blanche. If you leave, you will not find me here when you return."

Finally, all was explained, and the matrimonial sky became fair again. Unwittingly, Bishop Blanche, who was a saintly man, had nearly put asunder what God had united.

Of all the missionaries sent to the North Shore by Bishop Blanche, Father Hesry was certainly one of the most enterprising. No sooner had he succeeded Father Robin at Rivière-au-Tonnerre than he conceived the idea of endowing his new parish with a fine church. He undertook at least two trips to Quebec and other places every year. He acquired many and very generous friends everywhere, even in government circles. Upon his return to Rivière-au-Tonnerre he invited every one of his parishioners to participate in the construction operations. Some floated to sea logs cut in the forest, others went to work with the long saws still in use at that time. The more skilful erected the frame of the building and improvised themselves into carpenters and cabinet-makers, according to need, all offering a hundred days or more of work without any remuneration or for as little as a dollar a day. Some received gifts from the Department of Agriculture to reward them for their labour. Thus was built the church of Rivière-au-Tonnerre, which was much talked about thereafter. It still amazes visitors. In it one can admire, framing the main nave, a row of pillars whose circumference is made of ridges artistically chiselled by the pocket-knives of the local fishermen. It is an enormous mass, magnificent and original, but too high for the sweeping winds of the North. A beautiful temple, the surprised visitor will say, whose majesty invites to prayer and reflexion.

This enterprise demanded of Father Hesry extraordinary energy, courage and patience, much good will, also, from his parishioners, especially from the skilful artisans of the time, John Cody, James Boudreau, and others.

During a retreat of the Fathers, Bishop Blanche asked whether one of us would be willing to replace Father Pouliot, who was leaving Our Lady of Lourdes at Blanc-Sablon. Father Hesry raised his hand. This gesture, without doubt the only one seen in the silent hall that day, was never forgotten. Bishop Blanche said later to Father Hesry : "Go to Blanc-Sablon. Do not ask me for anything... On the other hand, you may do everything as you see fit." Father Hesry went to work with a happy heart. From then on he always had some chapel in construction. "My chapel of Blanc-Sablon, of Saint Augustine, of Romaine, of Tabatière, etc." He was always talking about his chapels. He thought of a rectory only when his last chapel was completed.

During all this period of chapel building, schooners or other boats which brought supplies to the government lighthouses had very many articles aboard addressed to Father Hesry including lumber, shingles, nails, bells, statues, and boxes of all kinds, many of which were filled with gifts for the poor. Finally, after having remained for months in the warehouses of pier Louise in Quebec, this merchandise reached its destination or, to be more accurate, edged a little closer to its destination, since it was unloaded at Natashquan or on an island more or less near the locality to which it was addressed. The following year or so these materials became part of a new construction somewhere. He distributed the clothes and other articles to the poor whenever an occasion presented itself in the course of his travels.

Father Hesry's *kometik* was a sort of long box made to order so as to protect an infirmity known only to a few friends and which forbade him long walks on foot. The Father's famous "carriole" was always loaded with an assortment of furs. He paid his parishioners for this precious merchandise, or it was often entrusted to him to be sold to merchants of Natashquan or Quebec, an unprofitable business wherein the charitable missionary was nearly always, in spite of his protests to the contrary, much the loser. His charity knew no bounds.

In the fall of 1936 Bishop Leventoux appointed him pastor of Ellis Bay, where he was venerated and esteemed by the local inhabitants until the day of his death. After a stay of twenty-one years at Blanc-Sablon, Father Hesry left his beloved Labradorian missions with tears in his eyes and fifty dollars in his pocket. At Havre Saint-Pierre his bishop had to advance funds that would allow him to continue his journey : his fifty dollars completely dwindled away in handouts to the poor encountered along the way.

Kind and courteous, he had the same smile for rich and poor alike and was as much at ease with a Canadian official as with his poorest parishioner. Nobody could refuse him anything : "It's for Father Hesry !" He travelled exempt of fare on all boats. He was so serene, so patient, so resigned that he could be held up two weeks, even a month in the same place without showing the least sign of impatience. His arrival anywhere was keenly welcomed. He always made two visits in each family every time he went to one of his missions, one upon arriving, the other upon leaving. The first visit was always pleasant but, when came the moment of departure, Fr. Hesry's lengthy leave-taking taxed the patience of his guide, who was concerned about covering the distance foreseen for the first day of travel. Fr. Hesry never left a mission without seeing everyone in particular, even if he had to return to the same house twice for someone overlooked or absent at a previous visit.

He was gifted with an eloquence not always in conformity with the laws of rhetoric, but so visibly inspired by his love of God and of souls that he was always listened to with attention. Father Hesry was struck down by illness in the church of Ellis Bay. He was delivering a sermon one Sunday at High Mass, proclaiming his hope in the resurrection of martyred Poland, when he was seen to collapse suddenly on the altar, nearly lifeless. He was transported to the Saint John Eudes Hospital at Havre Saint-Pierre where he died, and was buried in the cemetery of that village. One of the doctors who assisted him in his last moments said : "This missionary was a saint." All those who have known and loved Father Hesry will ratify this judgment.

While Father Hesry was building his great church at Rivière-au-Tonnerre, Father Blondel obtained Bishop Blanche's permission to build a rectory at Natashquan. This ardent missionary, whose fiery eloquence had drawn thousands of labourers before his pulpit at Brest in Brittany, was equally appreciated at Natashquan, on the North Shore, and throughout the Province.

He had vast projects, too vast indeed. He immediately ordered all necessary lumber from Quebec. Never had the village seen such great quantities of beams and planks. The best carpenters of Natashquan, Mr. Hilaire Carbonneau and his sons among them, set to work. Did the Father want to build a college or a monastery? The building was so vast that Father Blondel's successor immediately thought of reserving part of it for a little convent, which could easily have sheltered three Sisters and a dozen girls. This project, which would have been consonant with the needs of the eastern part of the vicariate, did not materialize, much to the regret of its promoter.

It is said that Bishop Blanche found the bill rather high, but he had given his word to Father Blondel and, besides, he had such a good heart! May we recall another project of this Father at Natashquan. This little easterly village was a very attractive fishing community. There was very little agriculture, of course. Why cultivate sand dunes when the only vegetation consists of a few tufts of marine grass hardened by sun and sea breezes and having none of the good soil of France or Canada? Yet, Father Blondel imagined that his new parishioners were too taken up by the sea and had neglected the land. He was thinking in terms of the paternal domain near Versailles, which had been so lavish in its yield. He therefore built a wire fence around a vast area of these immense dunes and soon, cows and a horse entered a stable not far from the rectory. In the fall, hay was cut from these sandy dunes but, alas, the haylofts were far from filled. The animals soon tired of this meagre pittance in the course of the long winter which followed. In short, the experiment was a complete failure and occasioned difficulties for the Father's successor, who had to liquidate this first effort at colonization before expenses ran too high. It was a lesson. Let us leave the too dry grass of the Labrador dunes to the breeders of lean cows.

We cannot fail to write a few words about an enterprise of Bishop Blanche. This Vicar Apostolic fully realized the good that was to be accomplished. Nothing could dissuade him, once he had determined the manner in which it could be done. No sooner had he taken possession of his extensive territory than he began to think about the best means of educating the children. One can imagine the difficulty of carrying a program of education in a region so vast, where the villages were scattered, separated from one another by enormous distances, and were, at least in 1903, sparsely populated and devoid of income.

He called upon the Daughters of Jesus of Kermaria who, like other Congregations, had been victims of the persecution of Combes. They were happy to permit him a few subjects who stayed on the North Shore until June 29, 1912. Their houses had prospered by then in Canada. The Sisters from Labrador were needed and would not regret their poor installations of 1903.

Without losing time Bishop Blanche then addressed himself to the Sisters of the Child Jesus of Chauffailles. These Sisters hoped that Bishop Blanche's influence with the other Canadian bishops would help them to establish themselves in Canada, as so many other Congregations had done in those troubled times. This hope was not realized. It soon became evident that no foundation was possible. Could Bishop Blanche have forgotten his promise ? Had he been unsuccessful ? Secretly, the Sisters themselves made inquiries. Then suddenly, it was learned that Rivière-du-Loup was ready to receive them. The Sisters of the Holy Child abandoned all their houses the first week of July, 1917.

From that date on, the white headdress of the French nuns has not been seen in any of the poor missions of the North Shore. Only the parish of Esquimaux Point and the three main industrial centres have continued receiving the services of teaching Sisters. Their influence over the children has left a profound impression on them, especially on the little girls. Even now one can see the good results of their work in the mothers who once had the advantage of being their pupils.

The Sister dedicates her life to children ; she assures more stability, more continuity to teaching in her locality. Her love of God and souls and all the virtues which she daily acquires through her religious exercises and close contact with Him who is "the Way, the Truth, and the Life" give her a superiority over the lay teacher, excellent though she may be, but more exposed to worldliness and less fortified by the divine source of devotion.

All the missionaries of 1903 who came from the colleges of Saint-Sauveur of Redon, of Versailles, and of Saint-Martin of Rennes took a great interest in the education of children. Father Blondel dreamed of opening a school for boys in his spacious rectory. A few Fathers gave lessons to the bigger boys in their offices. Father Le Strat, who later became vicar general of their Excellencies, Bishops J.-M. Leventoux and N.-A. Labrie, became, both at Manicouagan and at Pentecost, the first professor of Latin, French, and mathematics of the present Bishop of the Gulf of St. Lawrence. When one of the first missionaries of 1903 answered a sick call in the colony of Taillardat in September, 1946, he was surprised to hear the mistress of the house salute him thus : "How do you do, Father ! You are not a stranger among us. My husband was telling me yesterday, when he returned from the High Mass which you sang in our church, that you taught his father in 1903 at Manicouagan." Pleasant words to hear, evoking memories of a good deed once accomplished.

Everywhere, the missionaries brought a good deal of attention to the education of children. Father Regnault strove to establish, at Pentecost and in the surrounding colonies, good schools directed by competent teachers. One of them, Miss Elmire Bernier, has obtained a well-earned pension for a long and successful teaching career of 25 years in different missions of the North Shore. For twenty-seven years, Father Arthur Divet sought to accentuate progress in education at Seven Islands, the first locality to possess a school for boys directed, first by one school master, now by two. At Clarke City we find Father Charles-Eugene Robitaille continually occupied with the direction of the schools which he had built for the settlers of Seven Islands Bay. With time, the missionary of Rivière-au-Tonnerre succeeded in providing decent schools for even the smallest missions.

In pursuing our way towards the east, we can see proof of the persevering efforts of Fathers J. Le Strat, A. Gallant, J. Lapointe, O. Proulx and, O. Ouellet. Thanks to them, modern schools were opened at Magpie, St. John, and Long Point. Even farther, at

Baie Johan-Beetz, Aguanish, Ile-à-Michon, Natashquan, and Grande-Rivière, suitable schools are standing witnesses of the fine work of Fathers G. Blondel, L. Garnier, J. Gallix, J. Huland, and L. Lebel. One of them has more than thirteen schools to his credit, although he could not affirm that the first five or six are still standing. Funds were lacking then, and the schools were often miserable and not too solidly built.

Havre Saint-Pierre was favoured by the presence of the Vicar Apostolic and of the Saint-Joseph Convent. The pastors of this mother parish, Fathers Louis LeDoré and J. Le Strat, were envied by their colleagues. Similarly, Clarke City, Shelter Bay, Godbout, Baie Trinité, Franquelin, and Baie Comeau are important centres where the vigilant zeal of Fathers Robitaille, Lapointe, Alfred Poulin, and L. Bourque actually finds scope. A cordial understanding between the Fathers, the municipalities, and the forestry companies provides the best possible solution to the school problem. The Sisters of the Holy Cross and four lay teachers at Baie Comeau, the Sisters of Charity and a schoolmaster at Shelter Bay, the Little Franciscan Sisters of Baie Saint-Paul at Clarke City and other industrial centres, competent and well remunerated lay teachers, provide adequate education for the children.

A teaching personnel had to be found for all these schools. The convent of Havre Saint-Pierre supplied some teachers. Often, they had to be recruited on the South Shore. Moreover, God alone knows the difficulties the missionaries had to face when hiring teachers for very small localities. The young girls dreaded the isolation of the small villages and did not like accepting the meagre salaries offered. To remedy this state of affairs, petitions were made by a few Fathers to the Department of Education for the granting of scholarships to promising young girls chosen in these villages. They thus acquired qualified teachers, a procedure well worth being continued, as it has already produced excellent results. Seeing the little success obtained with the boys, as the young women-teachers were frequently unable to cope with them, a few missionaries, too poor to think of hiring a master, had recourse to evening classes. A store clerk, Mr. Jos. Labbé, a man of exuberance and good will, succeeded admirably at Rivière-au-Tonnerre but did not remain on the North Shore. A few intelligent young men were sent out to the Thomas Institute of Quebec City and returned reasonably well qualified. One of them, Horatio Duguay, died of appendicitis. Another taught for a while, then was also prevented by illness from pursuing his career. A missionary has written a strange letter about this young Ronald Cody : "I am experiencing one of the most beautiful moments of my life. This morning we brought the body of a young man to his last resting-place. He was twenty-five years old. He died like a saint, suffering much and edifying all the visitors. He was a telegraphist who owed his education to me and showed himself ever grateful for it. Eight years ago he had suffered horribly from severe cold weather and returned from the woods with frozen hands. A doctor who happened to stop by, but without any surgical instruments, had to amputate his fingers by repeated operations. His last martyrdom lasted three years. What beautiful things he used to say ! Really, I hope his memory will live on like that of his comrade, Horatio Duguay, that it will also do

BISHOP GUSTAVE BLANCHE, C.J.M.
First Vicar Apostolic (1905-16)

CATHEDRAL AND BISHROPRIC OF BISHOP BLANCHE AT SEVEN ISLANDS

some good, and that both of them will help me to bear my cross and bring relief to distressed families."

Father Hesry, doughty builder of chapels though he was, who consecrated all his very limited resources to them, was unable to give to the education of the children around Blanc-Sablon the impetus required. The teaching personnel, often recruited in the locality, was inadequate. A missionary who had already had six years of experience at Shelter Bay and Anticosti, Father Louis-Philippe Gagné, succeeded him in September, 1931. From the day of his arrival this Father, whose intelligent activity is well known all over the North Shore, set himself to the arduous task, the urgency of which he fully understood, of ministering to an area of three hundred miles. Soon, it was learned that a new recruit, Mr. Gerard Bouchard, was teaching in the village of Tête-à-la-Baleine (Whalehead). He was a serious young man, whose sojourn in the region did much good. His memory still lingers there. An outside woman-teacher was hired for Our Lady of Lourdes at Blanc-Sablon. A start had been made ; emulation and the desire for a better education grew. In the spring, an important bit of news circulated from hamlet to hamlet and from island to island : Father Louis-Philippe Gagné has left for Quebec, accompanying His Excellency Bishop J.-M. Leventoux. They were both received by the Honourable A. Taschereau, Prime Minister of the Province. An important issue was then debated in his office, that of whether a considerable group of French Canadians, pioneers of the Labrador fishing industry, was to be allowed to remain illiterate amongst their Protestant compatriots, much better favoured in all respects.

This interview bore excellent results. Strongly abetted by the Prime Minister's support and the constant collaboration of the Honourable Mr. Rochette, our Member in the Legislative Assembly, who was ever ready to help the missionaries, Father Gagné was able to go ahead with his project. With the Government grant he could now build schools and hire teachers. During the summer, double classroom schools were built at Blanc-Sablon and Saint Augustine, single classroom schools at Baie-du-Milieu, Souriaban, Baie-de-la-Terre, and Portage-d'Hiver. These last localities were so tiny that Father N.-A. Labrie persuaded the people of Souriaban to abandon this locality and join the main group, a transfer similarly desired by many missionaries in other areas, as they were unable to bring adequate spiritual help to certain parishioners because of their isolation or their very small number. After having achieved this first feat of school construction, Father Gagné accomplished another quite as difficult : he found ten teachers to take charge of the new schools. We shall mention the names of these first teachers, as it is they who gave impetus to a very necessary service and accomplished a real apostolate :

BLANC-SABLON : Mr. Walsh
LOURDES OF BLANC-SABLON : Miss G. Touzel
BAIE-DU-MILIEU : Miss Lavallée
SAINT AUGUSTINE : Mr. Thomas Boudreau
BAIE-DE-LA-TERRE : Mr. Léon Levesque
SOURIABAN : Miss Stella Boudreau
TÊTE-À-LA-BALEINE : Mr. G. Bouchard
PORTAGE D'HIVER : Miss A. Leblanc
ROMAINE : Miss A. Doyle

Mr. Bouchard was unable to adjust himself to the surroundings, but Father Labrie acquired a precious collaborator in the person of Miss Elmida Beaudin. Meanwhile, Father Gagné, who was thoroughly familiar with that area, believed that two missionaries were absolutely necessary to minister adequately to the souls in that district and likewise convinced Bishop Leventoux, who acted immediately.

The future bishop of the Gulf of St. Lawrence, Father Labrie, arrived at Baie-Rouge in September, 1932. Without losing any time he applied his remarkable talent of builder and organizer to the task of building a rectory and a school for this locality, as well as repairing the church of Providence off Tête-à-la-Baleine and building a new school at Romaine. Because of his health, Father Gagné was obliged to leave the missions where he had accomplished so much good. He then took charge of Godbout.

Father A. Poulin, nephew of Father N.-A. Labrie, succeeded him at Blanc-Sablon. The present church was built under his direction. When he became sole missionary of the area, this active Father decided to reside in Baie-Rouge as being a more central location. He immediately undertook the construction of a chapel at Tête-à-la-Baleine, the demolition of the old church at Baie-Rouge, and its reconstruction in a more appropriate spot, near the rectory. Four young Eudist missionaries, Fathers Gerard Labrie, J. Jones and M. Méthot at Our Lady of Lourdes, and Father F. Michaud at Baie-Rouge zealously continued the good work of their predecessors. Now relieved of the overwhelming task of new constructions, they were able to visit their missions regularly, preaching, teaching catechism, and visiting the sick, without neglecting the upkeep of their chapels and schools. Father Michaud succeeded in acquiring a little gasoline yacht, a very useful conveyance, indeed, in making the rounds of this immense territory.

As we have seen, from 1931 to 1945 an energetic drive was conducted by the missionaries for the furtherance of education in the eastern part of the vicariate. The best witness, His Excellency Bishop N.-A. Labrie, wrote : "The schools of this region have given excellent results. The parents have generously collaborated, and the children have shown themselves to be docile, assiduous, and intelligent. Thanks to these schools, a young man can now continue with college studies, and others can enter commercial schools. Many young girls follow classes at convents, and three have already obtained Normal School certificates. A great part of the credit goes to the teaching personnel, which has shown a zeal worthy of the highest praises. The last years have been less successful, perhaps because salaries have increased everywhere else and the sums at the disposal of these poor schools are no longer sufficient to permit equal competition with wealthier municipalities. It has become difficult to find teachers. We have great hope that Bishop Scheffer will make use of his fine organizing ability and will set them once again on the way to progress."

The Very Reverend Father Jehanno, former Superior General of the Eudists, came in August, 1932 to preach the annual retreat of the Fathers. Upon setting foot on the wharf of Havre Saint-Pierre he told Bishop Leventoux that he had just come across three things in a neighbouring mission : a wharf, a church, and an enthusiastic pastor. If the Very Reverend Father Jehanno, whose remark amused the persons assembled on the wharf, had time to travel all along the North Shore, he would have seen not one, but thirty churches or chapels built by missionaries, not only full of enthusiasm, but active and practical. All were builders of churches, chapels, schools, rectories, very much attached to their ministry, and ready to leave by *kometik* or by boat at the first call. This good Father was coming to encourage them in their work and did so with great talent.

It seems appropriate to close this general view of religious activities on the North Shore by drawing the reader's attention to an aspect of "Catholic Action" practiced by certain persons in villages that had, and still have, no resident priest.

Franquelin, as an example, is a little mill town nine miles north-east of Baie Comeau. It is perched on a hill, facing the rising sun, and protected on three sides by the Laurentians, which are very close to the Gulf in this district. An automobile leaving the wharf reaches it by climbing a hill. Seventy families live here in attractive little houses built alongside the road leading to the mill, each surrounded, during the summer, by gardens full of vegetables and flowers. A church, schools, stores, and a few more elaborate houses make Franquelin one of the most picturesque hamlets of the North Shore.

It had very modest beginnings. In 1918 it was merely a meeting place for lumbermen occupied with the cutting of logs in the winter and the loading of barges in the summer. At that time, a rather severe depression was making itself felt throughout the Province and especially along the North Shore. Men flocked to the lumber camps to earn a little money. At Franquelin, as well as at other lumber camps, they came in too great numbers. Many who came without money had great difficulty finding work ; others were forced to return and seek work elsewhere.

Two persons of this village, Adélard Thibault and his wife, whom everybody called "Mother Thibault", played the role of Good Samaritans and were always ready to be of service to the unfortunate ones. Mr. Thibault, a former contractor, kept a boarding-house. It would be difficult to enumerate all the charitable deeds accomplished by these two good Christians. Mr. Thibault welcomed any new arrival, found him work, whenever possible, or helped him a bit before his forced departure. "Mother Thibault" directed the boarding-house and accepted payment for the meals served, if the guests had money, but contented herself with the gratitude of the others, even inviting them to eat, if they were too timid. A Eudist Father has seen her gaily distribute fifty to sixty free meals at one time. "Mother Thibault" had, as can well be imagined, a great moral influence on her guests. To prevent swearing or the abuse of liquor, she entreated, flew into a temper, and even banished offenders from the table. Far from being annoyed or resentful, the men, good fellows at bottom, would submit, enjoyed such scenes, and teased her about them. Thus, alcoholics overcame their bad habits, and men who had drifted away from the church accompanied Mr. Thibault, known as the "Father" because of the functions he presided over at church. What good was done to souls in this way by a big-hearted woman who could have given everything and forgiven anything in order to be of service!

Twenty-eight years later, in 1947, as I was called upon to spend Holy Week in this parish, I was struck by the profoundly religious and moral character of the parishioners. How could such fervour, such perfect understanding among them have been maintained without the regular presence of the priest? The missionary of Godbout has hitherto not been able to visit Franquelin more than once a month.

During the epidemic of influenza in 1918, this village was deserted for serveral months. It came to life again with the arrivals of such families as those of Joseph Beaudin, Joseph Tremblay, Alfred Beaudin, J.-B. Légaré, Adélard Thibault, etc., the founders of Franquelin. It was from that date that Mr. A. Thibault played an important role among his fellow-parishioners. He asked Father Regnault, who was the missionary of this district at the time, for the unusual favour of keeping the Blessed Sacrament in the tabernacle of the humble chapel. His Excellency Bishop Leventoux readily granted permission after having assured himself that Mr. and Mrs. Thibault would constitute themselves keepers of the church.

Subsequently, a large number of the faithful assembled in the chapel every evening. At the regular hour, Mr. Thibault proceeded to the church, where he replaced the absent priest somewhat by leading the congregation in the recitation of the beads and evening prayers. Every Sunday, while Masses were being said in other churches, the good old man could be seen kneeling before the altar. When all the inhabitants had taken their places in the church, he would read aloud the sublime prayers of the Mass.

On Good Friday, at the very hour when the Saviour died on the cross, he presided over the Way of the Cross. Stores and offices were closed, and the entire population devoutly followed the venerated patriarch in this holy exercise.

Father Lucien Bourque, the present missionary of Godbout and Franquelin, has no worries with regard to this village. For a time he concentrated all his energy on the building of an attractive church, which he was glad to open for worship on Christmas, 1948.

The diocese of the Gulf of St. Lawrence has just lost an outstanding educator in the person of Miss Blanche-Emma Jomphe. Having become a prey to sickness she had to leave her pupils at the beginning of February, 1949. She died at Havre Saint-Pierre on April 21 at the age of thirty-seven, assisted by her relatives and friends, and edifying them by her admirable submission to the will of God and her joy at the prospect of receiving her reward from the Master whom she had so well served.

Her death was a great loss to parents, children, and all those who take an interest in education. For the past eight years she had given herself to the education of the children of Franquelin. They will long remember their benefactress, who spoke well of them : "I like my pupils of Franquelin ; they are good, obedient, and grateful." Miss Jomphe was in her twenty-first year of teaching when she died, thus sharing with another teacher, Miss Elmire Bernier, the honour of having devoted herself for such a long period of time to the education of the children of the North Shore.

Some of her last words merit being recorded for the edification of future teachers of the diocese.

"I spent five years with the children of Saint Augustine, a village in Labrador in the vicariate of His Excellency Bishop Scheffer. They were the best years of my life. There was very much to do over there, and the children profited very well by my teaching. Three of them actually became teachers and are now carrying on the work that I had started...

"Alas, we do not fully realize the greatness of our vocation. Some of us do not sufficiently put to use the fine education received from the Sisters of Charity of Havre Saint-Pierre. Once out of Normal School, they lose interest in the things of the mind and in questions pertaining to education...

"My greatest sorrow lies in the fact that I must, at 37, leave my beloved children to whom I would have liked to impart so much good. I would have liked to inspire them with the love of their maternal language and to help their mothers bring them up as good Christians. Is not my profession that in which a woman can best fulfill her role of educator?"

Beautiful thoughts, indeed, left as a precious testament by this much regretted teacher to those who will succeed her.

Permit me to recall, in concluding this chapter on the moral and religious life of the North Shore, an audacious undertaking of one of the missionaries of 1903. No sooner had Father J. Laizé arrived at Pentecost River than he began to print a little paper which met with a certain success and was much appreciated by its first readers. It was called *L'Écho du Labrador* and proposed to relate sundry news concerning this region and serve as a link and a stimulus among the missionaries, who were so isolated one from the other.

To unite the missionaries in spirit and make known the projects of each and everyone and the good accomplished in each community was the choice task of the *Écho*, in which all its collaborators vied with each other in ardour and enthusiasm in the effort to keep alive a beneficent apostolic emulation for the good of souls and the greater glory of God.

CHAPTER SIXTEEN

THE LEADERS OF THE FLOCK

I

(BISHOP GUSTAVE BLANCHE)

Church restored and bishopric built at Seven Islands
by Bishop Blanche in 1905 ;
destroyed by fire in 1915.

T HE name of Bishop Blanche has appeared frequently in these notes. He bas born in Britanny at Josselin, site of the famous shrine of Our Lady of Roncier. His was a profoundly Christian family which had produced a fine line of doctors and pharmacists.

Gustave Blanche studied at the Eudist college of Redon, an institution which enjoyed a wide reputation for the excellent education imparted to a great number of the sons of Brittany's aristocracy.

When, in 1870, the call to arms sounded through France, young Blanche joined the Breton Mobile Corps and distinguished himself by his outstanding bravery. He was noticed by his superior officers and one of them, General De Martenot, chose Second Lieutenant Gustave Blanche as orderly officer.

When the war was over, Gustave Blanche returned home and undertook the study of law. Soon, however, the young student felt the call to a different vocation and one day informed his mother of his desire to become a priest, a Eudist Father, if it pleased God.

Once his theological studies were completed, he alternately became prefect of studies and superior in Eudist colleges at Rennes, Versailles, and Besançon.

It was this distinguished priest that his superiors chose in answer to a request made by Archbishop O'Brien of Halifax for someone to organize education in the Acadian district of Baie Sainte-Marie in Nova Scotia. Father Blanche accomplished this difficult task with matchless courage and devotion and built a rectory and a college, only to see them destroyed by fire. Undaunted by this great setback, he proclaimed that, since everything was destroyed, the only thing to do was to start all over and submit to the will of God.

This ardent apostle became Apostolic Prefect in 1903 and first Vicar Apostolic of the Gulf of St. Lawrence in 1905.

Worried over the future of the Eudist colleges in France in 1903 because of the real religious persecution then going on, Father Le Doré, Superior General of the Congregation, left the Fathers free to choose between France, Canada, and Spanish Columbia. Many chose Canada. Father Blanche, the founder of all the Eudist houses in this country, was asked by his superiors to find some sphere of activity for his colleagues. The Bishop of Chicoutimi, Mgr Labrecque, who had met Father Blanche at the Saint John College, in Versailles, received him as a friend and brother.

In this interview the North Shore was discussed. Events thereafter happened in rapid succession. By a decree of July 13, 1903, Father Blanche was given the administration of the territory surrounding the Gulf of St. Lawrence and was named Apostolic Prefect of this area. Two years later, on September 12, 1905, His Holiness Pope Pius X, upon the requests of Their Excellencies the Bishops of the Province of Quebec, raised the prefecture to an apostolic vicariate and appointed the former Prefect as first Bishop of the Gulf of St. Lawrence. The news reached Father Blanche at Esquimaux Point, where he had brought Father Louis LeDoré to install him as pastor. It dismayed him. "I commend myself to your prayers," he wrote. "I see in all this the will of God. *Fiat* ! But I have never dreaded a responsibility as I do this one."

The consecration of Bishop Blanche took place on October 28, 1905 in the beautiful cathedral of Chicoutimi. Nothing was spared that could add to the solemnity of a ceremony seen for the first time in a still very young city.

His Excellency Bishop Bégin officiated at the consecration of the new bishop, and another benefactor of the Eudist Fathers, Bishop Blais of Rimouski, pronounced the sermon.

More than ever before, submission to Divine Providence was necessary to the new bishop, as new hardships were to befall him and even multiply themselves. One will bear a name well known in the solitudes of Labrador : isolation, isolation from community life, precious safeguard of religious life, isolation from the family, and isolation from the world for six months. Others were to arise from certain tasks which he willingly assumed. "As we lack servants," he once wrote, "I wake up the community every morning and light the stove, not an episcopal function, but one must get along here as best one can."

The episcopate of Bishop Blanche was overcast by the premature death of a few missionaries : Fathers Conan, Brézel, and Le Jollec ? Empty places appeared in the ranks. Promising subjects were snatched by death in the fullness of their youth. "People who do not know us would accuse us of imprudence. As for myself, I seek in vain the reason why Providence treats us so severely, but the more I reflect on the enigma, the more obscure it becomes. *Fiat voluntas Dei !*"

1903-1916 . . . Thirteen years of missionary work on the North Shore. Bishop Blanche decided to make his residence at Seven Islands. He had great confidence in this important and most picturesque locality built along the beach and facing an immense bay. Today it seems certain of a brilliant future because of the mines of the Hollinger Company. Most of the population is of Canadian or Acadian origin, good, polite, cordial, and religious folk. It is the ideal site for a little college, a juniorate, and a convent. Seven Islands ! to Bishop Blanche, it was the city of the future. In dreaming of the future greatness of his episcopal town, did the first bishop of the North Shore err very much ?

Nothing could dishearten this former soldier cut out for action and struggle. If he could not carry out his dreams for Seven Islands, he turned his energy towards other good works. He wrote letters to the Fathers to encourage them in the accomplishment of their duties, inviting them to thank God for graces received and to pray for the success of common enterprises. For Lent, he wrote pastoral letters in which was shown his apostolic anxiety for the good of souls. Under an appearance of majesty, of natural distinction which came from his education, his family, and his relations with several groups both in France and in America, he hid a heart of gold.

What more could be said of Bishop Blanche? That he was a Eudist, a true son of St. John Eudes, always first at the spiritual exercises of the community at Seven Islands and first for the morning meditation ; that he was a soldier with a great love of his country, which he had defended in battle at Champigny and at the siege of Paris ; that he also greatly loved Canada, happy to entertain these two loves so easily reconciled, that of France and his adopted country ; and especially, that he was a soldier of Christ, writing and preaching the good word, ardently defending our faith without fear and without affectation.

He died in Paris on July 28, 1916 while reading a report on his beloved vicariate to his colleagues, who were attending a general assembly of the Congregation. He was conjuring up a past filled with trials which he wished to forget in order to consider solely what appeared to him as the brilliant future of the vicariate in the offing. He had worked hard, and he had suffered physically and morally to a degree known only to God. His friends were not surprised, therefore, to see tears roll down his thin cheeks when he shook hands with them at the pier of Seven Islands, just before leaving for France. It was his last farewell to his vicariate, which he had loved and served wholeheartedly and for which he was to die while pleading its cause before his brothers in religion.

II

(BISHOP A.-P. CHIASSON)

The successor of Bishop Blanche, Alexandre-Patrice Chiasson, was born at Grand-Étang, Cape Breton Island, on November 26, 1867, of Olivier Chiasson and Angèle Haché-Gallant. In 1886, although barely eighteen years of age, he became a teacher at the Saint Louis of Kent College. Like his parents, who were now living at Rogersville, Mgr Richard, his pastor, sensing that the young man was called to the priesthood, advised him to attend the college of Sainte-Anne-de-la-Pointe-de-l'Église. One can imagine Bishop Blanche's happiness at receiving a pupil who was already a precious collaborator.

At twenty-seven, he was admitted to the Eudist Novitiate in Kerlois, Brittany. Four years later, on June 4, 1898, Patrice Chiasson, already a Eudist for two years, was ordained a priest at Rennes by Cardinal Labouré. For nineteen years he exercised a remarkable activity at Saint Anne College of Baie-Sainte-Marie, both as professor and director. He became its superior in 1908 and filled this important post very successfully until he was called to the North Shore by the Holy See in 1917.

After Bishop Blanche's death, days, months, even a whole year passed by with no mention of a successor. Great misgivings began to fill the minds of the missionaries along the North Shore. Would they have to abandon the missions to which they had become so attached? One of them, finally, having obtained an

BISHOP JULIEN-MARIE LEVENTOUX, C.J.M.
Third Vicar Apostolic (1922-38)

interview with Cardinal Bégin, heard these consoling words : "Your Congregation will remain on the North Shore." Some time later, in fact, Patrice Chiasson was appointed Titulary Bishop of Lydda and Vicar Apostolic of the Gulf of St. Lawrence. He was consecrated bishop by Cardinal Bégin at Saint Anne's College on October 18, 1917.

On November 27 of the same year, Bishop Chiasson arrived at Esquimaux Point. He was welcomed with understandable enthusiasm : an Acadian bishop coming to reside in the most Acadian village of the region seemed like a distinctive favour granted by Divine Providence to this important group of the martyred people, who had been driven from burning Grand-Pré in 1755.

At Seven Islands, the new bishopric and the church restored by Bishop Blanche had been destroyed by the terrible fire of 1915, which had also caused the death of a nun, Sister Émilienne. This was another cross for the Vicar Apostolic. Bishop Chiasson did not rebuild the cathedral and the bishop's residence at Seven Islands. Probably he did not have the necessary funds. He chose to live modestly in the village of Esquimaux Point 140 miles east of Seven Islands, in the old rectory of Mgr F.-X. Bossé, first with Father René Kerdelué, then with Father Le Strat.

A chronicle of the times states : "God has sent us a choice pastor. Ardent and energetic, Bishop Chiasson does not hesitate to jump into the little boats, man the oars, guide the rudder, or travel by *kometik*, even in the coldest weather of winter." A remarkable walker, this lover of sports and the outdoors very willingly travelled by this universal mode of transportation on the North Shore. He once chose to make a tour of the missions of Natashquan in the middle of winter? It was not easy to travel over the hills and bays of Napissipi, Pachachibou, Maskana, and Watichou! "It was bitterly cold," relates the Bishop's travelling companion, "and when we stopped for a midday lunch in Joseph Deraps' camp, we ate quickly, standing up, with the bread freezing hard in our hands. When we resumed our journey, water had risen on the ice and made slush with the freshly fallen snow, a hindrance to people in a hurry. As I was better used to Labradorian travel, I often left my seat on the *kometik* to run behind it so as to prevent any dangerous chill. Thus, I kept myself reasonably warm and alert and was feeling very well when, in the evening, we reached Johan Beetz and greeted his interesting family. Poor Bishop Chiasson! He immediately asked to be shown to a room in order to rest and warm his tired frozen limbs. For once, his good spirits were flagging. His ride in the *kometik* had momentarily taken away his enthusiasm for all sport!"

It was during his all too-short administration that the admirable Sisters of Charity returned to Saint Joseph's Convent. They had been asked, in 1904, to give up their establishment in favour of the Daughters of Jesus, who had accepted the direction of the little schools of the North Shore. The Sisters of Charity had left quietly and simply, and they returned in the same manner to work anew with the same zeal and devotion in their convent of Esquimaux Point. Their return was the work of a tactful move on the part of the spiritual leader. The heroic humility of these holy women is also to be commended, for they left the painful past behind them and took up their work, unhesitatingly, for the greater glory of God. The actual state of their work is proof that heavenly blessings have descended in recognition of these two gallant deeds : that of the Bishop requesting their return and that of the Sisters accepting it "with a joyful and willing heart."

The North Shore could have expected a great deal from this new bishop, so courageous, so mindful of his duties, and so competent in the work of education. His beneficent influence made itself felt very quickly in Saint Joseph's Convent, in which he was greatly interested and also in the little schools along the coast. His sojourn in the vicariate was very brief, and he had no time to realize any great enterprise. There was so much to be done ! But how, and with what means ? A rigorous climate, a long winter season, lack of fertile soil, everything was against him. Even the fishing industry was already on the wane. Bishop Chiasson was appointed to a higher post and later achieved the reputation of being one of the outstanding Canadian bishops. He was appointed Bishop of Chatham in 1920 and left Esquimaux Point on October 4 of the same year.

III

(BISHOP J.-M. LEVENTOUX)

Julien-Marie Leventoux, our third bishop, was born at Trélivan, a little village of Brittany situated on the banks of the Rance River opposite the peaceful and ancient city of Dinan. While still very young he was admitted to the Eudist juniorate at Plancoet. There, and later on at Saint-Sauveur College of Redon, as at the novitiate of Kerlois and the seminary of Roche-du-Theil, he displayed a remarkable intelligence, devotion to his work, and a robust faith. An excellent disciplinarian, he impressed the most mischievous by his meaningful composure. He was a professor at the Saint-Sauveur College of Redon when the departure of several missionaries for Canada was decided upon in 1903. Upon his arrival he was appointed director of the juniorate at Pointe-de-l'Église and pastor of the concessions.

It was from the Seminary of Chicoutimi that he left for the North Shore in 1905. The missions of Pentecost and Anticosti had the privilege of being directed by this distinguished priest. During his sojourn in these two missions his personality and influence projected themselves on his parishioners in various wholesome ways. Amiable and polite with everyone, he chatted with the people on subjects with which they were familiar, even using their own vocabulary to discuss fishing, hunting, or work in the lumber camps.

He was in his element in his frequent visits to the schools. No one was better qualified to examine the copybooks, correct mistakes, give a lesson in spelling or literature, and stimulate the pupils to work. There, as well as in church or in catechism classes, Father Leventoux was always on the lookout for possible religious vocations. If he did not succeed in multiplying vocations to the priesthood as much as he would have liked, it is to his credit that he watched over the development of a most outstanding one among those he guided, that of his successor to the episcopate, brought to fulfillment, also, those of the Eudist Fathers, Alfred Poulin, Albini Vigneault, Moïse Méthot and François Devost, and directed excellent Sisters to the cloister.

Although he was alone at Anticosti for many years, Father Leventoux rigidly adhered to a rule. He came down from his room at six o'clock every morning and spent some time in meditation. He then repaired to his confessional and afterwards said Mass. In the late afternoon he was again in church between four and six o'clock.

He was still at Anticosti Island when he was called to the dignity of a bishop. His nomination gave rise to an amusing anecdote. He had received no official news of the event, although the Fathers of the vicariate had been informed by a telegram from their Provincial and had immediately sent their congratulations and best wishes to their new chief. To his great surprise, all these telegrams reached him on the first of April, a day when he good-naturedly took part in "April Fool" pranks with the young people of his parish. These telegrams caused him much merriment, still remembered by some ; he believed himself to be the object of a well-organized joke on the part of his colleagues. A few days later, telegrams from bishops and other personalities and a formal letter, finally, from the Apostolic Legation, convinced him of the reality of his nomination. On October 28, 1920, this well-qualified missionary succeeded Bishop Patrice Chiasson with the powers of a vicar general. He left for Europe in 1921 and was appointed Vicar Apostolic on April 1, 1922. On June 11, in the church of Saint-Cœur-de-Marie in Quebec, he was consecrated by

Cardinal Bégin. Bishop Leonard of Rimouski delivered the sermon.

The following spring, Bishop Leventoux decided to to build for himself and his missionaries a suitable dwelling where they could all find accommodation during the annual retreat. For the construction and furnishing of this humble bishopric at Esquimaux Point he enlisted the services of his talented curate, Father Le Strat, who made an attractive residence of it. It has a pleasing aspect when, coming from the wharf, one beholds it at the entrance to the village, standing in a garden of lawns and flowerbeds.

On May 1, 1924 a village chronicler wrote : "Today, Esquimaux Point has legally and canonically changed its name. It will henceforth be known as Havre Saint-Pierre. Let us congratulate Bishop Leventoux for having brought about this change at the very outset of his episcopate." Havre Saint-Pierre, so aptly named, has been endowed by nature with all the properties of a good natural harbour. A boat may enter or leave, either to the east or to the west, without the slightest difficulty. The largest ocean-going vessels can manœuvre at ease in this inland sea, allowing tourists to admire the most picturesque and grandiose of Laurentian panoramas formed by the long chain of the Mingan Islands stretching over a distance of twenty miles. One can understand that it is quite an event in the village when one of these huge vessels is sighted gracefully entering the harbour through the narrow passage between the Mingan Islands and the mainland. Bishop Leventoux resided for eighteen years at Havre Saint-Pierre and left it periodically to attend meetings of the Department of Education in

Quebec, to travel to Rome and France, and to make confirmation tours in his vicariate.

Nothing much showed exteriorly during this episcopate, yet very fine works were quietly accomplished, all without publicity. A missionary was saying one day to Father Lebrun, then Provincial of the Eudists in Canada : "God has given us a good Bishop." "Yes," answered the Provincial, "I believe he will be the best of the three we have had, the one that will do the most for the North Shore." A certain inhabitant of Anticosti Island would have been surprised to hear his judgment of Bishop Leventoux preaching ratified by an eminent personality, who was leaving the Saint-Cœur-de-Marie church, where our Bishop had just pronounced the sermon : "This missionary expresses beautiful thoughts in a most harmonious language. He is truly eloquent and does not seem aware of it."

While he was still a missionary, Bishop Leventoux loved children and did all he could to help them get a better education. On becoming Bishop he took an even greater interest in education. At Saint Joseph's Convent he directed the pupils, encouraged them in their work, and read their monthly reports, adding wise advice when necessary. From the very first years of his episcopate he organized end-of-the-year contests for the older pupils. A profitable emulation was thus created among the schoolchildren. On the appointed day, he presided over the group himself, dictated the questions, and supervised their work. This contest promoted a spirit of friendly rivalry among the teachers and the pupils.

On March 19, 1935, his beloved Saint Joseph's Convent celebrated its 50th anniversary. Bishop Leventoux then made a glowing speech, which was printed in its entirety in the *Enseignement primaire*. He began by recalling the meagre means originally at the disposition of the North Shore for the intellectual development of the children. "Hardly a dozen little schools were to be found in a territory of more than six hundred miles in length. How many men, women, and young people were then unable, not only to read, but even to sign their names?" He then rendered thanks to God for having inspired, for the progress of education on the North Shore, such men as Mgr F.-X. Bossé, Vicar General Gendron, and Bishops Blanche and Chiasson, two notable educators, as well as the admirable Sisters who have succeeded one another as teachers in the schools. In 1925, it became necessary to think of enlarging the convent built in 1909, which had become much too small. Better still, thought Sister Sainte-Martine, its superior, who was also the enterprising sister of Bishop Labrie. Due to generous government subsidies obtained by her in that same year, Bishop Leventoux was able to bless the spacious new building which now stands as an impressive testimony to the success of the work begun fifty years ago. "If today on the North Shore of the Gulf of St. Lawrence," added Bishop Leventoux, "we have more than fifty schools and more than sixty classrooms, where eighty Sisters and qualified lay teachers are educating some two thousand children, do we not owe it to our convent of Havre Saint-Pierre? And how many young people have been able to acquire a more advanced education, thanks to the first lessons received in this convent?"

This admirable discourse, adequately summing up the development of education in Labrador, is eloquent proof of the importance ascribed to it by Bishop Leventoux. He dedicated himself to it whole-heartedly during his episcopate. It has been said that he did not go out enough, that he did not negotiate sufficiently with governmental authorities. Bishop Leventoux hesitated greatly before undertaking a journey. It was a great effort for him to set out for any place, but he left his missionaries free to do so, guiding them with sound advice, even accompanying them to parliamentary offices, if necessary. There, his unanswerable arguments and eloquence were sure to win the cause. Fathers Louis-Philippe Gagné and J. Taillardat, as well as many others, know that, due to his help, they have been able to accomplish much for education and colonization.

Many missionaries organized merry evenings of card games in their rectories, as they did not have any parochial halls. This was the principal means of distraction for many years before the advent of the radio and motion pictures. There was much enjoyment in the victories and defeats of the players and, at the end of an evening, there were prizes for the winners and laughs for the losers. They were real oldtime holidays, these noisy evenings where the missionary acted as host. In Rivière-Saint-Jean they still talk about these gatherings of young and old organized by Father Le Strat, who was the life of any party. The good Father believed, and rightly so, that he could thus preserve a brotherly spirit among his flock. For a long time, our Bishop took part in these reunions. Later, however, he preferred a quieter circle of friends, the "apostles", as they were termed by the more roguish. Then, he deprived himself of all exterior distraction.

Responsibilities weighed heavily on the aging Bishop Leventoux. In 1937 he asked to be relieved of his duties. This news saddened all the missionaries and inhabitants of the coast. The very good Father was beloved by all and, had the Fathers known of his intentions beforehand, they would have entreated him to remain with them.

Bishop Leventoux spent his last years at the Sacred Heart Rectory in Chicoutimi where he was a constant source of edification to his colleagues and their parishioners by his presence at all religious offices of church and community. He was too attached to the North Shore not to feel, in this retreat, a veritable nostalgia for the vast regions over which he had travelled. With what pleasure he would leave in François Devost's car or Father Taillardat's truck ! "You will surely not bring your companion back alive," people used to say to these two good Samaritans during the last years of his life, "he is feeble and ailing," but they always brought him back feeling younger and happier to have seen Ruisseau-Vert, Baie Comeau, Godbout, etc., once more.

Then came two years of confinement in a hospital room. The venerable patient received the best of care from the good Augustine Sisters of Chicoutimi's Hôtel-Dieu and from the doctors and nurses to whom he often expressed his heartfelt gratitude. After having received the last rites from Father Jauffret, he lingered on for eight days and was continually visited by his colleagues who prayed with him or entered into short

THE LEADERS OF THE FLOCK 271

conversations with him. From time to time it was possible to interest him by talking about the North Shore, the missionaries who were still working there, of Father Le Strat, his companion for so many years, and of Father Taillardat, who had organized his last extensive trip on the North Shore. Upon the request of the persons attending him, his hands for the last time blessed those present and absent, the members of his Congregation, his friend and successor, Bishop Labrie, and all the inhabitants of the North Shore, who will never know how much he had loved them. On September 3, 1946, the Bishop, who had so well understood his duty and had so faithfully discharged it, peacefully rendered his soul to God. He was in his seventy-eighth year.

IV

(BISHOP N.-A. LABRIE)

Let us pause, finally, before the sympathetic personality of the fourth bishop of the North Shore, his Excellency Bishop N.-A. Labrie. The few lines devoted to this illustrious native of the Canadian Labrador will add to the knowledge of this particular region and will, furthermore, throw light on some aspects of the ministry exercised by the Eudist Fathers since 1903.

Of all the villages scattered along the coast, Godbout is, without doubt, one of the most picturesque. First, there is the large bay where rise and fall the blue, deep waters of the Gulf on a long beach of russet sand, which is ideal for bathers during the summer. Bordering this beach is the road on which cars and trucks of the St. Regis Timber Company travel, following the original tiny path traced by the first residents of the locality. At the back a hill, covered with trees, rises in a gentle slope up to the mountains which seem to reach the sky. From their summits, one can see the waters of the St. Lawrence and the rolling land of the South Shore on one side, and on the other, the boundless forest stretching farther than the eye can see, a most striking panorama, variations of which can be viewed all over the North Shore.

In this village, so greatly cherished by Alexandre Comeau, the fourth chief of the apostolic vicariate and the first bishop of the diocese of the Gulf of St. Lawrence was born, on August 5, 1893, who, while still "a little boy," said Bishop Labrie on the day of his consecration, "heard the call of God. He had seen of the world only the paternal home situated in a region of green mountains by the side of the sea. The harmony of wind and waves had lulled his dreams. As a prelude to his sleep each night, he would repeat the holy names of Jesus and Mary and receive the kisses of an angel who called him 'my little priest'. When she made me say my prayers, I could feel this desire burn in her heart. Her confidence was absolute. Mothers have those intuitions which seem to force, so to speak, the will of God."

This woman, mother of fourteen children, who entertained such hopes in her heart for 'her little priest' reminds one of another : the mother of Cardinal Vaughan. Convinced that such a vocation was a special grace, she proposed obtaining it for her children by making an hour of adoration before the Blessed Sacrament every day. She kept this up for thirty years, and her prayers were granted. Her daughters entered convents, and six of her eight sons became priests : one, a cardinal, two others, archbishops. Do not such sublime sentiments in a mother, shared by a Christian father, and preserved by a family life where the members pray in common, provide the most favourable medium wherein priestly vocations grow? Happy and blessed are the families where God is thus first served. May the Divine Master multiply them in our too materialistic world, particularly on the North Shore where priests are so much needed.

Father Leventoux and Father Le Strat were happy to help realize the desires of parents so well disposed. The first lessons were given to this child by Father Le Strat, first at Manicouagan, then at Pentecost, where he joined Father J.-M. Leventoux. "I shall always remember Bishop Leventoux and Father Le-Strat with the greatest fondness," said Bishop Labrie further on the day of his consecration and then turned to the two in question : "We spent two wonderful years together in your rectory where you united your efforts to develop my mind and heart before guiding me to the Congregation which you have taught me to love."

The young Labradorian proved himself a brilliant pupil while attending the college of Sainte-Anne-de-la-Pointe-de-l'Église. There, one of his predecessors on the North Shore, Bishop Chiasson, taught him science. Then came the journey to Rome where he studied for four years at the Gregorian University. He was ordained on April 15, 1922 in the Latran Basilica, and after a visit to the principal Eudist houses in France, he returned to Canada.

On August 12, 1922, under the direction of Father Regnault, a great celebration was organized at the little village of Godbout. When Mr. Alfred Labrie's yacht was sighted coming from Matane, bearing his son, the new priest, his daughter, Sister Sainte-Martine, Father de la Motte, relatives, and friends, a whole flotilla of flag bedecked boats went out to meet it. As if by chance another yacht appeared to the east carrying Bishop Leventoux and Fathers Regnault and Le Strat. The flotilla also escorted these distinguished guests. One can imagine everyone's joy in this meeting of the newly-arrived with the people waiting on the shore. The following day a High Mass was sung in the open air, at the foot of the moutains and by the waters of the St. Lawrence. A long table was set out on the lawn for a banquet to which everyone was invited. Bishop Leventoux confirmed the children and blessed the great cross erected on the slope of the mountain facing the Gulf. (In 1930 Father Bourque repaired this cross, which is illuminated in the evening.) Frolicsome boat races over the calm waters entertained the assembled throng, and fireworks proclaimed afar the joy that filled all hearts. Evening prayer and the Benediction of the Blessed Sacrament ended this day of rejoicing in fervent thanksgiving to God.

Beautiful words were spoken that day by Father Le Strat, Father de La Motte, and especially by the new priest. Father Labrie thanked God for having called him to the priesthood. He expressed his gratitude to his good parents, who had such a decisive influence on his vocation, to Bishop Leventoux, whose opportune presence permitted a celebration for both the father and the spiritual son, to Father Le Strat, his first teacher, and to Father Divet and Father de la Motte. The celebration was all the more considerable, for few of the persons present had ever taken part in a similar one. "When I saw the little flotilla of Godbout manœuvering at the foot of these mountains of which I dreamed so often," said the new priest, "I thought of the ceremonies which drew my admiration in Europe, and I said to myself : 'I have never seen any more beautiful than this one.' They appealed but little to my heart ; this one wholly penetrated it."

In September Father Labrie went to Saint Anne's College where he taught for one year. Then, he became a missionary on this North Shore where he was born and where he is now called upon to play the role of a prominent leader. He was first appointed at Our Lady of Betsiamits, a mission made justly famous by the long and fruitful work of Fathers Arnaud and Babel and many other Oblate Fathers. A new church, built by Father Brière, was so much improved by him as to become one of the most beautiful of the region. Later, having been put in charge of Pointe-aux-Outardes, in spite of very limited funds, he improved the chapel and the tiny rectory. There, he had to travel over a vast territory, then devoid of means of communication. He was afterwards transferred to an even more difficult post.

One day, Bishop Leventoux, who was well aware of the ability of his former pupil, asked him to take charge of the most difficult mission in the vicariate. He shared, first with Father Louis-Philippe Gagné, then with Father Alfred Poulin, his nephew, those territories which have now been entrusted to Bishop Scheffer and the Oblate Fathers. In a little village, half hidden in the farthest corner of Baie-Rouge, Father Labrie spent five years, very much occupied with visits to his flock, scattered around bays over a distance of more than a hundred and fifty miles. He made his visits ordinarily by day and occasionally by night. His departure for the first winter mission was always set for the day after Epiphany, and it lasted for a month. The missionary was weary and his stomach more or less upset. Yet, no sooner had he returned from visiting the missions to the east than he had to turn his attention to those in the west : another eight or ten days of discomfort. Nevertheless, Father Labrie who, during the first year, was a guest of Adélard Cormier, had also to solve a problem which arose for most of the Eudist Fathers : that of building a modest residence. He drew the plans himself, directed the construction of the house, and helped the labourers throughout the day. Later, he painted his rectory as well as an experienced painter could have done. And now, the sick or the needy, visitors or chance passersby, all are welcome at the rectory of Baie-Rouge.

Father Labrie acquired a reputation as an intrepid traveller. He frequently snowshoed, alone, the twenty miles between Pointe-aux-Outardes and Pointe-Lebel. In 1943, when he was already vicar apostolic, he replaced one of his missionaries on a trip. At the set hour he was dressed in his travelling clothes, and his bag was ready. Agile, with the experience of a seasoned traveller, he took his place on his *kometik* and started off for the distant missions of Manitou and other places. To the missionary who apologized for imposing such

Photo Studio Audet

HIS EXCELLENCY BISHOP NAPOLÉON-ALEXANDRE LABRIE, C.J.M.
First Bishop of the Gulf of St. Lawrence

MISSIONARIES OF THE NORTH SHORE
AT THE CONSECRATION OF BISHOP LABRIE

a task on his bishop, he answered smilingly : "Don't give it another thought ! I was pleased to do it, and it gave me an opportunity to come out of this forced physical inactivity !"

When, at the beginning of April, 1938, Father Labrie was called upon by the Holy See to leave his parishioners to whom he had become so attached, he did not hesitate to hitch his dog team and travel two hundred miles over bays, portages, and mountains. Two days later, tanned by sun and wind and still alert, he boarded a plane at Natashquan for Havre Saint-Pierre.

News of this nomination fulfilled the wishes of his colleagues and of the whole population. Because of the great distance and difficulties of all kinds, his consecration could not take place at Havre Saint-Pierre, as he would have desired. On July 17, 1938 the Saint-Cœur-de-Marie church was again the scene for this solemn and imposing ceremony. Archbishops, bishops, colleagues, numerous members of the clergy, representatives from both the Federal and Provincial Governments, relatives, and friends filled it to capacity. His Eminence Cardinal Villeneuve was the consecrating bishop. Father Gautier, a Eudist, made a masterly synthesis of Catholic doctrine concerning authority in the Church. At the banquet, the Honourable Mr. Onésime Gagnon extended the good wishes of the Provincial Government to the new vicar apostolic and congratulated the Eudist Congregation for the good work it accomplished in this country, particularly on the North Shore.

When His Excellency Bishop Labrie arose, he was the object of a great ovation. In a moving speech, interrupted by applause, he expressed his thanks, first of all to God, the source of all good, then to the Eudist congregation to whom he owed so much, and finally to Bishop Leventoux and Father Le Strat. The conclusion of his address brought the listeners back to the North Shore : "Your Eminence, if I insisted on receiving this holy anointing from your hands, it is not only because of the legitimate pride which we take in your dignity of Prince of the Church, but also because you have received me with understanding kindness and encouraging words. Also, there is another reason which nobody probably suspects. It is that you are an Oblate of Mary Immaculate, and that between the Oblates and myself there is a certain affinity. Do not both our Congregations have a special devotion to the Most Blessed Virgin ? Then, the Oblates were among the first missionaries of the North Shore. It was an Oblate Father who united my father and mother in wedlock. A few years later, on a terrible winter day, my father and three companions were carried away by the ice of the St. Lawrence. To all seeming they were doomed. My mother, a horrified witness of this drama, thought of Father Arnaud and sent him a telegram. Very soon an answer came back : 'I am praying Mary Immaculate and her Blessed Mother, Saint Anne. They will not perish.' The following day, the castaways drifted ashore at Sainte-Anne-des-Monts." Bishop Labrie was referring here to an incident which is recounted at length in Alexandre Comeau's absorbing book : *Life and Sport on the North Shore.*

Two weeks after the consecration, four hundred and fifty miles from Quebec City, His Excellency Bishop Ross of Gaspé presided over the enthronement of our vicar apostolic in the lowly and nearly century-old church of Havre Saint-Pierre. A son of the North Shore was thus officially established on an episcopal throne by an illustrious colleague, who also belonged in some way to this region, having taken his first school lessons from Mgr F.-X. Bossé at Esquimaux Point.

The Clarke Steamship Company put its best steamer at the disposition of the guests of honour on this occasion. Its president, Desmond Clarke, announced that a scholarship was henceforth to be paid by the Company to the most deserving student, to be chosen by His Excellency Bishop Labrie, a charitable project which admirably corresponded to the greatest desires of the new spiritual chief of the North Shore. A thought expressed by one of the orators at the banquet, the Honourable Mr. Pierre Casgrain, struck all those present : "We joyfully greet, on this day, the two vigilant sentinels placed by the Catholic Church at the two outposts of the Canadian frontier, as though to forbid entrance to certain evil errors of the Old Continent." If Bishop Ross has done his share on the South Shore, one can be assured that Bishop Labrie has done his, first at Havre Saint-Pierre, then at Baie Comeau.

Our Bishop has since presided over certain celebrations on the North Shore. On July 13, 1941, at Havre Saint-Pierre, he had the happiness of ordaining Father Moïse Méthot. Eight days later, he took part in a Solemn High Mass sung by the new priest at Long Point of Mingan at an altar erected in front of the chapel, in the presence of a great crowd of relatives, friends, and parishioners. After the retreat of the Fathers in 1944, preached by the Reverend Father D'Amours, Provincial of the Eudists, Bishop Labrie obtained the cooperation of this Father, of all the Fathers of the vicariate, and of the parishioners of Rivière-au-Tonnerre in organizing a celebration for the 50th anniversary of Father Louis Garnier's ordination.

Our Bishop's time is now divided between pastoral visits, attendance at the meetings of the Department of Education in Quebec, and an interminable flow of correspondence wherein the most lowly are never forgotten. Several circular letters, authoritative studies of timely questions, such as vocations, education, and Christian family life, are addressed by him to the clergy and the faithful.

Momentous enterprises have been undertaken and are progressing well under the firm and constant guidance of our indefatigable vicar apostolic. The old convent of Havre Saint-Pierre has become a Normal School for the training of more competent teachers. The organization of primary teaching so as to allow pupils to follow the school programs of the eighth, ninth, and even twelfth year, the opening of a classical college, and offering the most talented pupils the opportunity of pursuing university studies, such are the aims which he is seeking to attain in the near future. Meanwhile, His Excellency is imposing heavy sacrifices on himself in order to provide for the education of the children of the North Shore. At least fifty are now studying in different institutions of the Province. All resources at his disposal are set aside by him to train priests, if it so please God, or choice citizens to form a society.

Charitable and social work receives particular attention : Bishop Labrie succeeded in making of the Saint John Eudes Hospital as charitable an establishment as possible, and pupils have been sent by him to study social sciences at Laval University in the hope that they will work, later on, in the best interests of the labouring class.

Another activity, both social and economic, has particularly interested Bishop Labrie, as well as all his fellow bishops : Cooperation. In 1943, groups of men in the fishing villages met to study together what means would provide their greater well-being both materially and morally. Fishermen's cooperatives and credit unions were subsequently established in the more important centres. A cooperative for electricity, the first of its kind in the Province, was formed to furnish electricity to several groups of fishermen. Is it not time to utilize the marvellous wealth of hydraulic power which Providence has lavished on the North Shore? Henceforth, the fisherman will no longer be isolated. His working companions are not strangers any more, but brothers and friends with whom he is in constant relation, studying with them the best methods to capture prizes from the deep by means of the line and the best ways to prepare fish. The former routines, which never allowed modification of methods that were a hundred years old, seem very obsolete now to the fishermen working in a cooperative establishment. They feel a greater human dignity, more independence, and more pride in their work, which will permit them to better their lives economically and morally. This progress, realized in all domains at an astonishing rate, has naturally influenced the Sovereign Pontiff to make a regular diocese of the apostolic vicariate of the St. Lawrence.

On August 11, 1946, a beautiful page was added to the glorious history of the Catholic Church in Canada.

His Excellency Bishop N.-A. Labrie took possession of his throne in his episcopal city of Baie Comeau. His Excellency Bishop Courchesne, Archbishop of Rimouski, presided over the ceremony in the new cathedral. He expressed his profound satisfaction in seeing a native of the district at the head of the new diocese and one so well prepared to give the necessary impetus to the new organization. Bishops, prelates, Eudist missionaries, the Superior General and the Provincial of the Congregation, priests of the diocese of the Gulf of St. Lawrence, the Honourable Mr. Onésime Gagnon, representatives of local industry, and members of the diocese from all over the North Shore met there. The joy that was in their hearts was reflected on their countenances. There was a general feeling of perfect harmony, a happy portent for the future, among the religious, civil, and industrial authorities, as well as among the entire population.

Captain A. Schmon recalled that, twenty-seven years earlier, a first Mass was sung on the veranda of his home at Shelter Bay. He stressed the cordiality of his relations with the Eudist Fathers, whose devotedness he has always admired, especially with Father Louis-Philippe Gagné, the former untiring pastor of Baie Comeau, whose influence on his parishioners had always been so beneficent and efficacious. Colonel R. McCormick said on this occasion : "The Almighty, in guiding my steps towards this rocky shore, has granted me the opportunity to offer as an example to all Canada, the cordial relations which exist here between employers and employees." The Honourable Mr. Onésime Gagnon thanked this great benefactor of Canada. His Excellency Bishop N.-A. Labrie was happy to pledge his efforts in union with all these men of good will for the great spiritual and material welfare of the people of his diocese.

At Baie Comeau, as in all other industrial centres of the North Shore, the worker is satisfied with his lot. He can see how the authorities do all in their power to improve his way of life in the little industrial city as in the middle of the forest. Above all, he knows that at the bishop's palace, at the rectory, and at the schools, he has sincere friends and loyal protectors to help him live and bring up his family according to the dictates of Christian morals, alone able to guide men to their ultimate destiny. It is these hopes which have inspired, for the happy future of the North Shore, the words, the writings, and the deeds of the new bishop of the Gulf of St. Lawrence. May God grant him health and the time necessary to keep on doing good and to carry out the noble projects he has undertaken.

CHAPTER SEVENTEEN

THE FUTURE PROSPECTS FOR INDUSTRY

W HEN, in 1944, Mr. T. B. Fraser was manager of Woods Operations at Shelter Bay, he witnessed an amusing incident which he enjoys relating.

"A young French-Canadian was harnessing his horse for the day's work. Nearby, a comrade, 22 years of age and only recently arrived from Labrador, was watching this task with lively interest. At his home in Labrador he had never seen any of the animals in common use in our woods operations. Suddenly, he said to the French-Canadian: 'I'd like to see your horse's feet'... The Canadian did not understand, so I had to act as interpreter. 'Show him', I said in French, 'your horse's foot'... The young newcomer drew near to look, as the teamster held up his horse's foot, which he had been told all horses wear nailed to heir hoofs and was amazed at sight of the iron shoes."

Today this young man, who until then had travelled on nothing other than dog sleds, has become a devotee of the airplane, which brought him to the woods operations and will carry him back home, in the short period of a few hours, when he wishes to return.

This little incident shows clearly that the north shore has ceased to be the "North Shore". Let us give

THE AUTHOR'S GOLDEN ANNIVERSARY OF ORDINATION (*August 11, 1944*)

THE FUTURE... 285

it its true name — the County of Saguenay — whose forest and mineral wealth are attracting so much attention and exciting so much eager desire.

The County of Saguenay and Anticosti Island together actually produce 25% of the pulp in the Province of Quebec, and 10% of the pulp prepared in Canada, while extensive limits still remain to be worked. On the rivers Bersimis, Sainte-Marguerite (Sacré-Cœur), Colombier, Moisie, Manitou, Magpie, Saint-Jean, Aguanish, Natashquan, Saint-Augustin, Saint-Paul, to name only the largest, the companies have rich reserves of timber for the future ; and this without including the hundreds of lesser watercourses whose shores are thickly wooded.

As is known, Baie Comeau is the principal centre of forest industry in this vast county. On rugged ground, amid overlying and criss-crossing rocks, in the heart of this North Shore forest, Colonel McCormick, proprietor of that renowned newspaper, *The Chicago Tribune*, aided by Captain A. A. Schmon and several other devoted collaborators, built the Baie Comeau Mill which, every day excepting Sundays, turns out 480 tons of newsprint paper. The genius of man, armed with modern machinery has succeeded in a remarkable enterprise — establishing a mill the daily operation of which is the admiration of all visitors, the expert as well as the non-expert.

A question may arise at sight of the immense quantities of wood daily transformed into fine paper. Can this industry at Baie Comeau expect a long life? It can be stated with certainty that the forest reserves of this region will last indefinitely, if protected against those dangers that lie in wait for them.

The enemy most to be feared is fire! — In 1820 and again in 1870 forest fires wrought havoc and destruction throughout the greater part of the country, from the Saguenay River to Labrador. Several areas, saved from this scourge, bear trees of an age of 200 years. Elsewhere, the age of fir and spruce is no greater than 125 years. We can ourselves remember still more recent fires which have ravaged and laid waste so many extensive forest areas. Let us hope that the precautions taken by the Government, the Companies, and all those employed in forest operations, will be increasingly intensified toward safeguarding a wealth so precious to our country.

We may assert without hesitation that it will be found necessary to apply to this industry, which has so wonderful a future, the rules outlined in a pastoral letter of His Excellency, Bishop N.-A. Labrie, on *The Forest*, a veritable code of forest exploitation.

The Bishop of the Gulf of St. Lawrence knows the Canadian forest, was born on the borders of its great woods, passed his schoolboy holidays in the shade of its great trees and on the shores of its lakes and rivers, and dedicated his life as a missionary to the fishermen and hunters.

He has, at the opportune moment, found time to make a complete analysis of the problems concerning forestry on the North Shore of the St. Lawrence and to launch an appeal for conservation, reforestation, and those methods of development most beneficial to the general weal, an appeal which Esdras Minville, forestry engineers, and all those who have their country's interest at heart, have endorsed unanimously.

This authoritative study, which so perfectly establishes the responsibilities of the public, companies, public men, clergy, and forest workers, will certainly not remain a "dead letter". Solicitous of their own true interests as well as those of the country, government and the companies should find in this study inspiration towards the preparation of suitable laws for the preservation, conservation, and even the eventual enrichment of the Canadian forest. In any event, for the welfare of all, the best possible use should be made of this national wealth. Let us thank God that he has endowed our Bishop with sufficient knowledge of science, with the will, and with the solicitude for the material and spiritual well-being of his flock, to set before the public the best means of attaining this end.

Following the enthusiastic reception recently accorded this letter throughout Canada, may we not now look forward to the realization of the Bishop of the Gulf of St. Lawrence's great project : the creation in its entirety of a new town, "Hauterive", just lately so named.

An enchanting site has been chosen, on level ground, overlooking the great estuary of the Manicouagan River. Not far distant the Laurentians are to be seen ; thereafter are vast plains broken here and there by little valleys ; all this imposingly encircling the site and environs of the future city.

Those who have visited this charming "corner of Canadian soil" will look forward with delight to the changes to take place there during the coming spring and throughout the following years. A cathedral, bishop's palace, hospital, seminaries, college, normal school for girls, and without doubt a school of sylviculture, long desired by all who dwell in this region where so many forestry problems await solution ;

forest settlements, co-operative camps, and now the hope of a stable population and the delivering of these workers from the painful separation of family members whose destiny is rather that they live together under one roof — the home : such are the great works for the success of which His Excellency labours unceasingly.

Soon, a broad highway will unite the new town with the industrial centre of Baie Comeau, situated some five miles distant, and will facilitate daily communication between the towns. Great are the hopes held for this "New Quebec on the banks of the Manicouagan."

The Prime Minister of the Province, the Honourable Maurice Duplessis, together with his ministers, will bear the enviable honour of having supported the worthy Bishop of the Gulf of St. Lawrence in this almost superhuman undertaking. And the Quebec North Shore Paper Company will be particularly and gratefully remembered in that they proved themselves so able in collaboration with the Bishop.

There can be no doubt that the settling down together here of greater numbers of people, and with a clear understanding of what is to the general welfare of the district, would create many more prosperous enterprises ; for example, the manufacture on the spot of all articles produced from wood : paper of every shade and grade, various nylon and plastic articles, etc.

May Divine Providence vouchsafe to hasten the fulfilment of these developments and grant that soon the new town will open wide its doors to workers from both shores of the St. Lawrence — workers weary of the nomadic, unstable life to which they have heretofore been subjected. For several years past the forests

THE FUTURE... 289

of Saguenay have grown to be of such value that we ought all to thank God for having placed so courageous a pastor in such favourable surroundings and for having associated with him such understanding and co-operative industrialists.

"One man", wrote His Excellency lately, "recognized the opportunities offered on the North Shore and gave proof of sufficient wisdom to invest his capital in a great undertaking. From this has come the only prosperity we have yet known, and its beneficial influence has made itself felt not alone in the County of Saguenay, but in Charlevoix, the length and breadth of the South Shore, and even to Quebec and Montreal, as commerce with these two great centres has been particularly favoured. Thanks to this, navigation and air-lines have prospered, and we have had the advantage of an open road as far east as Baie Comeau. One could never end in attempting to list all the benefits that have accrued from the manufacture of paper in Baie Comeau."

But, behold! at the dawn of 1949, at Seven Islands and at Havre Saint-Pierre, respectively 115 and 265 miles to the east of Baie Comeau, work of all kinds is attracting general attention, presaging for this part of Saguenay a radical economic metamorphosis.

The time is already long past that deposits of ilmenite were first noted at the mouths of the Bersimis, Moisie, Manitou, and Natashquan rivers, and many a Labradorian beach. A glittering black sand has filtered in with the ordinary sand and at times covered or even replaced it entirely. A needle or small blade, no matter how slightly magnetized, will attract and hold these particles. This magnetized sand comes through disaggregation from the anarthrous rocks which, in New Quebec, extend from Lake St. John to Labrador, at distances varying according to the waterways whose direction they follow. It may well be supposed that many minerals scattered throughout these rocks, from which river currents have carried so many particles to the sea, are still unknown and will attract future prospectors. Were not blast-furnaces once kept alight to extract steel from the sands of the Moisie! And, about 1914, did not a civil-engineer, a Mr. Mackenzie, find a million tons of ilmenite in several acres of sandy dunes bordering on the east of the Natashquan River! And now, 35 miles north of Havre Saint-Pierre, about Lake Allard and neighbouring lakes, considerable deposits of ilmenite have been analyzed and found by several engineers, among them Mr. W. W. Longley, to be of great value to industry.

Ilmenite is, in fact, a composite of titanium and iron from which is produced titanium oxide, the best quality white paint in the world. A precious metal may also be extracted therefrom : titanium, almost as strong as steel and as light as aluminum, besides possessing other valuable properties. This is the mineral that has occasioned the developments now under way at Havre Saint-Pierre. The existing wharf is soon to be lengthened and will then be linked with Lake Allard by means of a 35-mile railroad. At present the plans are that the raw material be transported to Sorel for processing into titanium oxide. Needless to say, this decision at first occasioned a very natural reaction amongst the population. The dreams of development, which until this time had so obsessed all minds and loosed all tongues, suddenly appeared to be vanishing. God

THE FUTURE... 291

grant that more favourable developments arise to give the inhabitants of this region greater opportunity. May it not be considered just and right that, if at all possible, these people be engaged throughout the year in the extraction and treatment of ilmenite, especially as Providence, by having placed these riches within their reach, would thereby appear to have granted them at least a share in its exploitation !

Will the people of Seven Islands be any better off than their friends of Havre Saint-Pierre because of the Ungava Mining developments?

As His Excellency the Bishop has said : "We know that, at first, it will be no easy task to create an industry capable of treating millions of tons of ore. Nevertheless, if the words of Mr. W. W. Durrell are correct, we may well hope that the two million unexported tons will be treated at Seven Islands. This foothold will lead us to the threshold of the day when, with an ever-growing industry near the source of supply, exports of raw material will diminish, to the eventual benefit of all in this region."

Picture to yourself the growth of Baie Comeau repeating itself at Seven Islands and at Havre Saint-Pierre. Who, even then, could imagine the immense sphere of activity in the Diocese of the Gulf of St. Lawrence open to seafaring men, to business men, to engineers, and to craftsmen of all kinds?

It is indeed difficult to form an exact idea of the industrial hopes that these mines and the seeking out and development of these minerals have given rise to.

In the December, 1948 number of *Fortune* there appeared an article entitled : "The Great Labrador Venture," with the following sub-title : "One of the world's richest bodies of iron ore lies in the northern waste. Canadian and U. S. enterprise join to bring it to market."

A name to be remembered in history is that of the man who discovered these deposits back in 1890 — the Chief Geologist of Canada, Mr. A. P. Lovv. After close study of the reports and maps of Father Babel, O.M.I., and the Jesuit Laure, two famed missionaries to the Indians, this dauntless man left Bersimis with five Indians and travelled throughout Ungava, making four tours, each lasting six months ; ascending rivers, descending others, crossing lakes by canoe or circling them, observing the rocks, and extracting therefrom precious minerals. The Indians and their customs, the forest with its trees, plants, flowers, rivers, and lakes ; all these A. Lovv saw and described in pages which form one of the most beautiful memorials any man may leave behind him.

The way was, therefore, already prepared for the next geologist, the well-known J. A. Retty. Guided by Mathieu André, who had brought the first piece of haematite out to Seven Islands, J. A. Retty courageously and successfully followed up Mr. A. Lovv's explorations. J. A. Retty and André made their first trip, in the year 1937, by plane as far as Lake Sawyer, some 800 miles into the interior. These researches by Joseph A. Retty, carried out with such praiseworthy perseverance over a period of more than ten years, led other well-known men : Jules R. Timmins, President of Hollinger Consolidated Gold Mines Limited and George H. Humphrey, President of the M. A. Hanna Company, to make a more precise estimate of this unsuspected and immense wealth. They found rock formations over a distance of 200 miles containing on an average 65% haematite, the best-quality iron mineral. 300,000,000 tons could be extracted from that area alone explored by Mr. J. A. Retty, and here a mechanical shovel may be operated with comparative ease. There is at the same time every possibility of the discovery of even rarer minerals.

Another Canadian, Paul Provencher, a Baie Comeau Forestry Engineer, has made four separate trips throughout this territory and has, through that most suitable medium, the camera, been able to acquaint the general public with this, as yet, almost unknown country. With his two companions, an Indian and a compatriot, he set out by plane and then, endeavouring to follow in the tracks of A. Lovv, wandering in the wilderness for two days, he was able to travel by canoe and afoot from Sangert to Hamilton Falls. The splendid photographs taken by Mr. Provencher, some of which are reproduced in this book, give but a slight idea of the beauty and variety of the coloured films shown by him in the United States and at the Royal Institute of Canada in Montreal. These unusual films were a great success, and we now eagerly await the appearance of the book in which the author, Mr. Provencher, intends to present the fruits of his artistic and scientific observations.

With these many explorations it now becomes understandable why so many millions of dollars have been set aside for this "Great Venture", as yet in its infancy.

The present headquarters of the recently discovered iron mines bears the very suitable name of "Burnt Creek". Here, there are comfortable camps with running water and electricity, suitable to all the most pressing needs. Similar camps have been constructed, over a three-month period, along a 70-mile long road capable of accommodating trucks, tractors, and mechanical battering rams, indeed, all such machinery as used in mining country. Two hundred and fifty selected men have been brought to this wilderness — hoping to earn much and spend little, and be able to keep in touch with their families by means of the modern radio station which is at everyone's disposal.

How has it been possible to accomplish such marvels? Because, ten miles from Burnt Creek there is an airfield on which, each week, often each day, giant planes alight and discharge men, food, and the materials necessary to the execution of this work.

Happily, to date there has been no serious accident in all this coming and going of aircraft between Seven Islands and Burnt Creek — a total round-distance flight of 650 miles.

However, airplanes, which will continue to be used, will be unable to cope with the transportation of minerals. Therefore, work has been started and is, indeed, almost completed, on tracing a route for a railway line starting at Seven Islands, following the Moisie River, then, one after the other, its tributaries, the Nipissis and the Wacouna, arriving at the height of land, winding around a succession of lakes, and traversing the plains, for a total distance of 350 miles, in which no insurmountable obstacles has been encountered. This line is to be constructed as soon as conditions warrant.

Moreover, in a corner of the bay famous since the days of Jacques Cartier, at Pointe-aux-Basques, deep water wharfs are being planned.

In the light of these events a change is to be foreseen throughout the length and breadth of this vast region, more especially so when the resources Providence has here placed at the disposal of industry are taken into consideration.

Some 70 miles from Burnt Creek, north of Lake Knob, at Eaton Canion falls on the Kanepiska River, 70,000 H.P. is available for development when the preliminary work requires it. Naturally, it is to be expected that, in a not too distant future, the directors of these industries will take into consideration the almost limitless possibilities of power development to be found within a relatively short distance of Seven Islands.

Should the 3,000,000 H.P. easily developed from the rivers Manicouagan (1,500,000 h.p.), Bersimis (500,000 h.p.), Manitou (500,000 h.p.), and Magpie (500,000 h.p.) be found insufficient to operate the mighty mills required at Seven Islands — the point at which they could be most centrally located — there could be added to this, for the benefit of other future industries as well, the 7,000,000 H.P. that could be developed at Hamilton Falls.

As Bishop Labrie has said : "May those who wish to develop this great country not restrict themselves solely to the extraction of raw materials, but interest themselves also in the development of our immense hydroelectric power resources. Such development, together with the decentralization of large masses of people and the creation of new towns, socially and scientifically organized, would serve not only this region, but would contribute greatly to the prosperity and progress of the whole Province."

It may be objected that Seven Islands is at least 320 miles from Quebec City and there would, therefore, be great difficulty in reaching these riches. However, there already exists the much-used water route of the Gulf of St. Lawrence, well-known to all mariners, over which control becoming daily more scientific makes shipwrecks a rarity in spite of the many shoals and sand-banks.

On this inland sea the County of Saguenay has five of the most magnificent seaports : Baie Comeau, Godbout, Seven Islands, Mingan, Havre Saint-Pierre. From these ports ships of all sizes can set sail for Quebec, Montreal, the South Shore, Gaspé, Sydney, Halifax, and the United States of America.

Navigation is assured for at least nine months of the year, the other three months alone remaining ill-suited to regular sailings, chiefly because of the ice which blocks the harbours in February and March and the floating ice in the month of April.

The enormous increase in coming and going of pulpwood barges is well known, these ships plying between ports of the North Shore and others in Canada, the U.S.A., and Great Britain.

Although the embryonic roads already in existence between Seven Islands and Baie Comeau (this latter now linked with Quebec by a suitable road) permit of the passage of automobiles at various points, there still remains much to be done before this section of Saguenay is provided with the highway which would appear to be indispensable to the traffic in prospect. In any case, it is admitted that the terrain is favourable to the use of the most modern machines along this North Shore, and many are convinced that the time has now come to build a national highway. This is a necessity from every point of view ; and there exist no serious grounds for objection. The new towns of Havre Saint-Pierre and Seven Islands must be linked with Quebec, as Baie Comeau has been for the past two years. Not only does "Business" cry out for this route, but the devotees of the open-air life, ever seeking healthy change in the tranquillity and solitude of the wilderness, have been looking forward for some time past to enjoying its many advantages. Such a road would run at times along the shores of lakes abounding in fish, wind over rocky heights, and skirt the edges of sandy russet beaches. There are many such beaches, some apparently boundless, others bordered by rocky cliffs which give them shelter, still others flowing back into verdant plateaus. Here one may take one's ease, gather wild strawberries or other tasty berries and, in July and August, swim in the salt water of the Gulf.

In this country fishermen may try for salmon on many rivers and take fish of unusually large size. If some streams offer only 8 to 10-lb. salmon, others offer 10 to 20-lb., specimens. On the Moisie, one of the largest and most beautiful of these many rivers, and at Bersimis, salmon weighing 30 to 35 lbs have been landed, and even up to 50 lbs.

As for trout, they abound in all the lakes and at the mouths of all rivers and leap avidly for the fly, exhausting even the most ardent fishermen by their abundance.

A short time ago, in a Quebec newspaper, Damase Potvin posed the following interesting question : "Why does not our government create, on the Island of Anticosti, one of the most beautiful of national parks ?" Here is the ideal spot for a park par excellence, this stretch of land set by God at the gateway to that majestic watercourse, the St. Lawrence, up which for centuries past have come those voyageurs from the old world of Europe and Asia to the new world of North America.

Where has nature been more lavish with its beauties? What an inexhaustible reserve for fur-bearing animals and venison! This island is even now the resort of faithful visitors during the best season of the year, those carried away in anticipation of the sport there to be enjoyed.

All these are the industrial and vacationing potentialities which are now bringing new life, a veritable rebirth, to this section of Canada. Vast forests, still rich in wood of the best quality for paper manufacture; untold mineral wealth just being discovered; sea-ports such as are under way at Seven Islands, quite as large as that of Gaspé; sportsmen's paradises; is all this not sufficient to attract the attention of our leaders to such national wealth and lead them to develop it to the great benefit of Saguenay, Quebec, and the whole of Canada!

www.ingramcontent.com/pod-product-compliance
Lightning Source LLC
Chambersburg PA
CBHW052211240426
43670CB00036B/113